D0149266

Readers' Comments

"My husband and I were just starting our own business when we read *Blue Mountain*. We were able to draw and learn from the many experiences and lessons shared by Susan in this wonderful book. It kept us inspired, lighthearted, and determined.

"In the autobiographical section, I was impacted by how people like Susan have changed the world for women today. It was fascinating to realize that it was only a short time ago that things were so different, and to see how women had to fight against such prejudice." — *K.J. and E.J., Carmel Valley, CA*

"Reading Susan Polis Schutz's *Blue Mountain* provided me invaluable advice at a time when I most needed it. As a 23-year-old aspiring filmmaker a year out of college, I have encountered challenges that have caused me to waver about my chosen passion. But *Blue Mountain* reminded me that passion, commitment, and moral integrity can make a difference. Because of Susan's lessons, I have regained confidence in my choices." — *A.C., New York, NY*

"*Blue Mountain* shows the importance of persevering and never giving up. Dreams are important and Susan shows they can come true. After reading this book, I gained courage to send my writings to a few places for publication, and if I get turned down, I'll send them somewhere else." — *B.S., Hopewell Junction, NY*

"It's so easy to blame circumstances for failure instead of taking control. *Blue Mountain* is a tremendously valuable lesson illustrated in business but applicable in life! This is a must-read for my children, who are now venturing out on their own, to show the proactive approach to dealing with the inevitable challenges instead of giving in to them." — *R.G., Boulder, CO*

"Hats off to you, Susan, for blending your business story with your life and family history all wrapped up into an uplifting read. I learned about the importance of balance and of blending family with work. You are living my dream. This has been by far the most inspiring book I have read in a long time." — *M.P., Frederick, MD*

Tributes

"It's hard to make sense of the business world today, especially in this era of loose ethics and overwhelming greed and in an environment when few are prospering and fewer still are happy in their jobs. In Susan's captivating and honest book...her journey provides the reader with a critical map of how to build a compassionate life in all its many aspects."

—**Kara Swisher**, *Wall Street Journal* columnist;
author of *aol.com*

"Throughout the story, Susan does a great job of showing how each experience teaches a critical life lesson. This book can really teach people to shape their own lives and achieve their dreams.

"*Blue Mountain* is not just a great personal story but a riveting social history as well, showing the struggles of the civil rights era, the Vietnam protests, and the women's movement through Susan's own experiences. Susan and Stephen's winding path to business success...is a fascinating tale of how an enterprise evolves from vision to viability."

—**Joseph P. Kennedy II**, former member of Congress;
chairman, Citizens Energy Corporation

"Stephen and Susan Polis Schutz show us how we can all turn our dreams into realities when we use the *Blue Mountain* principles they generously share with us. They have the rare ability to uplift people from feeling down to feeling joy at the top of the mountain."

—**Spencer Johnson, M.D.**, author of *Who Moved My Cheese?*

"*Blue Mountain* is the opposite of *The Big Chill* because it's about hippies growing up, becoming hugely successful, and instead of losing, holding on to the starry-eyed idealism of their youth."

—**Judith Viorst**, author of many bestselling books, including
Alexander and the Terrible, Horrible, No Good, Very Bad Day and
Grown-Up Marriage

"I think there is a feeling one MUST sell out or be crushed. Susan and Stephen didn't and are strong: There are almost NO stories like this today.

"Everyone thinks whatever the large corporations want, they will get, so go along.

"America needs to believe again...Susan and Stephen are fantastic role models that did it 'their way.'"

—**Pat Schroeder**, former member of Congress;
president, Association of American Publishers

Other Books by Susan Polis Schutz

Come Into the Mountains, Dear Friend
I Want to Laugh, I Want to Cry
Peace Flows from the Sky
Someone Else to Love
Yours If You Ask
Love, Live and Share
Find Happiness in Everything You Do
Take Charge of Your Body (with Katherine F. Carson, M.D.)
Don't Be Afraid to Love
To My Daughter, with Love, on the Important Things in Life
To My Son, with Love
I Love You
One World, One Heart

We welcome your comments regarding this book at
our special Web address: http://www.sps.com/dreams

From living out of a pickup truck to a billion of their greeting cards sent...
this is an amazing SUCCESS story
with insights you can learn from

Blue Mountain

The story of Blue Mountain Arts Publishers,
BLUEMOUNTAIN.COM, and
two accidental entrepreneurs living their dreams

Susan Polis Schutz

Includes the lessons they learned as entrepreneurs
and a separate autobiographical section

Blue Mountain Press®
Boulder, Colorado

Author's Note: The names and physical descriptions of the following persons, and the locations in which events involving them took place, have been changed for purposes of this book and are not intended to refer to actual persons with the same or similar names: Messrs. Ames, Greenwald, Hudson, Jacobson, Lausch, Wedge, Wright, Revson, and Limon; Mses. White and Edson. In addition, the "managers" referred to in Chapter Eleven are composite characters and are not intended to refer to actual persons. Finally, although quotations of statements made by the participants in judicial proceedings are drawn from the transcripts of those proceedings, the other dialogue is based on the author's best recollection and is not intended to be a verbatim reproduction of the actual words used.

Copyright © 2004 by Stephen Schutz and Susan Polis Schutz.

Library of Congress Control Number: 2003021495
ISBN: 0-88396-695-6

CREDITS appear on page 357.

Certain trademarks are used under license.

Manufactured in the United States of America.

First Printing: 2004

Library of Congress Cataloging-in-Publication Data

Schutz, Susan Polis.
  Blue Mountain : The story of Blue Mountain Arts Publishers,
BLUEMOUNTAIN.COM, and two accidental entrepreneurs living
their dreams / Susan Polis Schutz.
      p. cm.
   ISBN 0-88396-695-6 (hardcover)
  1. Blue Mountain Arts (Firm)—History. 2. Publishers and
publishing—Colorado—Boulder. 3. Literature
publishing—Colorado—Boulder. 4. Electronic
publishing—Colorado—Boulder. 5. Greeting card
industry—Colorado—Boulder. 6. Schutz, Susan Polis. 7. Schutz,
Stephen. I. Title.

   Z473.B628S38 2004
   070.5'09788'63—dc22

                                                        2003021495
                                                               CIP

Blue Mountain Arts, Inc.

P.O. Box 4549, Boulder, Colorado 80306

Blue Mountain is dedicated and written with a lot of thankfulness and love to my husband, Steve, who is my perfect partner in life, my three amazing children, my mother and brother, and to the Blue Mountain family.

Acknowledgments

I want to first thank my husband, Steve, for helping me remember so many details and for being my chief editor throughout the entire time I spent writing this. He has read the manuscript many, many times and made significant suggestions every time. Steve is the inspiration for this book, but most importantly, he is the love forever in my life.

I thank my children for their extremely diligent and important input to this book and for being the most wonderful children in the world. I love them more than anything.

A special thank-you to the following people for spending so much time on this manuscript and for providing substantial comments, criticisms, advice, and encouragement: Lesley and Spencer Johnson, Marjorie and Mort Shaevitz, Karen Bidgood, Patti Wayant, and Jorian.

Also, I am grateful to the following people for reading the book and offering helpful feedback and important suggestions: Robert and Rae Polis, Lee Levine, D'Arcy Randall, Jody Handley, June Polis, Matthew Polis, Pat Schroeder, John Purvis, Harry Melkonian, David Black, Samantha Stevenson, Rebecca Milanski, Andrea Pierotti, Barbara Stuck, Kris Wilson, Gloria Andujar, Barbara Cunningham, Helene Steinbuck, Joan Weiss, Myrna Estes, Bob Gall, Ellen Golden, Robert Golden, Kara Swisher, Judith Viorst, and Joe and Beth Kennedy.

So many professionals told me that you cannot combine a business story, an inspirational story, and a personal story in one book. A business story is about people. People have personal lives. They should be human beings first, business people second, and if there is an inspirational message that can be gleaned from their lives, this, too, should be told.

Contents

Introduction

Most people do not realize that the story behind the famous bluemountain.com website actually began over thirty years ago when my husband, Steve, and I founded our publishing company, Blue Mountain Arts.

It is a story that started when Steve and I hand-printed our first posters and sold them around the country while living in the back of our pickup-truck camper. Eventually our poetry greeting cards became the number-one selling card line in America.

In *Blue Mountain* I write about our lives and how we overcame obstacles while learning to build and manage a growing business.

I speak about how we stood up in court to two of the largest corporations in the United States to fight for our company's survival. I describe these lawsuits in detail because they had such a strong impact on us.

In the late 1990's, our family was swept up in the insanity of the dot-com craze with our electronic greeting card website. I chronicle our whirlwind entanglement in the fast-moving world of the Internet and how we quickly realized that we did not belong there.

I write with joy about how important our family is to us and how we never compromised our ideals or our love for one another.

Many people have told us that our story is inspiring, funny, enlightening, and even suspenseful. They said that they admired the way Steve and I successfully pursued our personal and professional dreams. And they asked the inevitable question: "So why don't you write a book and tell us how you did it?"

Steve and I then realized that the knowledge we gained might help others bypass some of the pitfalls and hurtful mistakes we experienced and turn their dreams into realities. This is why, after years of living privately, we felt *Blue Mountain* should be written.

We learned something valuable every time we took a step forward or backward. As you read this book, you will encounter numerous lessons, which appear at the beginning of the chapters.

The first and most important lesson we learned is that you must follow your passion. For Steve and me, our dream was to work together by combining our love for each other with our love for writing and art.

We wanted our creations to help people communicate their feelings and promote understanding and peace throughout the world. Thus, Blue Mountain Arts was born.

Having been "flower children" in the 1960's, Steve and I started out knowing absolutely nothing about the business world, and though we often stumbled and fell, we were able to turn most of our failures into successes. In this book, I speak frankly about many of our mistakes. I remember them well because they have been the best teachers we have ever had.

We learned that it is essential to believe in yourself, but you must also be honest about your strengths and limitations. You must ignore all the naysayers who will try to discourage you. You must trust your own instincts and be willing to take risks.

Steve and I learned to concentrate and spend time on what was most important to us. If we became engaged in an activity that didn't fit our ethical criteria or that just didn't feel right, we tried to end our involvement in that activity. We discovered how fragile life is and that there isn't time to do things that we don't believe in.

For the last (purple) section of this book, I have written a personal memoir that complements the history of Blue Mountain Arts. These autobiographical anecdotes include growing up in Peekskill, New York in the 1950's; living and teaching in New York City; exploring the hippie and feminist philosophies; falling in love with and marrying Steve; and giving birth to and raising our children.

Steve and I worked hard to intertwine our family life with our careers so we could share all areas of our lives. We have managed to live our dreams.

I hope this book will encourage you to create your own mountain of dreams.

Susan Polis Schutz

chapter one

David and Goliath: The Beginning of a Nightmare

"Susan, what's wrong?" Steve asked. He'd only seen me cry a few times during our marriage, and I was sobbing now.

I couldn't talk. I pointed toward the Hallmark store, shaking my head and wiping my face.

Minutes before, Steve and I had been strolling through a Southern California shopping center, enjoying the day and looking for a card store. Even after fifteen years, it was still exciting to discover our Blue Mountain Arts cards and books. We often go to stores incognito to straighten out our displays and organize the cards. We also watch people read our cards. I love seeing their faces light up when they realize they're not alone in their emotions.

On this sunny Saturday afternoon in April 1986, Steve waited for me in the mall while I went into a card shop. I immediately noticed that three of our cards were out of place. I picked them up, intending to put them back on the Blue Mountain Arts display rack, but I couldn't find our rack. Usually it is right in the front of a store, and our cards have such a distinctive look that they're impossible to miss.

I wondered why the store had only three of our cards. Most stores carry at least twenty-four different designs.

I turned over one of the cards to see the code numbers on the back and gasped. It read: "Personal Touch" by Hallmark.

These were not our cards, but to me they looked the same, with nearly identical features, including textured paper, a deckle edge, a stripe of color next to the deckle, long unrhyming poetry on the first and third pages, a nature illustration, and the inside page left blank, as well as other identifying characteristics. These cards even had enlarged first letters on each poem, another distinguishing feature of Blue Mountain Arts cards.

I read the poetry, but the words didn't make sense to me.

The cards seemed like a cheapened version of our cards. I visualized rows of computers putting together imitations according to some massive database marked "Greeting Cards." The cards were there, but the emotion, the essence, was gone.

Steve and I had spent years creating every aspect of our cards, but these cards weren't made by Blue Mountain Arts, the publishing company Steve and I founded in 1970. They were made by Hallmark, the largest manufacturer of greeting cards in the world. How could this be? I shivered.

A thought leapt into my head. It was a rumor I'd heard a month before and quickly had discounted. "The Hallmark salesman just told me not to carry your cards anymore," a storeowner told my mother, June Polis, who was the sales manager of Blue Mountain Arts. He told her that Hallmark was coming out with a knock-off line. At the time, I didn't believe him and discounted this information.

I lingered in the card shop, struggling for composure. "Maybe there are only three cards like this," I thought. I opened a display drawer. Piles of airbrushed cards that seemed to look just like ours lay in the drawer, dozens of shadows of our life work.

The sight of so many of these cards sent me over the edge. I grabbed a handful of them out of the drawer, flung them on the floor, alarming the cashier, and ran from the store to tell Steve.

"Let's go to another shopping center and see if there are any more cards," Steve said, stroking my hair. We hoped this would turn out to be just a dream.

We went to five other shopping centers and found several dozen different Hallmark cards that we thought looked exactly like ours. It wasn't a dream. It was a nightmare.

"I'm calling Mr. Hughes!" I exclaimed, spotting a pay phone. Mr. Hughes, co-chairman of Hallmark, had recently visited Steve and me, and he had seemed so nice.

"He didn't have anything to do with this," my heart was telling me. "He'll say it was a big mistake, apologize, and they will stop making the cards."

"Oh, come on, Susan," my mind retorted. "Be realistic."

I was torn between asking Mr. Hughes for an explanation and cursing at him. I dialed Information.

"Susan, you can't call him now." Steve gripped my hand. "Let's find out what they're doing. We don't want him to know we're mad. Yet."

"Kansas City," I said to the long-distance operator, ignoring Steve. "I want the number for Hallmark." I was livid.

I wanted to talk to Mr. Hughes. I felt so helpless. It was as if an insurmountable power had taken control of my life. I had to find out what was going on.

"Don't worry," Steve said. "We'll contact a lawyer. We'll fight them. They don't know how strong-willed we are, Sue."

I looked into his blue eyes and then at the solid, determined line of his jaw.

"How can we fight Hallmark, Steve? We don't even have a lawyer. It's all over. It's the end of Blue Mountain Arts," I choked out through returning tears.

I searched Steve's face. Was he just trying to calm me down? Did he really believe we could battle Hallmark? His eyes reflected a strength that never failed to awe me.

I hung up the phone.

On the drive home that day, furious thoughts raced through my head. I began to replay in my mind what had happened a few months earlier when Mr. Hughes's secretary had called us to set up a meeting with him.

"Why does he want to meet us?" I asked Steve, who shrugged.

We invited Mr. Hughes to come to our home. For the occasion, we dressed as conservatively as we could bear. I wore leather boots and slacks with a wide leather belt on my hips, and Steve wore tight-fitting jeans, a western shirt, and bolo tie.

What on earth would we talk about with him? The world of huge corporations seemed so distant from our homegrown Boulder company.

Mr. Hughes didn't disappoint us. He arrived in a private jet and took a limousine to our home. His custom-made tweed suit and impeccable hairstyle embodied refinement.

"I've been a great fan of yours for a long time," he said, shaking our hands while we gazed at his perfectly manicured nails. "It's so nice to meet you at last."

"Thank you" was all we could muster. Impressed by his warmth, we led him into our home studio where we served lunch.

As I picked up my napkin, Mr. Hughes asked, "What are your plans for the future?"

Steve choked on his first bite of salad and looked at me for help. We never made plans. For better or worse, we mostly did things spontaneously, learning as we went along. We never had any long-term planning sessions.

"Well," I said, scrambling for an answer, "I'll always continue writing poems. I also want to spend more time with my children."

This didn't seem to be the answer Mr. Hughes wanted, so he rephrased his question. "What are your plans for Blue Mountain Arts?"

"We love creating poetry and art together, and we love Blue Mountain Arts," Steve said. "What we've done in the past is exactly what we'll be doing in the future."

"But when companies become a certain size, problems always arise," he said. "You two might be happier just creating without a business to manage."

He asked us how many cards we made, and when we told him two hundred, he seemed very surprised.

He then asked us how a card company like ours could be so successful with so few cards. He told us that Hallmark had over eleven thousand designs.

He discussed Hallmark's organization, and to our amazement, he confessed they'd been suffering a "creative shortage." His polished manner took on a sheepish cast.

He mentioned how Hallmark had developed a corporate bureaucracy that made it difficult to keep up with the times.

He said that Hallmark's creativity was inefficient, uninspiring, and unimaginative and that they were trying to keep up with the public's current needs and tastes.

"Your cards satisfy a communications need, and your look is distinctive and recognized."

He paused a moment.

Then he told us that Hallmark could set up a creative house under our management.

Mr. Hughes mentioned that many large companies buy small companies, and the original owners continue to direct the creativity without worrying about the business. He gave us examples of several companies that Hallmark had recently purchased.

Our expressions must have given away our thoughts because he redirected the conversation at once.

"Is there anything Hallmark and Blue Mountain Arts could do together?" he asked us.

I shrugged. "I really can't think of any reason in the world why we'd want to do anything else or work for anyone but ourselves."

We were happy and fulfilled following our passions independently— in our own way. And we didn't want to compromise this at all.

We socialized for an hour or so, enjoying our meal and one another's company. We introduced him to Jared, our little son, who had been playing in the room next to our office. Mr. Hughes appeared to be the epitome of the country gentleman, despite his apparent shock at our independence and demeanor.

As we finished our dessert, Mr. Hughes looked into our eyes, and for the first time since we'd met him, he let down his guard and asked, what seemed to me, a completely unrehearsed question.

"How did you do it?" he inquired, nearly whispering. He wanted to know how our products were able to "sell" so well.

Steve and I exchanged glances and smiled. That answer was simple, but I could imagine why the head of an enormous company like Hallmark might have difficulty understanding it.

"We're not creating a product to sell," Steve said. "We're creating something we love."

Mr. Hughes, eyebrows raised, looked at us in disbelief as we described the importance of our family and our basic philosophy of life. It seemed that he was expecting us to use key business words, such as "marketing" and "profits," with an emphasis on "money." Instead, we were using words and phrases like "love," "nature," "expressing our feelings," "creativity," and "helping people communicate."

When our meeting was over, Mr. Hughes called his pilot. I remember thinking that he looked uncomfortable, confused, and considerably less polished than he had when he arrived.

We shook hands again. Before entering the limousine that would take him back to his corporate life in Kansas City, he turned and said, "If you ever change your mind, please call me." Relief showed on his face as he waved goodbye.

Steve and I reentered our home, both thinking that even though we came from a completely different world than Mr. Hughes, we had made a new friend. We were pleasantly surprised at how likeable he had been. But more importantly, we were comfortable in our knowledge that we wouldn't give up management of our greeting cards to Hallmark or anyone else. "Who knows?" we both thought, "Maybe Mr. Hughes will go back and implement a plan that will bring creativity back to Hallmark."

*   *   *

"A plan was implemented all right," I thought as we drove home from the mall after seeing the Hallmark Personal Touch cards. We concluded that Mr. Hughes was not at all our friend. The thought entered our minds that perhaps the purpose of his visit had been to "size us up." He might have surmised that we were two laid-back, lucky artists.

We were glad that we had seen the Hallmark cards when we did, so we could address the problem before the cards became more widely distributed. If we hadn't routinely visited stores, we might not have been aware of them.

We had learned over the years how essential it is to get out into the real world and personally observe our customers.

However, we surely did not expect to see this. I was devastated. Steve hugged me. What would I do without his strength and love?

The battle of David v. Goliath, as the press would later call it, had begun. We were about to enter a war to preserve our past and determine our future.

Always keep focused on your goals, and work hard to get the job done.

* * *

It is important to be happy with the goals you are pursuing.

chapter two

Come Into the Mountains, Dear Friend

Come into the mountains, dear friend
Leave society and take no one with you
but your true self
Get close to nature
Your everyday games will be insignificant
Notice the clouds spontaneously forming patterns
and try to do that with your life

Knowing that we had a huge battle ahead to fight for Blue Mountain Arts' survival, my mind flashed back to the laborious, yet exhilarating, birth and growth of Blue Mountain Arts.

In late 1969, after Steve and I had gotten married, we left Princeton University in New Jersey to start a new life in Boulder, Colorado. Steve had just earned a Ph.D. in physics and would be working at the Environmental Sciences Services Administration studying solar physics. I would be freelance writing for magazines and newspapers.

Steve and I felt much more creative surrounded by the beautiful mountains than we did in the crowded streets of the East Coast. I soon realized that I could never go back to live in New York City like I had planned, so I began building my career in Boulder, sending out hundreds of query letters every month to magazines. I also started to write for a local magazine and newspaper. Every day, I walked to the post office to see if I had received acceptances or rejections for my magazine article ideas. Then, no matter how much work I had to do, I met Steve for lunch. We wanted to spend all our time together, not just our nights.

Sometimes an event occurs that changes the course of your life. It may arise spontaneously or develop out of a strong interest or passion. It was a love for writing, for art, and for each other that was at the heart of Steve's and my first creative project. This project eventually led to the beginning of our publishing company, Blue Mountain Arts.

One day, after motorcycling near the majestic foothills of Boulder, I wrote a poem titled "Come Into the Mountains, Dear Friend" for a friend in New York City who was having problems. I thought that if she could be closer to nature, she might feel better.

Steve told me that my poem was beautiful and that it would help my friend.

Then he uttered the words that started us on our life's calling: "I've got a great idea. When I come home tonight, I'm going to illustrate this poem and we'll make it into a poster."

I thought it sounded like a wonderful idea; we could create something together. A poster would combine my writing with Steve's art. Steve's job didn't afford him much opportunity to pursue his hobbies of painting and drawing, and we hadn't been able to spend as much time together as we had wanted to.

When Steve got home that evening, he hand-lettered my "Come Into the Mountains, Dear Friend" poem.

The next day, Steve made a list of the materials we'd need to make a silk-screen poster, and we went to a lumberyard, hardware store, and art store to buy wood, silk remnants, silk-screen paint, and a squeegee. We drove forty miles to a paper distributor in Denver to purchase five hundred sheets of paper at three cents a sheet, as opposed to the twenty-five cents per sheet we'd have to pay at the art store in Boulder. The supplies and paper came to forty dollars, a hefty price for our meager budget.

Steve nailed the pieces of wood into a rectangular frame, stretched and attached the silk to the frame, hinged the frame to a flat piece of wood, and the silk-screen was finished.

I loved watching Steve work at moments like this: the way his brow furrowed with concentration and the intensity in his blue eyes increased as he measured the exact size of the frame. I thought Steve could do or make anything he wanted to, and I wondered how he knew so much about so many things.

That night, Steve drew a silhouette of himself gazing up at a mountain. We cut out stencils of the mountains and lacquered them to the silk-screen. The stencils allowed paint to flow through certain areas of the silk while blocking others. We blended blue and pink paints together to form a soft sunset background, and then we squeegeed purple paint across the silk onto the poster paper to form the mountain.

When the ink started to dry, we placed the stencil of Steve's silhouette onto the paper, trying different positions to see where it looked best. When Steve placed it about one-third the distance from the left side, we immediately said in unison, "That's perfect." If we'd asked fifty people where to place the stencil, we might have gotten fifty different answers, but Steve and I knew that if we put it elsewhere, the design would look off-balance.

Perhaps our agreement was a result of similar instincts or our closeness as a couple—I don't know. But even today, after designing thousands of greeting cards, books, and calendars, as well as offices and rooms in our home, we recognize how unique and important it is that Steve and I have the same sense of design, proportion, symmetry, and feeling for art. If we did not share the same artistic eye or had strong contrary opinions, working together could have been tumultuous, hurting our relationship rather than strengthening it.

The next night, using black paint, we silk-screened my "Come Into the Mountains" poem together with the silhouette of Steve. When I lifted the first completed poster from the screen, I gasped. I hadn't been able to imagine exactly how it would look until I saw it with my own eyes and held it in my own hands. The colors, the picture, the poem—they worked together to create an image of peace in the mountains.

Together we had transferred an intangible idea, through our poem and illustration, onto paper. It was an extraordinary experience, and we wanted to do it again.

So later that night, Steve hand-lettered another poem—one I had recently written to him while we were hiking together.

When Steve got home from work the next day, he drew a silhouette of the two of us holding hands. Several days later we completed making a poster that represented our love for each other.

Our friends liked our posters, and they suggested we sell them to stores. Steve and I brought samples to Hatch's, a bookstore in the local shopping mall.

I walked into the store. The walls were covered with black light, fluorescent posters with bright, bold designs that included paintings of rock stars, such as Jimi Hendrix who was very popular at the time.

Our pastel-colored posters bore poems about nature and love. They would not fit in with the psychedelic pictures on the walls!

Despite my doubts, and much to my surprise, Mr. West, the store manager, accepted twelve of our posters on consignment.

"I'll hang one poster up on the wall and take eleven more," he said. "If they sell, I'll pay you. If they don't sell, you take them back."

His proposal sounded fair enough, so we went to our apartment to retrieve twelve posters and delivered them to Mr. West. On the way home, we stopped at an organic grain store to buy cereal, and the owner agreed to take two of each poster on consignment as well.

Then we drove to the tiny mountain town of Nederland and stopped at a sandy area off the road. We attached the posters to our car, posted a "For Sale" sign, and waited for the customers to line up.

An hour later, one car stopped.

"Is this the way to Central City?" the passenger shouted out the window.

"Yes," I said, disappointed.

For five more hours, we watched people flash peace signs out their windows, honk their horns, and smile at the two hippies in the leather headbands and flower-painted car. But no one bought any posters.

"I wonder if one of our posters will ever be sold," Steve said.

Two weeks later, Steve and I were browsing in the nonfiction section of Hatch's Bookstore when a man grabbed Steve's arm. It was Mr. West. We had been avoiding him because we didn't want to hear the news of our miserable failure as poster artists.

"I've been trying to find you," he said breathlessly. "I sold out of all your posters, even the one on the wall, but I didn't know how to contact you. I owe you thirty dollars, and I want twelve more posters."

We were very pleasantly shocked.

As we motorcycled home to pick up more posters, we discussed ideas for new designs.

Steve and I work so well together. He edits my poems and I suggest changes to his artwork. We've always created collaboratively. If we don't agree with each other, then I have the final say about my poems and Steve has the final say about his art. We work toward the same goal: to convey a feeling via a poem, with a soft, sensitive illustration and background. Since we trust and support our critics—each other—we have more confidence in the final result.

Steve and I loved our new hobby, but we couldn't continue to silk-screen in our small apartment. We rented a small, red-brick house on a street with many old homes. Because we couldn't afford the rent, we soon sublet most of the house and moved into the basement.

Our new dwelling had a red cement floor, and like most residents of a studio apartment, we did our best to create "rooms." Our "bedroom" consisted of our bed, stereo, and tape recorder. A toilet and tiny shower stood a few yards away; beyond that, a sink and a counter with a hot plate constituted our "kitchen."

We hung five rows of clothesline at one end of the basement to save floor space, and we were ready to begin our silk-screen hobby in our new studio/home.

For several hours we trekked back and forth across the long room, pouring, squeegeeing, and hanging posters to dry, until we'd finished the backgrounds on 250 posters. I didn't have the stamina to go on any longer, and the paint smell was giving me a headache. Steve cleaned the screen, and the next morning, I neatly stacked all the dry posters so when Steve returned home from work that evening we'd be ready to continue silk-screening.

Before we started to silk-screen that night, I opened a window to prevent the fumes from exploding, and the wind dried the paint on the screen, causing it to clog. It was such a mess. Steve took the silk-screen outside, rubbed it clean with a chemical, and after a couple of hours we were able to silk-screen again. Well into the night, a little dizzy from the paint fumes, we decided to rest outside in our double sleeping bag (Steve had sewn two sleeping bags together). We crept out to the backyard, drank a few beers, and watched the stars twinkle in the clear, black sky. The night was magical, and I knew the creation of our posters was the start of something special.

At three o'clock in the morning, after coffee and a cold shower, we started silk-screening again. We finished five hundred posters by six that morning. The labor-intensive process was tiring, but the end product made it worthwhile.

A couple of hours later we went our separate ways to work: writing, studying, and wondering what the other was doing. It was a different world from the one we had constructed in our basement. There, among the drying posters, paint fumes, and silk-screens, we had created the perfect work environment: one where we could be together doing something we enjoyed.

That morning I packed up 110 posters, grabbed a cup of coffee, and drove to the University of Northern Colorado Bookstore in Greeley to find out if anyone outside of Boulder liked our posters.

As I drove, I watched the beautiful scenery pass by. I felt as though I were the only person in the world. I pulled over to the side of the highway and stared at the mountains. I walked to a fence and saw hundreds of cows grazing on acres of land.

I could have admired the scenery forever, but I had to get to a meeting: my first real appointment selling our posters.

"Is Mr. Gadeken in?" I asked the secretary at the university bookstore.

"Yes he is," she said. "But he has an appointment with a salesman."

"*I'm* the salesman."

She eyed my jean shorts and T-shirt and called for the manager.

Mr. Gadeken and I talked for about an hour. I told him that Steve and I had recently moved to Colorado and how we had made the posters. In the midst of our conversation he said, "I think the college kids will love them. I'll take fifty rolled. When can I have delivery?"

I told him I'd be back in a little while.

I raced out to the car, and in ninety-five degree weather, I rolled fifty posters, placed them in bags, made out a sales slip, entered the sale into our log, and carried the bundle to the bookstore. Mr. Gadeken laughed when he saw my armload.

"You really do it all yourself, don't you?" he said. Then he asked me to help him find a good location in the store for our posters.

Buoyed by the delight of my sale, I drove to another college town, Fort Collins. Mr. Roley, a kind-hearted man who owned a large, attractive gift and card store, bought several dozen of our posters.

By the end of the day, I had sold eighty-six posters, and this time everyone had our phone number in case they wanted to reorder. I called Steve, and we made arrangements to celebrate at Señor Miguel's, our favorite restaurant.

I started the long drive home, stopping once more to soak up the scenery. I felt so good. I had written, designed, and created posters with the person I loved. Though our audience was tiny, the idea of having a following at all was exhilarating.

I wanted to expand our new hobby. Excitement and determination charged through me. The possibilities were limitless! I felt successful, happy, independent, and so in love with Steve. As I looked up at the mountains, my eyes filled with tears of joy.

come into the mountains , dear friend
leave society and take no one with you
but your true self
get close to nature
your everyday games will be insignificant
notice the clouds spontaneously forming patterns
and try to do that with your life

— susan polis schutz

Our "Come Into the Mountains, Dear Friend" silk-screen poster, 1970.

Silk-screening our posters in our basement studio/home, 1970.

Expect to fail, learn from your failures, and then ignore them. Focus on your successes.

* * *

Turn negative situations into positive ones.

chapter three

Hopes and Dreams

Men are told by society
that they always have to be strong
and put on a tough exterior
to block out all sensitive "unmanly" feelings
It is drilled into men from birth
that they are leaders
that they must achieve
that they must succeed in a career
Men are judged their whole lives
by the power they have
and how much money they earn
I would hate to have
such overwhelming pressure
threatening my entire life

For the next couple of months, Steve went to his physics lab each day while I wrote magazine articles. In my spare time, I tried to sell our posters by knocking on every possible store door. Most nights we stayed up late creating new designs for S&S Creations (the name we printed at the bottom of our posters). For all I know, we might still be making posters as a hobby if my father hadn't had an operation in 1970.

One day in early fall, my mom, June Polis, called me from my parents' apartment in Peekskill, New York. In a troubled voice, she told me that my dad had just gone into the hospital to have an emergency thyroid operation. Steve and I flew to New York, posters in hand, thinking we'd give some of them to family members. Immediately upon arriving, we rushed to the hospital near Peekskill. The smell of hospitals—medicines, disinfectants, and sickness—makes me depressed and lightheaded. My sense of smell is extremely sensitive, and I remember most places I've been to by their scents.

I spoke softly to my father, who was hooked up to tubes and machines in intensive care, and tried to control the sadness that overcame me. I was watching my father drift in and out of consciousness, sad that he was ill, that we were in a hospital, and that his recent years had been so joyless.

My father was 5'7" with a broad build, fair skin, and thin, straight, gray hair combed back with Vaseline. His big dimples emphasized his keen, cynical sense of humor. Dad was the sixth and youngest child of Russian immigrants, and he was the only one of his siblings born in America. Intelligent, sensitive, conservative, creative, and philosophical, he graduated from Columbia University and then Brooklyn Law School, but he never took the Bar exam or practiced law. Instead, he started a wire-plug business with his brother. When the business began to fail, he moved the factory to Peekskill, New York, a very small, country town where I was raised, ninety minutes from New York City. When he couldn't afford to pay the rent, he moved the business to the basement of our house. I remember helping him spin spools of colored threads around wires in the 1950's, before plastic-coated wires were available.

When I was a child, my father and I listened to Cincinnati Reds games on the radio together. We played catch every day, and he taught me how to throw hardball. He encouraged me to play sports, work hard, and be tough. My parents never bought me dolls (probably because they knew I wouldn't play with them), and I've always been grateful to them for not treating me as most other parents treated their daughters back then. When I was older, they probably would have preferred that I acted more like a "proper" young woman, but I don't think they realized that they had raised me to be strong and independent.

I have many happy memories of my dad singing while he played the mandolin or banjo, going for long drives in the country together, and sleigh riding in the winter. But after his business failed and he lost all his remaining money in the stock market, I remember him mainly as a depressed, sad, but loving man. He became a victim, succumbing to what our relatives call the "Polis syndrome of depression": a nagging sense of pessimism and hopelessness. Most probably if he had gone to a doctor for his depression he could have been helped. But back then depression was a stigma and it was hidden. He floundered around for years with no real interests, no particular goals, and little motivation to work. His self-esteem deteriorated with his inability to pay household bills. I worried that he might never again experience true happiness.

We sat with my dad for a couple of hours, and all of a sudden, a weak David Polis awoke and smiled at the sight of us. We had tried to brighten up the dreary hospital room by hanging some of our posters on the walls and being as cheery as possible.

At midnight, long after visiting hours ended, Steve and I were about to go to sleep in my parents' apartment when the phone rang.

"I love your posters!" my father exclaimed into the phone. "I showed them to my doctor and he wants one! Do you have one you could sign for him? I could sell a lot of these posters. What time will you be here tomorrow?"

For the first time in years, Dad sounded excited about something. I had always wished he had something to do to get his mind off himself and his problems. Could S&S Creations resurrect my dad's excitement? Could we give him something to look forward to?

The next morning, we arrived at the hospital to find my dad in a wheelchair, showing off the posters to a patient in another room. When Dad came back to his room, he told us that the patient wanted to buy the mountain poster for his daughter.

"Everyone loves your posters," he said, showing his dimples in a wide grin. "I can't wait to get out of here."

My mother and I stared at the seemingly reborn man before us. Dad always made a habit of discussing his aches and pains, but this morning, not once did he mention them.

Later in the day, Dad took me aside. "I have something for you. It's a poem I wrote last night."

Tell the world I'm out
I want to meditate
I want to learn who I am and why I am here
I want to meditate and think about the wonders of nature
I want to be free to feel the meaning of life

"I feel better than I have in a long time," he said. "It's because of your posters, Sue." He smiled shyly. "Maybe my poem could be a poster, too.

"When I get out of the hospital, ship five hundred posters to me, and I'll sell them as fast as they come in."

The change in my father overwhelmed me. Mom had always said he'd once been a prosperous and enthusiastic businessman who played tennis, was in a band, and dressed stylishly. For the first time, I saw what he must have been like back then. In a matter of days, I watched thirty years of gray depression fall away from his face.

Steve and I now had a very important reason for making our posters: my dad. His new attitude encouraged us to make the posters into a real business.

"Go sell your posters while you are on the East Coast! The stores'll sell out of them in no time," Dad insisted.

We decided to listen to him. We rented a car, and as we bade goodbye to my parents, Dad called out to me, "Call me after every sales call! I can't wait to hear how many posters you sell."

Before embarking on our "business trip," we stopped to swim at the Blue Mountain Reservoir right outside Peekskill. As we splashed and played in the cool water, the tension of the week started to drain away. Steve mentioned that the name "Blue Mountain" reminded him of Colorado. At the same moment, we realized we'd just found a meaningful, new name for our business. We would be Blue Mountain Arts.

Our first stops were the "head shops" in New Brunswick, New Jersey. Head shops were a new phenomenon then, popping up in cities and towns across the country. They all seemed to have four traits in common: They were small, cluttered, opened at whatever time the young owners woke up (sometimes at noon), and closed late at night. Often colored beads, black light posters, candles, and avant-garde clothing were draped over or sat on every available surface. Marijuana paraphernalia came in all forms: paper, ceramic, glass, and wood. Everything in a head shop seemed to be for the purpose of getting high, enhancing the experience of getting high, or appearing to be high.

The first storeowner we visited loved the posters, but couldn't afford to buy any. He offered a trade, and we dashed to the clothes racks.

After a few moments, we found a gray, double-breasted, tweed jacket with silver buttons. Steve tried it on, and he looked like a rock star. I kissed him.

"You've got to have this jacket," I said, and the owner offered it in exchange for twelve posters. We gave him fifteen and ran to a phone booth to share the news with my parents.

"It's about time you owned a jacket," Dad said to Steve, laughing. "Remember, save one of each poster for samples. If you sell more posters than you have, tell the stores you'll mail the posters to them."

At a bookstore, we sold two posters and bought lunch with the money. Then we decided to split up, with Steve on one side of the street and me on the other. We visited head shops, gift stores, and bookstores. Several more storeowners bought our posters, but most looked at us as if we were from Mars.

We then went to the Seton Hall University Bookstore where the buyer studied our "Come Into the Mountains" poster.

"You spelled 'spontaneously' wrong," he said.

We'd spelled it "spontaneonly." We had printed five hundred posters that contained a spelling error! Embarrassment colored my cheeks as I realized we'd sold misspelled posters, but fortunately no one else ever mentioned to us that they noticed it.

Our next stop was Princeton, New Jersey. A gift-store owner bought five posters, and when Steve told him he had a Ph.D. from Princeton University, the owner laughed.

"What's a Princeton Ph.D. doing selling posters?" he asked. "I thought you fellas were all stuffy and academic."

We left Princeton happy, laughing at the man's confusion. Steve, with his long, dark hair, thick mustache, and easygoing attitude, didn't even come close to the typical 1960's Princeton student.

Our appearance, which had gotten both of us into trouble over the years, now worked for us when we sold our posters. People knew we were down to earth and believed in what the posters said, and our enthusiasm became infectious. I knew, though, that the posters themselves were the key. Their messages transcended people's doubts and differences, proving to me that everyone has the same basic emotions, needs, and feelings. Whether in the head shops of New Brunswick or the gift stores of Princeton, people seemed to identify with our messages.

The next morning, after sleeping in our car, we drove to stores near the University of Pennsylvania and sold out of the rest of our posters. Remembering my dad's advice, we kept a few posters as samples so we could show them to the Penn Bookstore.

The manager's wife greeted us at the door. She loved the posters and introduced us to her husband. The couple, like us, wanted to spend all their time together. When the husband was offered the management job, he insisted that his wife become the buyer for the gift department. They spoke of their plans for the store with enthusiasm. I love it when people are so excited about their goals.

We confessed that we, too, wanted to spend all our time together and that Steve had thought seriously about leaving physics. They were the only people who didn't think we were crazy and encouraged us to work together. I smiled. We left the store with our first order to be mailed and two new friends.

After a mad dash to the airport, we missed the plane to Denver. Looking on the bright side, we decided that we might as well take the opportunity to drive to Boston to sell our posters.

We heard every type of rejection: "The buyer isn't in"; "We don't have money to buy"; "We don't want to carry posters"; "No one wants to read poetry on a poster"; "I only carry posters with pictures, not word posters"; and on and on. After four intense, long days of selling, we realized that for every eight stores we called on, only one would buy our posters.

Right after each rejection, we'd quickly go to more stores until someone finally liked the posters and bought them.

Instinctively, we would ignore the many failures and focus on the positive encounters.

Our next stop was the Harvard University Coop in Cambridge. The Coop's several floors of merchandise were overwhelming. It resembled a department store more than a bookstore, but we swallowed our misgivings and marched in to meet the manager.

"Hi. I'm Mr. McDonald. What can I do for you?" he asked in his New England accent. We showed him the posters, and he showed them to a young buyer.

I held my breath as he read each poem.

"I think Harvard students will buy them," he said. "They're refreshing and original. Please send me one dozen of each design, and make sure I know how to contact you if I need to reorder." He invited us into his office, and we spent an hour chatting with him. He was so enthusiastic and friendly.

"Steve, can you imagine!" I shouted as we left Harvard, "Harvard's going to sell our posters. This is unbelievable!"

We drove to the airport, stopping at several more stores along the way. This time we managed to get on the airplane to Colorado ten minutes before it took off.

Instead of being disappointed when we had missed the airplane to Denver, we were happy to have had the opportunity for another day of selling. Despite the fact that by a large majority most stores did not want or even like our posters, we didn't give in to rejection, but persevered until we found storeowners who did like our poetry and art. As long as the situation was something we had control over, we always had a positive attitude and were able to turn things around for the best.

My dad's goal for Steve and me to sell our posters in the East was realized. Most importantly, my dad, who went into the hospital physically sick and mentally unhappy, would come out of the hospital a new person full of Blue Mountain hopes and dreams.

Most tasks take much longer to do than you think they will.

* * *

Assume that things will go wrong, especially when you are in a rush.

* * *

Work is not "work" when you enjoy what you are doing.

chapter four

No Sleep

One thing Steve and I learned right away was that "if a wave comes, go with it." So when a woman called to offer us a last-minute chance to be a part of the National Stationery Show, we jumped at the opportunity.

My dad, looking out for our long-term interests, had called to enter us in the show, but had only succeeded in getting us placed on a long waiting list in case someone cancelled. He had told me that the Stationery Show was one of the biggest trade shows of the year. It was being held in what was then the New York Coliseum at Columbus Circle, with three floors of manufacturers showing their posters, greeting cards, and stationery products. All the major companies would be there, along with salespeople, distributors, and other people in the industry. Storeowners and buyers would be there to observe and buy the products they liked.

When he heard we'd been offered a space, he was thrilled. "Call her back immediately and say yes!" Dad exclaimed.

I called the woman and accepted her offer despite the five-hundred-dollar entry fee—our total income from all our poster sales. My dad said that we were lucky to get the booth.

Steve and I had no idea how a trade show worked, nor did we know anything about the greeting card industry. But we did know that this would be a great learning experience. Because Steve had to work in his laboratory, I would have to go alone, but the National Stationery Show, as my dad said, was not an opportunity we could miss. I could meet new people, see how other companies function, and maybe even sell enough posters to pay for the cost of the show.

The next day while Steve was at work, we called each other every hour because we realized we couldn't possibly fill a big booth with only five posters. We discussed our ideas for creating posters with new poems and photographs.

On the weekend, we went into the mountains and took over a hundred black-and-white photographs, selecting three to make into posters. For one of them, Steve placed the camera on a huge rock and set the self-timer. As I ran along the edge of a cliff, he pressed the button, then ran to be in the picture with me. The pose resulted in a lovely image of Steve and me running against a background of perfect cotton-ball clouds. Steve attached a yellow filter that deepened and dramatized the cloud tones. We brought the photos and poems to a local printer.

"Are you kidding?" the printer said when we asked him to print five hundred copies. "I can't get that done in a week!"

We turned to walk out.

"Wait," the printer said. "I'll give it a shot."

We picked out a matte paper and a deep, reddish-brown color for the ink, which would make the pictures look softer. I left my poems to be superimposed on the photographs.

A week later, when we returned to get our finished posters, we saw that they had been printed in black ink, giving them a harsh, dark look.

"You made a mistake." I said. "We can't sell posters like this. They look awful! I'm leaving for New York City in three days! You have to reprint these by tomorrow!"

"That's impossible."

"If Steve and I can silk-screen hundreds of posters by hand in one day, then I am sure you can print these posters on your machine!"

"I'll reprint two of the designs, but you'll have to keep the third one in black."

"Well, I guess that's okay," I said, satisfied.

The crowd at the National Stationery Show would have thousands of designs from which to choose, and ours had to be as good as they could be to stand out and epitomize our vision.

We left the printer and rushed home to make a poster from my dad's poem, "Tell the World I'm Out." Steve hand-lettered the poem and drew a man climbing to the top of a mountain surrounded by purple sky.

With just five days left before the show, we set to work silk-screening new posters. The paint had hardened from the day before, and Steve couldn't clean the silk, so we went to the store and bought a chemical that was supposed to remove the paint from the screen. The chemical didn't help at all, and when we accidentally spilled a few drops, it dissolved the red paint off the floor. Steve finally had to stretch another piece of silk and remake the film. When we finished running the one hundred foregrounds, we realized the copyright symbol had smudged on every poster, so I had to hand-letter the copyright information at the bottom of each one. We wondered if we'd ever be ready. Everything that could go wrong did! And the preparation list was endless.

We would come to realize that most tasks take much longer to do than you think they will. And you have to assume that things will go wrong, especially when you are in a rush.

We had decided to make our posters into greeting cards. We gave the designs to a silk-screener in Denver, because we thought that a professional silk-screener would do a more efficient job than we could. But when we went to pick up the cards, the ink was light, the cards were smudged, and the overall quality was terrible. We would have been embarrassed to have our names associated with these cards, so we knew we'd have to remake them ourselves. We had very little time left to silk-screen at least one hundred copies of six different greeting cards.

As we cut out the stencils for the greeting cards, a neighbor poked her head inside the door.

"How about going out with Rich and me?"

"Sorry, Katy, but we're really busy," Steve said.

"You're always really busy. Don't you ever stop working and have fun?"

"We're having lots of fun!" I said. She shook her head, and we didn't even hear her leave. Not only was it fun, but I loved the way the card-sized posters looked and couldn't stop admiring them.

I typed order forms with the wrong price and had to redo them. Steve had designed a metal display rack for our cards, but the manufacturer never mailed it to us; eventually, my father drove to Briarcliff Manor to pick it up and bring it directly to the National Stationery Show.

We went to get the final photograph posters, but they weren't finished—I'd have to stop by on my way to the airport the next day.

In the meantime, we had another idea. We had recently found a light-brown, parchment-like paper that we thought would be a lovely paper for greeting cards. We decided that Steve would use brown ink and hand-letter some of my poems onto this paper. After the ink dried, we hand-folded the paper into small greeting cards. We were so excited to see how attractive these cards looked. We glued some of the cards to pieces of wood we had shellacked, and we then had greeting cards, posters, and wood plaques with our poetry and artwork on them.

Finally I'd had enough. We had only averaged about three hours of sleep a night all week, and I desperately needed some rest before the show. During that hectic week, the only reason we were able to work so intensely, churning out creation after creation, was because we enjoyed what we were doing.

As I was about to fall asleep at five in the morning, Steve suggested that he hand-letter the poems and illustrations onto parchment paper scrolls.

"That's great, Steve...." I couldn't even think about making anything else.

"You go to sleep. They'll be ready for you," he said.

"I can't go to sleep without you," I protested feebly. "I'll just rest in bed and wait for you...," I said as I fell asleep.

Later that morning, we carefully packed eight cartons with posters, greeting cards, wood plaques, order forms, and a portfolio with the original parchment scrolls Steve had just hand-lettered. I was ready to go to New York City.

Despite my excitement about the show, I didn't want to leave Steve. We promised each other that we would never be apart again.

I boarded the plane to New York where I was about to experience the many different facets of the greeting card and poster business.

If you blame all setbacks on external circumstances, you are fooling yourself. Accept responsibility for what you do.

* * *

Not everyone will like everything you do. Don't let negative comments deter you from reaching your goal.

chapter five

The National
Stationery Show

My plane from Colorado arrived at Kennedy Airport and had to circle the city for two hours because of a rainstorm. After the plane landed, I carried one box at a time from the luggage area to the bus terminal, rode the bus to the old Coliseum building where the trade show was being held, and nearly screamed when I saw that it was closed. I sat down on the boxes, tired, wet, and hungry, and then went to a nearby phone booth to call my brother, Robert Polis.

"Robbie! Can you pick me up? I'm soaked, and I have eight boxes of cards and posters with me, and they're getting wet."

"Okay!" my brother shouted, laughing. "You're lucky I have a car."

Indeed I was. I hung up the phone and was thankful that at least some New Yorkers owned cars. Forty minutes later, Robbie, his wife, Rae, and I carried the eight boxes up to their apartment.

The next morning, we carried them back down again. Robbie and Rae dropped me off in front of the Coliseum, and I wondered how I'd get my boxes upstairs to my exhibition booth.

I had no choice but to leave seven of the boxes on the street—which, in retrospect, was probably not the smartest thing to do—while I brought one up the escalator. A guard stopped me.

"Ya can't carry boxes of merchandise into da show," he said. "Ya hafta register with da drayage company, and it'll cost ya about fifty bucks."

"I can't afford that," I said, shifting the weight of the box in my arms. "I brought these boxes from Colorado. I have to get them into my booth." I didn't care how big the guard was, and even if I'd had fifty dollars, I didn't think I should have to pay for someone to carry my boxes.

"Ya don't break da rules in New York," he said as he accompanied my box and me onto the down escalator.

I wasn't about to give up. I opened a box, took out ten dozen cards, and climbed the escalator again. The guard tried to stop me, but when he realized I was carrying only loose items, he backed off. Buoyed by my small triumph, I wandered around the building until I found booth number 3706: Blue Mountain Arts.

The booth looked like a cave: three blue-curtained walls on a cement floor with no tables, no displays, no signs other than the one with our company name on it, and nothing to fill the huge space. Other companies had ordered tables and chairs in advance, and their booths looked so attractive and professional. Someone told me that if I found some extra tables lying around I could use them. I started laughing uncontrollably. Our small collection of cards, posters, and scrolls would look ridiculous and lost in such a large area. I had to think of a way to fill the booth.

In the meantime, though, I had to get our products up to the booth. For the next four hours, I gathered individual cards and posters in my arms and carried them up the escalators, past the guards, to my booth, then walked back down to the street again. I wandered around at times looking for new escalators so I could avoid the scrutiny of the guards. I made about sixty escalator trips.

Once I'd brought up all the contents of the boxes, I dragged four abandoned, splintered, wooden tables to the booth, bumping into people and drawing stares.

I left the show and ran to Woolworth's across the street, figuring I could spend about five dollars on decorations and still have enough left over for food. I bought blue crepe paper, tape, and ribbons, and called my longtime friend from Peekskill, Helene Amiel. Helene was smart, creative, and aggressive. I knew that she could help me.

Helene and I met each other when we were in the fourth grade, and we became good friends shortly after that. We did everything together: traded comic books, went bicycling, double-dated, went to parties, shared a room our freshman year of college, and just hung out, discovering life. We indulged our serious sides together as well, reading and discussing our favorite authors and attending lectures and plays in New York City. Helene was now an educator with the New York City school system.

By the time Helene arrived, piles of posters, plastic bags, and stacks of loose cards surrounded me. She took one look at the booth and laughed.

"Boy, we'd better fix this up," she said.

Helene and I decorated the booth with long, blue ribbons, to which we stapled the cards. We hung these from the top of the booth, creating a greeting card curtain. Then, as I hammered crepe paper to the table, Helene attached some to the walls.

Suddenly a burly man with sunburnt skin and light-brown, curly hair approached us. "Whaddya girls doin' there?" he yelled.

Helene almost fell off her chair. "We're decorating this booth. What's it look like we're doing?"

"Exhibitors are not allowed to hang anything on da walls or da tables!"

"But everyone has stuff hanging from the walls," I said.

Recognizing our innocence, the man relented. "Honey, in da city, only da official decorator can do that. Ya could be kicked outta da show if they catch ya doin' this. It'll cost ya twenty-five dollars a half-hour, and there's a minimum charge of two hours' work."

"That's ridiculous!" I said, thinking Helene and I could do it in fifteen minutes.

When he finally left the booth, I asked Helene to go after him and distract him while I finished attaching the crepe paper to the tables. If he didn't *see* me decorating the booth, I reasoned, he couldn't know I hadn't paid someone else to do it. I hurried around the booth, hanging more cards and erecting displays, and fifteen minutes later, Helene was still chatting with the man.

"What the hell did you talk to him about?" I asked later.

Helene laughed. "I told him I was a teacher. I asked him to explain the rules. He asked me out. I think he forgot about the booth."

As we were about to leave for the day, a man in uniform entered the booth, holding a box of matches. I nearly screamed, but like a typical New Yorker, he talked so fast I didn't have time to.

It turned out he was from the fire department, and he wanted to make sure my crepe paper didn't burn.

"Are you crazy?" I cried. "Of course it'll burn!"

"Then ya gotta take it down."

"What?"

"Look, Kid, anything attached to da wall or table hasta be fireproof. My job is to test all material in every booth."

"Fireproof material? I've never heard of that!"

"Ya gotta call a company that makes fireproof material for trade shows. And I gotta watch ya take down da crepe paper."

Fifteen minutes later, the booth was back to being sterile and ugly.

Fees to carry boxes, fees to hang things on the walls, and now fireproof material...no one—not the guards, the drayage company, or the fire department—would keep me from making my booth presentable.

That evening, I remembered that my Uncle Paul on Long Island manufactured and sold theater curtains. It seemed likely that they would be fireproof. I called him, and at six the next morning, tired from all the excitement and lack of sleep (I had spent most of the night gluing cards to cardboard), I picked up five large pieces of a pretty, deep-pile, blue-velvet, fireproof curtain. I went to the Coliseum two hours before the show opened, and while no one was watching, I placed the blue velvet on the tables and even managed to hang one piece on the wall.

My mother came in on the early train, carrying an open carton of eight gardenia plants in her slender arms. Within minutes, her plants lent our booth some warmth to surround our poetry and art.

But the family wasn't done chipping in just yet. Rae, Robbie's dignified, sweet, and nonjudgmental wife, who supported us as much as she supported him, suggested the night before the show opened that we design signs to provide information about our products. Bright and early that morning, Rae and Robbie brought several signs that Rae had hand-lettered to our booth, and Robbie hung them on the back curtain.

Robbie looked as cute as ever. He has a small frame, olive skin, wavy brown hair, and dark brown, sleepy eyes. When he smiles, his dimples light up his face. With his cynical sense of humor, he could make any situation fun—even this one.

The five of us—my mother, Robbie, Rae, Helene, and I—stood in the first official Blue Mountain Arts trade-show booth. I wore my new pink and blue, tie-dyed T-shirt, bell-bottom jeans, and brown leather sandals. I even wore a bra, which for me was dressing up.

Full of pride for overcoming all the silly obstacles, we were now ready for our first National Stationery Show to begin.

As I drank my sixth cup of coffee, I watched people walk right by me. I didn't know what to say to them, so I sat back down and waited for customers to come inside my booth. Much like that day that Steve and I tried selling posters on the side of the road in Nederland, three hours passed before I realized I would have to do something, anything, to make someone look at Blue Mountain Arts.

I turned my attention to the couple in a nearby booth. They, too, had cards and posters, and they managed to get people to come into their booth. I listened to their pitch.

"Hi, how are you? We just came in from Long Island. We make some interesting cards, and they're selling fantastically. You should really try them in your store."

I went back to my chair, depressed and losing heart. They sounded like carnival pitchmen. I didn't mind selling to people, but not if I had to sound phony to get them to even look at our creations. I couldn't bring myself to lure people into the booth, but sitting there looking grumpy certainly wasn't doing me any good either.

I wondered if the National Stationery Show was just a big mistake. I missed Steve.

I wrote a poem to Steve:

> *I sit here*
> *bored*
> *I don't feel like talking*
> *to the people here*
> *I don't feel like looking*
> *at this place anymore*
> *I sit here*
> *lonely*
> *realizing that it's not*
> *people or places that*
> *make me happy*
> *It's you*

After writing this, I decided I had better make the best of my situation at the Stationery Show. Steve and I—not to mention my family and friends—had invested so much time and work into this show that I couldn't let it fail. Clearly, I would have to stand in front of my booth and look interested in and excited by all the activity. Helene, dressed in tight, black-leather shorts and a jacket, went off to explore some of the other booths, while I stood in front of mine, trying to muster enthusiasm.

I listened to other vendors' conversations and hoped for some glimpse of genius to assist me.

Across the aisle, a couple displayed an astrological gadget. The owner, a bald man with a protruding belly, consoled me.

"I've been entering trade shows all my life, and it takes a while before you know people here. Once you do, they come back year after year," he said as he watched the passers-by. He peered with bulging eyes at every person that passed, checking their nametags for department store names, convincing some to have their fortunes told.

"There aren't that many storeowners here today," the woman said to me. "It's raining. They're just not coming out today."

They were kind, and I knew they were trying to make me feel better, but that didn't sound right to me. If storeowners wanted to attend this once-a-year event, why would a little rain stop them? I walked around the show and concluded that the crowded booths sold interesting products, and the empty booths sold unappealing items. The couple who had blamed the weather for the lack of customers in their booth sold a bizarre gadget that presumed to tell the future. Who would want to buy that?

Many exhibitors told me that they were having a "great" show. I later realized that some of the exhibitors who were having a "bad" show mentioned the rain, the lack of parking, or whatever excuse their minds conjured up for their misfortune. However, it was really that their products did not fulfill the needs of the storeowners and their customers.

I learned that if you blame all setbacks on external circumstances, you are fooling yourself. If people didn't like our products, it meant that we were not communicating our message properly. We could blame nothing but our own creativity.

As I mused about the quality of Blue Mountain Arts, I felt a hand on my shoulder.

"What are you doing?" I snapped.

A young, chubby man with curly hair grinned. "Oh, I didn't mean to startle you. I was just putting this pin on you." He held up a yellow smiley-face pin.

"I don't want to wear your pin," I told him. He drew back, startled, and left my booth. I watched as he put his pin on everyone who entered the aisle, then lured them into his booth.

I stood before my booth, caught in a dilemma. I didn't want to be obnoxious, like the smiley-face man, or phony, like the couple next to me. Then again, my nonchalant approach certainly was not luring customers to my booth.

"What would I want if I were a customer here?" I wondered. I'd be most attracted to a friendly, sincere vendor, as opposed to an overbearing salesperson. I'd want to talk to someone who let the focus be on a product, not a gimmick. So that's what I decided to do. I stood in front of my booth and smiled in a friendly way. Soon, saying "Hi" to people became very natural.

Eventually, a well-dressed man in a gray, wool suit walked into my booth. We talked for about five minutes, and I learned that he was the owner of Scranton's Bookstore in upstate New York. He sat down and ordered one hundred dollars' worth of cards and posters.

"These are different. I'm in a college town. I think they'll do well there."

"They actually do very well in colleges," I said as I fumbled for my carbon paper and order pad. "I sold the posters to the University of Northern Colorado, and they sold right out." My hands shook a bit as I wrote the order. "I'm sorry I'm so nervous, but this is my first order."

"Well, it's refreshing to see a new face here. Are you representing the company?"

"What do you mean?"

"Are you the New York salesgirl?"

"Oh, no," I laughed. "My husband, Steve, and I own the company. I write the poems, and he does the illustrations. We sell, ship, and do everything."

He seemed surprised by that revelation and asked me how to reorder if the posters and cards sold out. He signed his name to the order, and as he left, I smiled widely, ecstatic. Our first trade show order!

By this time, Steve's intelligent, pretty sisters, Arlene, a chemist, and Janet, a teacher, had joined me and offered to watch the booth while I went to get another cup of coffee. While I was gone, Janet—thrilled about our new venture—sold cards and posters to a couple of stores.

People were coming in and out of the booth regularly now, admiring our work. I wanted to call Steve and tell him about what was going on.

"Mom, do you think you could watch the booth for a few minutes? I want to call Steve."

"Go! Call Steve!" she said, shooing me away.

"She'll probably sell more than I have all morning," I thought as I dashed to a pay phone.

When I returned a half-hour later, Mom confirmed my prediction.

"The owner of a twenty-five store chain was here! He wants to see the owner of Blue Mountain Arts!" Mom was excited as she scanned the aisles for him.

An exhibitor poked his head into the booth. "I can't believe the Fifth Avenue Card Shop was in your booth," he exclaimed breathlessly. "Did they buy?"

"Please let me know when that buyer comes back," said another. "I've got to meet him!"

I'd never heard of Fifth Avenue Card Shop, but they certainly had.

"Is the owner in yet?" a small man in a three-piece suit asked as he approached our booth.

"Here she is," my mother said.

"Where?" he demanded. He stared at me. "This is the owner? Such an owner?"

My mom introduced me to Mr. Cohen who said, "Well, what the hell. Okay. I wanna know what's the biggest discount you'll give me if I order for all my Fifth Avenue Card Shops."

I had never given a discount before. "What were you thinking of?"

"Well, I must have a twenty-five percent discount over your regular discount," he said.

"It's a deal," I said, later realizing that I probably shouldn't have agreed so quickly, especially without finding out what the standard discount was.

"I still can't believe you own the company," he said when we entered my booth. "How old are you—eighteen?"

"I'm twenty-six."

"You look much younger. Write up the order. I'll buy for half my stores, and if they do well, I'll buy for the others. I want them packed in tens."

As he signed the order, he noticed one of his buyers walk by our booth. He called her in and introduced us.

"This girl writes poetry," he said to her.

"Oh, I have a son who writes poetry," she said. "He lives in Colorado Springs."

She wrote down his name and number and gave it to me. We spoke at length about her son, whom she adored. Steve and I always had imagined that successful business people would be cold and distant, but here I was witnessing firsthand the warmth and kindness of the owner and card buyer from one of the largest card-store chains.

As they left the booth, Mr. Cohen asked, "Just tell me one thing: Why on earth did you price the cards at forty-five cents? In my thirty years in the business, I've never seen that price on a card."

"I don't know," I answered. "All the other cards are either twenty-five or fifty cents. We decided that this price would stand out."

He wished me the best of luck, and they laughed as they walked away.

I wondered why he had seemed so surprised that I owned the business. Why shouldn't I? On the other hand, I conceded, I did look young, and the other vendors, salespeople, and customers wore dresses and suits. I preferred looking different, though; it showcased how different our cards were from everyone else's. But just in case customers might think I was too unprofessional, I resolved to dress a little more formally in the future.

An attractive older woman with long, gray hair pulled back with a scarf entered my booth. She owned a resort gift shop in a ski area. She spent an hour with me, reading every poem and telling me how she had spent some time in a Colorado convent. She placed an order for several parchment cards and wandered off into the Hare Krishna booth.

"Do you know who that woman is?" another exhibitor asked. "She is Baroness Maria von Trapp. You know, *The Sound of Music*? The governess who taught music and married the Baron?"

"This is so glamorous!" I thought.

At around twelve-thirty, I watched a young woman march toward my booth followed by a small army of ten men. I loved the fact that, for a change, a woman was the general. As the team from Spencer's Gift Shops walked by, the exhibitors converged on all sides. She glanced at my posters and said she'd come back the next day.

I was starting to enjoy the Stationery Show. The only thing that could have made it better was if Steve had been with me.

A dignified-looking woman approached me and laughed when I asked if she owned a gift store. She ordered two dozen of every card, and after she left, several booth owners descended upon me, practically drooling with eagerness.

"Didja land her?"

"Did she order?"

"What's the big deal?" I asked.

"Don't you know where she's from?"

"Carson something, a store in Chicago."

The man laughed. "That 'Carson something' is Carson Pirie Scott, one of the best department stores in the country. It's even better than Marshall Field's."

"Marshall who?" I wondered. As soon as word got out that she had bought our cards, a steady flow of card manufacturers and storeowners came in to see what had attracted this important buyer to our booth.

The next morning, I woke up early and dressed in a long, maroon, velvet skirt and pink blouse with embroidered flowers on the high collar. As I sat down to drink a cup of coffee in my booth, I leafed through all the orders. I couldn't believe our success!

"I saw your cards yesterday, but you were busy with a customer. I'd like to rep you in Chicago," said Phil Gelman, who seemed to come out of nowhere.

I jumped. The man had entered my booth while I wasn't looking.

"How are you paid?"

"I'm paid at the end of every month," he answered. "You pay me fifteen percent of my sales at the end of every month."

"What if the store hasn't paid me yet?"

"You still pay me, and if the store doesn't ever pay, I return the commission to you."

"I don't like the part about paying you before I'm paid," I said.

"That's the way everyone does it," he said.

I told him I would let him know. It just didn't sound right to me. I decided to do research on this matter even though he appeared to be very honest and forthright.

After Mr. Gelman (who soon became our first representative) left my booth, a small, energetic young man bounded in.

"Hi, Doll! I've got something for you!" He handed me six orders.

"Where did you get these?"

"I'm Dan Weston. Don't you remember me?"

I did. I remembered that I had called several stores in Michigan asking them for the name of an honest representative, and each one of them had recommended Dan Weston. I then sent Dan a letter asking him to represent Blue Mountain Arts in Michigan, but he had lost some of our samples.

"I told you in our last phone call I wanted to show the cards to a few accounts of mine. And here's what they thought!"

I stared at the orders. He'd sold one thousand dollars' worth of cards and posters! I asked him how I should pay him, and the method coincided with what the Chicago representative had told me: fifteen percent of the month's sales at the end of each month. Dan volunteered to help me in any way he could, and he had the kindest, most honest eyes.

I couldn't get over how nice everyone was. I surveyed the booths around me, amazed at the sudden growth of our little company into a business that was in a trade show and had a sales rep. I went to the refreshment stand and bought a donut to celebrate.

When I returned to my booth, a heavyset woman wearing a lot of makeup, jewelry, and a turban on her head was waiting for me.

"What is your relationship to this company, young woman?" she asked.

"Well, I'm the owner, and I also write poems."

"Really! Tell me a little about yourself."

I told her about Steve and me and how we had started making cards. She produced and hosted a radio show in New York and invited me to be a guest on her program. I eagerly accepted her offer.

We shook hands and made logistical arrangements. I couldn't believe it. I was about to experience show business. However, I would soon realize that I had made the right choice in not following my childhood dream of becoming an actress.

Right after the trade show closed for the day, Helene and I went to the radio station. I sat down with a panel of guests that included a professor and the head of a philosophical organization that studied ethics, and within minutes we were "on the air." Though well-meaning, the producer-host took herself a bit too seriously. She called her three guests "virtually intrinsic people," and when we got around to talking about anything controversial, she steered the conversation back to happy topics. I fumbled my way through my first live radio interview, but the high moment of the program came during the commercial break. First they played an ad for prune juice, followed by one for soft toilet paper.

I looked at Helene, who was sitting quietly in the corner, and burst into laughter. No matter how hard I tried, I couldn't speak without laughing for the rest of the show.

Helene and I left the radio station giggling, and I sighed with relief that my show business debut hadn't been on television.

The next morning I had breakfast in a coffee shop in Greenwich Village. I noticed a college bookstore nearby, and I sold posters to this shop. I met the earthy owner, Len Riggio, who seemed to me to be the quintessential New Yorker. Full of pragmatism and energy, he owned about six college bookstores at the time, which was enough to impress me. That same year, he bought a local Barnes & Noble bookstore. Little did I realize that he would expand Barnes & Noble into one of the world's largest bookstore chains.

At the end of the next day, which was the last day of the Stationery Show, we took down our booth decorations. I thought about the whirlwind I had just been through. Steve and I had created so many different avenues for our poetry and art, and I had been through the rigmarole of setting up my booth, meeting the storeowners, and making my first publicity appearance on radio. I couldn't help but feel giddy at the new success of Blue Mountain Arts.

During the Stationery Show, several hundred storeowners had come into our booth. Of course, not all the feedback was positive. More people disliked our cards than liked them. They told me in no uncertain terms: "They're too small"; "No one wants poetry on a greeting card"; "There are too many words"; "I don't like double-folded cards"; "It doesn't say 'Happy Birthday'"; "The price is crazy"; "They're just so different from other cards"; "The colors are too dull..."

Over the next thirty years, I'd hear the same negative comments again and again ad nauseum. Though people's criticisms hurt us sometimes, we never allowed their words to discourage us.

My confidence in our works—and in our mission—overrode the doubters and their remarks. And I still believe to this day that if we continue to create products that people buy to help them communicate, then we've succeeded.

Try to do what you enjoy, despite the risks.

* * *

When you follow your passion, you want to do the best job you can and your chance of success increases. Pursuing what you like to do is a "success" in itself.

chapter six

Land of the Free

"Bert! What are you doing here?" I stared out our front door at my young cousin. Though he was no longer the ten-year-old boy I remembered, I recognized his sweet, friendly face immediately. His long, thin, brown hair rested on his shoulders. True to my father's side of the family, he was soft-spoken and mellow, with a biting, self-deprecating sense of humor.

"Just passing through," he said. "I thought I'd look you up."

I laughed. One thing Steve and I had learned was that when you live in a small, hip town like Boulder, anyone who's ever heard of you will call you if they are in or near Colorado, be they fifth cousins three times removed or the daughter of your aunt's best friend. And in the early 1970's, plenty of people "passed through" Boulder.

The hippie movement was ending, and many ex-hippies, hippies-to-be, and people looking for a better life arrived in Boulder hoping to find salvation in the mountains and outdoor life. Thus it was that Bert Polis—my first cousin whom I hadn't seen in fifteen years—joined Blue Mountain Arts.

Bert had been wandering around the country and had just arrived in Boulder. I welcomed him into our small basement apartment, and we talked late into the night. He'd been a teacher, he said, but had recently quit. He planned to travel, make money wherever he could, then go back to graduate school. He needed time to find himself.

When Steve and I showed Bert our posters, we all thought of the same idea at once: Bert could earn money by selling our posters as he traveled.

A week later, we loaded five hundred posters into the trunk of Bert's old car and bade him goodbye as he headed west. He had potential as a salesperson. He was likeable and had a trusting face, but despite his attributes, we didn't expect him to sell many posters. He seemed more interested in socializing and having philosophical discussions than working, so we were shocked when he called us a month later.

"I've sold posters to the University of San Francisco, Mills College in Oakland, Carmel Drug Store, and Shakespeare & Company in Berkeley," he reported, reeling off the names. "In June alone, I sold $550.85 worth of posters, and I'm meeting the neatest people. I went out to dinner last night with the owner of a bookstore, and I'm partying tonight with the buyer for a head shop! This is so much fun!" His achievements were impressive and showed us that California had a terrific audience for our message.

A year later, Steve had to attend an astrophysics conference in San Francisco. I didn't want to spend time away from him or pass up an opportunity to sell some posters in California, so I decided to join him.

While Steve was at the conference, I walked along Telegraph Avenue, the main street in Berkeley's university district, with our posters in hand. In many of the stores I stopped in, owners and buyers remembered Bert and placed orders for more posters and cards.

No matter where I went in California—Santa Cruz, Berkeley, San Francisco—the atmosphere was free and unique. I loved the college campuses in California. Students congregated outside studying, nibbling on their lunches, throwing Frisbees, talking in small groups, and listening to fellow students play their guitars. At San José State University, I attended a student art fair, and at UC Santa Cruz, I sold posters to the student store. The manager even helped me carry the posters from my car to the store.

After the conference ended, Steve and I traveled all over Northern California, selling our cards and posters in artists' communities, such as Carmel and Monterey, admiring the landscape in every city. We were in awe of the beauty of the Northern California Pacific, with its wild and dramatic waves crashing against the cliffs and rocks. Steve created a painting of a cypress tree that stood near the ocean, a painting that later became the cover of my second book, *I Want to Laugh, I Want to Cry.*

I wrote to Steve:

*The ocean brought me peace
the wind gave me energy
the sun warmed my spirit
the flowers showed me life
but you made me feel love*

We were attracted to the free California lifestyle: the "do your own thing" attitude that prevailed no matter where we went.

During our short time in California, Steve and I drove more than eight hundred miles and sold over one thousand posters and cards. On our last night there, my father called from Peekskill.

"Ever hear of Waldenbooks?" he asked. "Guess how many posters I just sold to them?"

"I—"

"One hundred of each design! That's our biggest sale yet! I told you that you had a winner!"

Not only was this the largest order we'd ever gotten, but my dad's voice sounded incredibly uplifted, strong, and confident. He was so happy.

Dad's call was a great end to our trip. What a night to celebrate! We were in California, land of freedom. Life at that moment was perfect!

On the trip back to Boulder, Steve and I decided that we didn't want this freedom to end. The next day, he would tell his boss at the government research lab where he worked that he wouldn't be applying for a job with them after his two-year position ended.

Needless to say, Steve's colleagues weren't as excited about our plan as we were, but when the time came for Steve to leave, they graciously threw him a going-away party.

"Are you sure you know what you're doing?" Steve's associate, Connie, asked him at the party. Connie was a very smart physicist at a time when there were very few women in this field. "You'll be throwing away all the years you studied to get a Ph.D. You'll have trouble getting back into physics," she warned Steve.

"Connie, if I really wanted to, I think I could," Steve said. "But right now, I don't think I'll want to return. I'd prefer to study physics as a hobby."

"You don't know the government. Once you're here, you have a job for life. It's absolute job security, but once you leave, that's it. Besides, even if you were able to come back to your job, you'd be a year behind in the physics world. How could you catch up?"

Steve explained that if he stayed in physics, he would only see me at lunch and at night and that we'd never be able to travel around America. He told Connie, "Now's the time for me to do what I want, and that's what I intend to do."

Connie shook her head, but held Steve's hand. The idea of Steve and me traipsing around the country selling posters worried her.

The wife of one of the scientists approached me. "You know, Honey, when I was a newlywed wife, I had to live apart from my husband," she said. "He had an important government job to do, and I let him do it."

"I'm not a newlywed wife," I said. The word "wife" sounded so much like "slave" to me. It didn't describe our love or our relationship. I was not a wife. I was a woman married to Steve. We wanted to spend our lives together, not sacrificing, but sharing and being together.

"But one of you has to make sacrifices," she continued, sounding more and more like one of the sitcom moms of the 1950's. "He's the breadwinner, so you should be the one making sacrifices."

"He's not the only breadwinner," I said, feeling myself get angry. "I make money as a writer, and I'll be earning more with time." I explained that we wanted to build a career together, whether it involved working as waiters, making jewelry, or selling our poetry and art. I told her that we didn't need a lot of money to be happy, just enough to eat and pay the rent.

"Oh, you're just young and idealistic," she said, looking so smug in her certainty. "You'll change."

Steve grabbed my arm and led me away before I could say something I'd later be sorry for.

"You know, there are physics conferences all over the country," another physicist said. "If there's enough money, the government will pay for you to attend them. Wouldn't that be a better way to see the United States?"

"No," Steve answered. "Susan and I want to see the country together at our own pace." Steve said that we didn't want anyone telling us when to come and go, and that he didn't want anyone demanding that he attend meetings and publish papers. Steve loved physics, but he wanted to study physics where and when he wanted to, and on his own terms.

Steve and I wanted total freedom from everything and everyone. We'd been in school most of our lives, with rules and time schedules and people telling us what we could or couldn't do. We were tired of this. We didn't want people to guide our lives anymore.

Connie came over to wish us luck. We knew her advice was heartfelt, coming more out of concern for Steve than any personal bias against his leaving physics. We also knew that we'd miss her. Everyone else in the room thought we were crazy. Perhaps their attitude stemmed from their own fears: fear that they hadn't fully lived their own lives, fear that we would prove a free life could be a happy one, or fear of the unknown. On the other hand, maybe they were just happy doing what they were doing.

As we kissed Connie goodbye, a well-known physicist stumbled over to us. He was clearly a few drinks over his limit.

"Well, you two hippies, be off with you!" he shouted. "Be off with you to see the world," he continued, gaining volume and conviction with each sentence he spoke. "I hope you find it better than I did…writing four papers a year so I can continue in my job. Damn the university and the laboratories! You don't even know the half of it.

"Be off with you," he said, snickering. "A toast to Stephen and Susan. They're smarter than anyone in this room." He threw back his glass of whiskey, and someone led him outside.

As Steve and I left the party, we heard the eminent physicist shout, "Freedom to the hippies!" and saw tears slide down his cheeks.

We didn't need any more encouragement than that.

Without knowing it, we had discovered one of the "keys" to our ultimate success: We were willing to pursue something that we really enjoyed doing, despite the risks.

We wanted to spend time traveling around the country. We could pay for the trip by selling our posters. We wanted to be with each other at all times. We wanted to continue to write and draw together. And we wanted to give my father the opportunity to be active and involved in our adventure. We weren't worried about the future. We wanted to live a life that we designed. And the time to begin was now.

*We cannot
listen to what
others want us
to do
We must listen
to ourselves
So start right now
You can live a life
designed by you and
for you*

If you are in a situation that doesn't feel or look right to you, you should remove yourself from it as quickly as possible.

* * *

It is essential to identify the most important and critical aspects of a business, and then focus on perfecting them.

* * *

If you make a mistake, immediately admit it and try to rectify it.

chapter seven

Our Home and Office on Wheels

Lean against a tree
and dream your world of dreams
Work hard at what you like to do
and try to overcome all obstacles
Laugh at your mistakes
and praise yourself for learning from them
Pick some flowers
and appreciate the beauty of nature
Be honest with people
and enjoy the good in them
Don't be afraid to show your emotions
Laughing and crying make you feel better
Love your friends and family with your entire being
They are the most important part of your life
Feel the calmness on a quiet, sunny day
and plan what you want to accomplish in life
Find a rainbow
and live your
world of dreams

"Hey Sue, the desk's gonna fall!" Steve yelled from inside the camper. "Slow down!"

I drove along the bumpy dirt road high up in the Boulder mountains at a speed of less than five miles per hour. The long steel desk stuck out from the back of the truck at least a foot, and Steve used all his strength to keep it from sliding out. We'd found the desk advertised in the Boulder newspaper for thirty dollars and wanted it to be part of an office we had created in the corner of our basement apartment.

Two hours later, we arrived home. Steve's arms were covered with bruises, but the harrowing ride was worth it.

We placed the gray, metal desk next to a bookshelf made with bricks and plywood that we had brought with us from college. We put this furniture on a red rug remnant. A rope clothesline hung from the ceiling above the silk-screening apparatus to the opposite side of the basement above our bed. When we hung our posters with clothespins on this long clothesline to dry, we couldn't walk across our living quarters. Instead, we had to crawl.

Right after creating our home office, we invested in an office on wheels. Using all the money we had saved, which was $750, we made a down payment on a bright-yellow pickup truck with an empty camper shell on the back.

Once we started preparing for our first trip, we realized how much work lay ahead of us. We had to silk-screen five hundred posters of each design, make order forms for storeowners, and fix up our truck as an office and home on wheels. Fortunately, our trade show experience had prepared us for a lot of work, but this time we realized that we couldn't do it all by ourselves. We decided to hire our first Blue Mountain employees.

Peter, a high-school boy who had mowed our neighbor's yard, looked like a biblical figure with his honest eyes and long, dark beard and hair. He arrived at our basement apartment with three of his high-school friends: Scott, Martin, and a cute, short girl with red hair and bright, blue eyes named Midge.

For the rest of the evening, we silk-screened, collated, and rolled posters, chatting about poetry and life in general, taking breaks to play the guitar and recite poetry.

"Your poems are soooo real and...," Midge said.

"Who wants a cold drink?" I changed the subject because I never knew what to say when someone complimented me.

Everyone was thirsty because our poorly ventilated basement filled with paint fumes was extremely uncomfortable on such a sweltering day.

"I hope poetry and art always guide our lives," Midge toasted.

We worked straight through to five in the morning, and Midge still asked if she could work for us again.

"We couldn't have done this without you. Of course we'll hire you," I said, "but first we have to sell enough posters so we can pay you."

"We loved doing it," Midge said. She told us that she had hated every job she had ever had, but this was like working for a philosophy. She thanked us for letting her help us.

Once we realized our basement didn't have nearly enough room for our posters, paint, silk screens, and paper, we rented a little room in a building across town. We didn't understand why the landlord had given us such a great deal on the rent, fifty dollars a month, until we arrived at the building and realized we'd rented the space surrounding the only bathroom in the entire building. Everyone in the building passed through our "office area" on his or her visit to the bathroom.

At last, the time had come to prepare our pickup truck for the trip. Steve built a bed and shelves out of plywood inside the camper shell, and I set about stacking posters, clothes, books, towels, pots and pans, and other necessities onto the shelves. We hung a poster on the wall and another on the ceiling, secured a portable radio to a shelf, and covered the cold metal floor with rug scraps I had gathered from several rug stores. I glued one last rug over the glass door for privacy.

To this day, I'm still not sure how we lived comfortably inside that truck, but we did. We used the space well—a result of living in so many dorm rooms and small apartments, I guess—and the freedom of having a home on wheels outweighed any claustrophobia we may have experienced. Our living space was tiny, but we had all of America as our backyard. When we needed some air, all we had to do was step outside the truck, and we'd see a mountain, a desert, or an ocean. We didn't need anything more than the bare necessities to enjoy such an unrestrained life.

Once again we worked through the night, reviving ourselves with an early-morning, cold shower. I tied a braided piece of leather around my forehead, and Steve wore his curly hair down to just above his shoulders. Wearing our matching jeans (they had an embroidered design sewn on the outside of the leg), tie-dyed shirts, and sandals, we got into the truck, bade farewell to Peter, Midge, and Scott, and headed for the military town of Colorado Springs with Bob Dylan blaring on the radio.

We wanted to get to Colorado Springs as soon as possible. We didn't have any money, and we knew that if we sold a few posters, we could at least pay for dinner. We were pretty carefree and didn't worry about the possibility of complications or emergencies.

Two hours later, we arrived at this pretty mountain town. I entered a large gift store, our posters in hand, and despite my nervousness, the owner loved how the poetry blended with the art. He ordered a dozen of each.

"You can bill me in thirty days," he said, and my heart jumped into my throat. Thirty days?

"I could give you a discount if you pay now," I offered. I was embarrassed to tell him that I had no money, and if I had learned anything up to that point, it was that a discount always helps a storeowner make a decision.

"Do you need the money that badly?"

"I'm living in a truck."

The manager laughed and paid me seventy-five dollars out of the cash register.

Steve also sold some posters, and we ended up that evening with one hundred dollars in our pockets. Steve called Peter to tell him the good news. We could hear Scott, Martin, and Midge cheering in the background, and I had a feeling they'd all have jobs very soon. I thought about what Midge had said. We weren't just selling posters; we were selling a philosophy, a philosophy we believed in. We were having so much fun, and the possibilities seemed unbounded.

We drove another hour to a campground and cooked a steak on our portable grill. Thousands of stars illuminated our impromptu picnic, and we enjoyed the night, not letting go of each other.

The next day, we traveled to the Colorado towns of Pueblo and

Trinidad, selling our posters wherever we went. We drove by what is now known as The Great Sand Dunes National Park near Walsenberg, Colorado. It was breathtaking, and we pulled over for a better view of the magnificent mountains of sand. Nature is so overwhelming, and we're such a tiny, fleeting part of it.

We'd planned to drive over Raton Pass to New Mexico, but a snowstorm closed the pass. We parked the truck on the side of the road where, protected in our sleeping bags against the freezing weather, we slept until the slushy sound of trucks moving through snow awakened us. As soon as the pass opened, we battled bumper-to-bumper traffic on the usually deserted road.

We drove straight to southern New Mexico, basked in the warm weather, and admired the light-brown adobe houses with red tiled roofs. We sold posters to stores in college towns, like New Mexico State University in charming Las Cruces, and promised ourselves we'd return to this serene state.

After New Mexico, we headed east to El Paso, Texas. I looked at the long, desolate strip of highway and thought that the isolation of the mountains was nothing like the stretches of desert solitude. We pulled over to inspect the large brown plants that blew across the road. The brush and tumbleweed seemed so exotic that we loaded some of them onto our truck as souvenirs and then continued on our journey.

"What's that noise? Why is the truck shaking? What's going on?" I shouted, snapping out of my reverie. Steve struggled to regain control of the truck and pulled over to the side of the road. He jumped outside to investigate and came back looking grim.

"We have a flat."

"That's just great. How are we supposed to pay for a new tire?" We'd spent most of the money we'd made on food and gas.

I looked through the windshield at the black line of pavement that extended to the horizon and, to my great relief, saw a gas station. Our truck wobbled to the gas station, and we called my parents. We told them what happened and asked them if they could wire us money. Then we hitchhiked one hundred miles to the Western Union office. By the time we'd hitched back to the truck, the gas station had closed and we fell asleep in the truck.

Tap… tap… tap… tap… tap…

I shot up out of the sleeping bag, nearly banging my head on a shelf, and opened the door to find a very startled gas station attendant rapping on our door.

"What're you folks doin' here?" he asked, peering into our dark camper.

Once we explained our situation, we paid him for the new tire, and he quickly put it on our truck. This left us with five dollars. We then headed for San Antonio. We realized we'd have to work even longer hours in the future so we could set aside money for emergencies.

From San Antonio to Fort Worth to Dallas, we stopped at every store we deemed appropriate to sell our posters. Texas felt bigger than all of America.

The moment we arrived in Dallas, we visited the book depository near where President Kennedy had been shot. Seeing the actual building brought back every shred of shock and horror we'd felt at the time we were in college when the president was assassinated. His optimistic attitude called for a celebration of freedom and youth. "Ask not what your country can do for you—ask what you can do for your country." His words helped shape and inspire my generation's philosophy and desire to work for changes.

Steve and I then toured the rest of Dallas. The city seemed oddly incongruous. Interspersed among the expensive department stores and boutiques in the downtown area were inexpensive, trendy head shops. The responses to our posters varied from that of a young storeowner who bought one poster—for himself—to that of an owner of a huge head shop that sold hundreds of different shaped pipes (from animal- to triangular-shaped ones) who snickered and said, "Are you kidding? The people who shop here don't want poems on posters." As usual, most stores were not at all interested in purchasing our posters, but there were enough to keep us satisfied.

While driving around Dallas, we picked up a hitchhiker carrying a salesman's case. He sold handmade plastic pipes that looked like light bulbs to head shops, and he thanked us for the ride with a gift of a purple pipe.

Next we drove to Arlington, Texas, which is right outside of Dallas. There we ended up in the weirdest situation we'd been in up to that point. Every fledgling business owner deals with deadbeats, but Arnold Revson was one of a kind.

Short, thin, and bent over, wearing a baseball cap with a bone attached to the brim, Arnold was the owner of a magazine store in Arlington. He asked us if our presentation could wait for a moment while he took care of some business. He was interested in our posters, so we waited for an hour in his shop, observing the merchandise: magazines, newspapers from around the world, black light posters, pipes, ashtrays, and clothes. After keeping us waiting, he apologized for the delay and ordered a dozen of each poster while boasting about how much business his store did.

"Oh, man, you know what?" he said as we brought in the posters. "I don't have the cash here. I got a checkbook at home, though. You can get the money there."

We followed him in our truck, arriving at a large, old apartment building. Cars filled the parking area, and loud music and voices poured from the windows of the apartment. Arnold welcomed us into the living room where he and a group of friends passed around marijuana in an elaborate pipe. He bragged to us about his plans to open more magazine stores, but his slight incoherence made me anxious about our situation. He and his friends typified everything I didn't like about the drug culture: people who acted loud and obnoxious because either they were high or they thought that was how they should act if they were high.

Steve and I were not at all comfortable in Arnold's house. We had to get out of there. We should have just left for good, but I was pretty stubborn.

We later learned that if you are in a situation that doesn't feel or look right to you, you should remove yourself from it as quickly as possible.

An indeterminate amount of time later—it felt like hours—Arnold staggered out of a room, eyes red and bleary. "I can't find my checkbook," he mumbled. "Stop by the store tomorrow. I'll be in at ten."

"Let's leave this town right now," Steve said.

"No," I said. "I want to collect our money. He has our posters."

We parked our truck at a closed gas station and fell asleep.

The next morning, two men with thick, red necks approached our truck. As they let out hearty laughs, they asked us rather loudly, "Who're you?"

One man polished the barrel of a rifle with a handkerchief as he spoke to us.

"What's that for?" Steve asked.

The man laughed. "For shootin' niggers and hippies."

I gasped, horrified. Was he serious? I hated the word "nigger" and I hated guns, and the combination was too much for me. The men laughed loudly at us as we locked the doors and sped out of the gas station, expecting to be shot.

Again, Steve wanted to leave the area that moment, but I insisted that we get our check first.

We returned to the store, but Arnold wasn't there.

"Sue, you've seen all the guns around here," Steve said, in an aggravated tone. "That character probably has a half dozen guns under his counter. Let's forget it and leave."

When Arnold finally showed up, I raised my voice and said, "I waited for you for two hours. Please pay me so I can get on with my trip."

Arnold opened the cash register. "Sorry, I don't have enough in here now."

"Then give me back the posters."

"I took them home. But I'll tell you what. I'll date the check for tomorrow."

I smiled, snatched the check from his hand, and ran to find Steve. I knew Arnold would come through.

Finally, we left Arlington and went straight to Austin, home of the University of Texas, where the university bookstore manager not only bought our posters, but also said that he'd recommend them to other college bookstores.

Austin reminded me of Boulder. Steve and I went to different stores trying to sell our posters. I found a terrific bookstore that had a copy of a book I'd been trying to find forever: Anaïs Nin's biography. Steve and I loved good bookstores, and we always browsed in the best ones we could find in any new city we visited. I felt at home in this university town. I sat on the grass in a park, reading *Rolling Stone*, as I waited for Steve. At the end of the day, he'd sold sixty posters and I'd sold thirty, earning us $135. We celebrated by staying in Austin to attend a concert by several folksingers.

The next morning, in Houston, I found a branch of Arnold's bank and went in to cash his check. The teller made a phone call, signaled to the manager, and brought me into her office. My stomach sank.

"I'm sorry, Honey," she said. "That guy's bad news. He closed his account two months ago and has passed thousands of dollars of bad checks since then."

I was furious. After all he'd put us through, I'd given him the benefit of the doubt, and he'd still cheated us. I called the police and asked for the top person in charge of prosecuting "bad-check writers." The receptionist referred me to the district attorney's office.

I spent two frustrating hours on the phone trying to get in touch with the district attorney. When I've been wronged—or if anyone's been treated unfairly—I tend to lose track of time and protocol. I'll do anything to fix the problem.

Finally I reached his secretary. "Does he know you?" she asked.

"I have information about a crook for you."

In a few moments, a deep voice came on the phone. "This is District Attorney Wade. Can I help you? Tell me about your crook."

I told him everything that had happened.

"How much is your check for?"

"A lot. Seventy-five dollars."

The phone clicked and we were disconnected. Undaunted, I called back.

"I was just speaking to District Attorney Wade and got cut off."

"Who are you?" his secretary asked.

"Susan Polis Schutz, from Colorado."

"Just a minute."

I heard the secretary murmur something and then a deep voice laughing.

"District Attorney Wade stepped out for the afternoon."

"When will he be back? He didn't tell me what to do about my bad check."

"District Attorney Wade told me to advise you to go back to Colorado," she said, and hung up.

I told Steve what had happened.

"Whom did you talk to?" he asked.

"District Attorney Wade."

"You actually talked to him? Do you know who he is?"

"He's District Attorney Wade."

Steve explained that Wade was the famous D.A. who was involved in the controversial investigation of the Kennedy assassination. "He prosecuted Jack Ruby!" Steve said, starting to chuckle.

It turned out that he was the "Wade" in *Roe v. Wade*, the famous abortion court case. He obviously had a lot more important things to deal with than the loss of our seventy-five dollars.

Before long, Steve's chuckle progressed to roaring laughter, and I finally joined him. I had done all I could; Arnold Revson was a lost cause.

"I can't believe you spoke to District Attorney Wade. You're really something," Steve said fondly. "Let's get the hell out of Texas and never come back."

With that, we pushed the accelerator past eighty until we crossed the state line.

* * *

We spent the next two months traveling across the Midwest selling our posters and experiencing real America. Until I traveled by car, I never had a sense of how big our country is and how interesting each region is.

We drove through Kansas, Missouri, and Nebraska, amazed at the long, expansive rows of corn and wheat, the enormous sky that seemed so flat, and the many little towns. Out of almost one hundred stores that we called on in Kansas City and St. Louis, only one liked our posters!

When we came to Hays, Kansas, we were a bit taken aback with the surreal little college town. The girls wore flared skirts with cotton blouses, and their hair was styled high above their heads in ponytails; the boys' hair was combed into greasy pompadours and they dressed like Jerry Lee Lewis. The fashions hadn't changed since the 1950's, and Steve and I must have looked bizarre in our jeans and tie-dyed shirts. They stared at us, and we stared back at them.

But the startling visual contrast was deceptive. Though we might have looked different from these students, after traveling and meeting so many people, I knew we all shared the same feelings, and our poetry spoke to basic human emotions. The Fort Hays State University Bookstore buyer loved our posters and bought quite a few.

We returned to Boulder with eight hundred dollars. We spent the next two weeks silk-screening another several hundred posters and then left for the West Coast to sell them.

We traveled to Salt Lake City, through Nevada, to Sacramento, Santa Rosa, Berkeley, San Francisco, Oakland, Santa Cruz, San José, Fresno, Bakersfield, Pasadena, Los Angeles, and Long Beach. Just as the Californians basked in the ever-shining sun, Steve and I did, too. After running out of posters, we again drove back to Boulder.

During our trips, we'd worked out a complicated method for shipping our orders. When we ran out of posters, we mailed our handwritten orders to my mother. My dad would give his orders to her, too. She would then enter them in an accounting book, bill the stores, and mail the orders to Peter in Boulder, who would ship the posters and cards to the stores. Steve's dad, Morton, went to Peekskill once a month to balance the books.

Eventually, we realized we needed someone in Boulder to keep track of every order. My mother already had a full-time job, and even though she never complained, I knew she didn't have time to continue helping us. Also, mailing orders from our location to Peekskill to Boulder took at least a week—not exactly the most efficient way to do business.

So we hired a very capable woman to bill and process our orders. She filed the orders in rows of shoeboxes and could locate any order in seconds. We rented an office in downtown Boulder, and we also moved the shipping area to larger quarters. I marveled at the way our company had grown. But I couldn't think about that for too long because we had a lot of posters to sell. So right after training our new employee, Steve and I traveled east to Nebraska, Iowa, Illinois, and Indiana. From there, we went to Michigan, where we visited the French Paper Company.

We'd recently silk-screened poems and illustrations on a beautiful, light-brown, parchment-like paper manufactured by French Paper. We spent days selecting the exact shade of paper we wanted and were disappointed to find that the last two boxes of paper we'd bought were much lighter than what we'd originally chosen. It looked sun faded, and the brown ink color we'd painstakingly chosen didn't stand out properly. After the Denver paper distributor refused to exchange this paper for the right color, we carefully piled all the sheets into our truck. We would just take the paper back to the Michigan manufacturer on our upcoming trip.

The French Paper Company seemed huge, and as we toured the facility, the detailed process of making paper amazed me. Our tour guide was none other than Mr. French himself, so we took the opportunity to show him the off-colored paper.

He laughed when he saw his paper stacked neatly in our traveling office. We showed him the shade we selected and compared it with the lighter shade. To our surprise, he said, "This paper is way too light. It's embarrassing. This paper isn't the quality that we usually make." He admitted his company's mistake and immediately rectified the situation by agreeing to exchange the paper. In the process, rather than losing our business forever, he gained a lifetime customer.

Twenty years later, our masterful Blue Mountain Arts' purchasing agent, Patty Brown (who has been with the company for over twenty-six years as of 2004), told us the French Paper employees still talk about our visit. We were the "two hippies who got Mr. French to take back cartons of light paper and even help them carry the paper from the truck to the factory."

We sold our next-to-last card and poster in Indianapolis and ended our three-month trip with one sample of each poster left and an unparalleled sense of accomplishment. We'd visited over twelve states, talked to hundreds of people, and were ready to return to our basement apartment.

In our business, the universal message of our poetry and art was the critical aspect, but the quality of the presentation also had to be as perfect and beautiful as possible. We spent a lot of time choosing the exact type of parchment-like paper and the exact shade of ink. It might have seemed silly at the time to return paper that didn't have the right coloration, but to Steve and me, it was very important that our products looked the best that they could.

Again, without realizing it, we had discovered another key requirement for success in business: It is essential to identify the most important and critical aspects of a business, and then focus on perfecting them.

Learn who you are and what you want in life.

chapter eight

Our First Book

The world turns around, new people grow up, and still the inhuman forces that society imposes against the individual are present. I believe that we can eliminate these evils through love and friendship.

Come into the mountains, dear friend, to seek out the beautiful things in the world so that you can use these positive forces to create a new and better world.

~Introduction to
Come Into the Mountains, Dear Friend, 1972

Once word about Blue Mountain Arts began to spread, to my astonishment and awkward pleasure, readers began sending us fan mail.

"Your poems express what I feel, but cannot say," wrote a girl from California.

A couple from Colorado Springs told us, "Because of you, we have just started not only to get to know each other, but we're getting to know ourselves."

"I have the poster 'Come Into the Mountains,' but now what? Your poems and Steve's illustrations say what I really feel inside but I can't get out. I need more of your words because I'm on the brink of discovering who I am," wrote another fan.

Apparently I wasn't the only person who couldn't articulate my feelings aloud. I don't write poems to be dissected. I don't use complex analogies or allusions. I attempt to write poetry and lyrics that make my feelings understandable. I use simple and clear words so people are able to relate to them.

Steve and I had received hundreds of letters from people asking if we had a book of our poetry and illustrations. Normally, I would have shrugged off the praise, but we realized that the underlying meaning of these letters was not just that people liked our work, but that our work helped them. Loving books as we did, publishing our own book appeared to be an exciting, natural, next step in expanding our creative horizons.

Knowing we couldn't possibly silk-screen an entire book, we visited a Denver printer to find out everything we could about how books were printed.

Many hours later, we went home and immediately started to design our book. The book had to make a statement. It had to look prettier than and stand out from other books on the shelf. We sat cross-legged on the floor, fifty of my poems scattered around us. We named the book *Come Into the Mountains, Dear Friend*, and I arranged the poems to reflect the progression of my thoughts.

Come Into the Mountains, Dear Friend is a poetry book of my philosophy. I believe people should "come into the mountains," either literally or figuratively. We are often trapped in a cage of our own creation, and thinking quietly in a natural setting can help us free ourselves. We all need to break away from the harsh world and learn who we are and what we want in life so we can open up honestly to others. Only then will it be possible to share our emotions, feelings, goals, and lives in meaningful relationships. By improving our individual lives, we can improve the world.

If our book helped a few people, perhaps they would spread the goodwill to more people, and the ripple effect would grow larger and larger.

Steve illustrated each poem in the book with soft, one-color nature drawings that captured the feelings of the poems, and we selected an appealing typeface called "Libra." We brought the poems and illustrations to a typesetter and photographer.

In the early 1970's, typesetting a book was a complicated process. Today, computers do most of the work, but back then a person would sit in front of a large machine manually typing each letter. The machine would carve the type into a metal plate, which would then be run through a printing press.

Next we talked with a printer who convinced us to print six thousand copies of our book. We had no idea what we'd do with so many books, but we decided to listen to him anyway. We figured we'd have enough books to last us a lifetime.

As we drove home from the printer, I sang along with Don McLean's song, "American Pie." As he saluted goodbye to rock 'n' roll, my mind danced between dreams of *Come Into the Mountains* becoming a bestseller and worrying about finding a place to store six thousand books that probably wouldn't sell anywhere.

We traveled to Denver again and again that fall to tell the pressman to run the ink heavier! Finally, on October 1, 1972, we were thrilled to watch the machine cut and bind the printed sheets of paper that would comprise our book. We held and inspected the first completed copy to come off the binding machine.

A real book of our poems and illustrations! It smelled of fresh ink and looked so attractive and different from any book we had ever seen. It was a bound volume for people to read, but to Steve and me, it was so much more. It was a very personal record of our feelings and beliefs at that moment in time and something we would hold sacred for the rest of our lives.

We brought our book to existing customers, and two weeks later, the storeowners astonished us by telling us that *Come Into the Mountains* sold quickly! Buoyed by our local success, we called for an appointment with the country's then-largest bookstore chain, Waldenbooks, in Stamford, Connecticut. We flew there two days later.

John MacCleron, the cultured, handsome, twenty-eight-year-old poetry buyer, warmly welcomed us into his office. We chatted about Shakespeare and F. Scott Fitzgerald, and when he finally asked to see our book, I excused myself and went to the ladies' room. I was apprehensive about being in the room while he read my poetry.

"I like this book," he said when I returned. "I like what it says, and the artwork is appealing, too. I think it'll sell. Send me three thousand copies."

I almost fell out of my chair. "What?"

"I said send me three thousand copies. You do have that many, don't you?"

Shocked and elated, Steve assured John that we had all the copies he wanted. Then we invited him to lunch with us. While we were eating, he described the publishing industry to us and suggested that we go on a book tour to publicize *Come Into the Mountains, Dear Friend*. When the bill for our lunch came, Steve reached for it, but John insisted on paying. He told us that Waldenbooks buyers were not allowed to accept gifts from publishers. If we paid for his lunch, it would violate this rule.

John and Waldenbooks instilled in me a faith in the book industry. They genuinely appreciated books, and they were honest!

On the airplane back to Denver, Steve and I held hands and read a news story. There were details about the *Washington Post* investigative reporters, Bob Woodward and Carl Bernstein, who had recently reported on a "secret fund" that was used to pay for illegal activities against the Democratic Party. Watergate had begun.

Over the next few months, we followed the increasingly disturbing news about Watergate. Nixon's top officials had tried to discredit Democratic candidates through "dirty tricks," including forgery, electronic bugging, and false leaks to the press. The White House spokesmen denied the accusations, but Woodward and Bernstein continued to report their findings.

First Vietnam, now Watergate! Our generation wanted so much to get away from this corrupt world. That's why we set up communes and dressed and acted differently than our parents. We wanted to create a new world.

It was our hope that *Come Into the Mountains, Dear Friend* would help spread love to a world that needed it desperately

* * *

On September 2, 1973, we were ecstatic to read the first newspaper article ever published about us. It was a two-page, full-color story in the Boulder *Daily Camera* written by Margaret Banman that included photos of Steve and me and our *Come Into the Mountains, Dear Friend* book:

> [The] introduction to Susan Polis Schutz' first book of poetry is also an introduction to the poet. She tells more about herself, her thoughts and feelings, with every poem in the book. *Come Into the Mountains, Dear Friend* has made Susan a best-selling author in less than a year. In only three years, she and her artist husband Stephen have built a nationally-known publishing house, Blue Mountain Arts, from a spare-time hobby....

This local article was followed by a two-page spread in a national magazine, *The Saturday Evening Post*, which printed six of my poems surrounded by a mystical photo of a woman gazing at the moon with a tree in the background.

I was giddy with excitement. This was the first time I realized that my childhood dream of becoming a well-known author, as well as my current desire to help people with my message, might possibly come true.

Don't just look to the past to see what HAS been done. Look to the future to see what CAN be done.

* * *

If you believe in something, you must stand by this belief despite all the people who try to discourage you. You can't let anyone destroy your dreams. You must remain strong and confident.

* * *

Don't get impressed when someone talks big and brags. Always check out a person's reputation before entering into a business relationship with him or her.

* * *

It is okay to make mistakes as long as you learn from them and do not make the same mistakes over and over again.

chapter nine

Difficulties

B$_y$ 1973, Steve and I had published posters, cards, and a book. We employed about ten people, including our parents. Once our business had outgrown our basement and the little office we had rented, we realized it had outgrown us, as well. Our families could only help so much, and Steve and I were acting as sales reps, creators, and managers all at once.

After our three-month tour of America, we tried to figure out what our next steps would be. We needed a team of sales reps, not just one or two who volunteered for the job. We needed someone to manage the sales reps—assuming we ever got more than a few. We needed someone to transcribe and ship the orders and someone to help with certain creative aspects. Basically, we needed to hire people to help us in all the different parts of our business.

Steve and I tended to learn as we went along, and our naïveté worked both for and against us. If we had been more familiar with the "can's" and "cannot's" of the printing industry, we may not have pushed printers so hard to print our products the exact way we wanted them. Had we been more familiar with the greeting card industry, perhaps we wouldn't have put poems and pastel illustrations on our greeting cards. Because everything was so new to us, we only saw the future and what could be done, not what had been done.

On the other hand, our inexperience also led to some business mistakes and painful, though valuable, learning experiences.

We began showing our posters and cards to sales representatives, hoping we could build a permanent sales force for Blue Mountain Arts. Our initial efforts were not very successful. We heard the same complaints that we were used to hearing.

"I don't really like your cards," said an Indiana rep. "The colors are so dull. No one wants to read such long poetry."

"Your cards don't look like anything out there," a California rep said. "The messages are too personal. Why don't they say anything on the inside?"

"Poetry and nature illustrations will never be popular," a Southern rep told us.

"A card has to have a specific occasion. You can't just leave the inside blank," said an Ohio representative.

They went on and on with an infinite number of negative comments. No matter where they were from, most reps clearly didn't like our poetry or art. But we persisted anyway because we knew that enough people did relate to our cards.

And we were just as picky as the reps. We wanted to hire reps who were known and respected, who weren't too aggressive, and who really liked and believed in our messages. Because our cards were so unique, we knew genuine enthusiasm was vital to selling them.

In order to hire a Colorado sales rep, Steve and I placed advertisements in two newspapers: the *Denver Post* and the Boulder *Daily Camera.* Steve expected hundreds of applications; I expected twenty. We received one!

As we waited for the applicant in a restaurant called the Pancake House in Boulder, I saw a jolly-looking salesman with strands of gray hair sticking out from under his white fedora get out of an enormous Cadillac. In about five minutes, all three of us realized he was not the right person to become a Blue Mountain Arts sales rep. He thought we were ridiculous, and we thought he was. After he left, I laughed and we ordered German apple pancakes and discussed a better way of finding sales representatives.

We went to the library and studied the yellow pages of ten large cities, writing down the phone numbers of gift stores in each city. We then went home and called the stores and asked for the names of "good, honest reps." I called the recommended reps and followed up with letters that included samples of our posters and cards. A week later, I called the prospective reps, and not one of them wanted to sell our products!

Wherever we went, people tried to give us advice on a product they didn't understand. They knew all about greeting cards, but they only knew about birthday cards, anniversary cards, and cards for other special occasions. They had never heard of our non-occasion cards. They tried to talk us out of our creative undertaking simply because it was so different.

I wasn't discouraged. I was mad. I wondered how many people with new ideas have given up their dreams because unimaginative people discouraged them.

We knew people identified with our messages. We'd witnessed it firsthand in the small towns of America, and we were more determined than ever to continue creating our posters and cards.

In our search for reps, we learned another very important lesson: If you believe in something, you must stand by this belief despite all the people who try to discourage you. You can't let anyone destroy your dreams. You must remain strong and confident.

We were sure that, eventually, we'd find reps that would be happy to sell our creations.

So when a man named Charles Hudson called from Miami and offered to represent us, we immediately said yes. He sounded professional and pleasant on the phone. He told me that he was a Boy Scout leader, had two children, and had set sales records for various other companies that he had worked for. I was so impressed that I didn't bother to call anyone to check out his reputation.

A week after we hired Charles, he called back. "Susan, I just sold a complete display of your cards to each of the first four accounts I called on. They were so easy to sell. Everyone loves your cards."

He told me to send out the cards with display racks that day because his customers wanted them immediately. He told me to mail them to his home, and he would deliver them to the stores.

He said, "I'm not just a salesman. I really care about my customers and the merchandise they sell. It's very important that I personally set up the display rack in the front of their stores."

Dizzied by his breathless delivery and sales success, I packed the orders and shipped them to his home address. The next day, Charles asked for four more racks of cards. He said he'd get a check from the storeowners as soon as he delivered the racks to the stores.

That was fine with me. I was happy that our sales rep was so enthusiastic, but Steve knotted his eyebrows. "We don't even know the names of the stores that bought these racks," he said. "It seems unprofessional."

We mailed him four more racks on the condition that we would get paid before sending any more.

Several days later Charles called again, bubbling over with excitement. He'd sold six more racks in two days, he said, and he'd mailed the storeowners' checks to us. I promised to airfreight six new card displays, but I silently decided to wait for our checks.

Two days later, Charles called to ask where the six card displays were, and I said we needed more time to get them ready. "Things are going extremely well," he said. "But hurry! I promised the stores next-day delivery. Now don't let me down, Honey. Put them on the plane tomorrow morning!"

I felt an awkward kind of pressure, and I didn't like it. We went to the mailbox every day that week, but no checks arrived. On the sixth day, I called Charles. There was no answer. On the seventh day, I called again, but the number had been disconnected. I called Information for all the surrounding suburbs, but there was no Charles Hudson.

A sinking sensation came over me. Had Charles Hudson stolen our eight displays of cards? I called the Miami police, and when they went to Charles's address, they discovered that no such number existed on that street. People who lived on the block said that recently there had been a large truck parked on the street, and it had been receiving hundreds of packages.

We'd been duped.

The next day, Steve visited Michael Wright, the owner of a Colorado soap company, to discuss sharing a booth with his company at a couple of trade shows. Coincidentally, Michael told Steve that he'd sold a hundred thousand bars of soap through a terrific, new rep named Charles Hudson. He'd had to hire four new people just to make enough soap to ship to him. He was so excited about this huge order. Poor Michael.

We didn't want Charles Hudson to take advantage of more innocent business people, so we wrote a letter to a trade magazine explaining what had happened. We asked to hear from other companies that had shipped products to Hudson, hoping to catch him in action.

We heard from several other companies that had shipped to Charles Hudson, and one company said they were presently shipping to a Don Greenwald who asked to have his products shipped to his "home" address.

I called Greenwald's number and recognized Charles Hudson's voice. As soon as I said my name, he hung up. I called the local police, but by the time they arrived at his temporary address, he was gone. That was the closest we ever came to finding him.

We'd lost one thousand dollars' worth of cards and displays, but our business recovered easily. The soap company wasn't so lucky, though, and went out of business. I tried locating Hudson for weeks, but he was clever and deceitful, and it became clear that we would probably never find him. Finally, Steve convinced me to forget Hudson and concentrate on positive things. Steve was right. It was time to move on.

At the time, the experience we had with Mr. Hudson had a big impact on me, but I later realized that most people are honest and he was the exception.

This incident was exceptionally annoying because it reminded us of some of the lessons we had learned before, but had forgotten: Business always has to be conducted properly and professionally. If someone wants to change the rules, and it doesn't sound or feel right to you, stay away from that person.

Don't get impressed when someone talks big and brags, and always check out a person's reputation before entering into a business relationship with him or her. And this last lesson was especially germane: It is okay to make mistakes as long as you learn from them and do not make the same mistakes over and over again.

Being able to rise above adversity can make the difference between success and failure.

* * *

It is important to understand your own strengths and weaknesses.

* * *

It is essential to have the right person in the right job, a person whose strengths match up to the requirements of the job.

chapter ten

The Perfect Sales Manager

"Sue, how on earth can I make a living selling greeting cards?" my mother said when I asked her to be the sales manager for Blue Mountain Arts.

By late 1973, I'd finally found some representatives who liked our work and our messages. Bernie Wisdorf and Don Haberman, two clean-cut, cute, young guys, would sell Blue Mountain Arts in Minnesota and Nebraska; Manny Avalos, in California; and Bea and Arthur Gordon, in Colorado. But we still couldn't find reps on the East Coast.

A New England storeowner told us about Madco, a well-known sales organization in Boston. Since Madco was a professional group, and I realized that Blue Mountain Arts needed to look more professional, I made a sales presentation book, which I sent directly to Mike Drukman, Madco's highly respected president and owner. For more than a month, my letters and phone calls went unanswered. Finally, I wrote a letter to Mike and sent it to his home address. In the letter, I told him it was unfair of him to keep the sales presentation book I'd spent five hours compiling. If he didn't want to sell Blue Mountain Arts products, I told him he should return my book.

Three days later I received a special delivery package: my sample notebook, with no explanation. I called Mike again. This time, I got him on the line and asked him what he thought of our cards and posters.

"Well, they're okay," he said. "I'm not sure how we'll do with them."

"Does that mean you'll represent us?"

"Well, I can only sell Blue Mountain Arts if I can have an exclusive in all of New England and New York."

"Someone's already selling to religious stores in Massachusetts, but you could sell to every other kind of store," I said, reasonably.

Mike said that he couldn't skip religious stores because it would be too complicated. He needed to be able to sell anywhere he wanted to.

"Forget it," I said, abruptly ending our conversation.

A few moments later I realized I should have handled the phone conversation a lot better. I didn't have to cut him off so quickly, and maybe we could have worked something out. Instead, I let my temper get the best of me.

When someone says something I find unreasonable, I tell him or her honestly how I feel, sometimes in unprofessional language, and by doing this I mess up the situation.

It is important to understand your own strengths and weaknesses. My temperament was not conducive to working with salespeople. Salespeople have outgoing personalities; they know when to say negative or positive things to impress or influence people one way or another. I could not play word games. Nor would I make an effective sales manager. A person in that position has to love interacting with people and be a diplomatic politician of sorts. Sales managers have to be magnetic; they must possess enormous tolerance, yet be firm, patient, friendly, and understanding. They have to have a strong intuition about motives and know when people are misrepresenting themselves.

I had none of the qualities necessary to be a good sales manager.

My mother, on the other hand, had all of them. So I phoned my mom and offered her the job as Blue Mountain's sales manager.

My mother, June Polis, is an admirable, softhearted, but tough woman. She skipped a grade in high school and graduated at sixteen. That same year, her father died suddenly at the age of forty, so instead of going to college, my mom got a job modeling at a department store to help support her mother and seven-year-old sister, Ivy. Her warm, brown eyes, outgoing personality, erect posture, slender figure, and impeccable taste in clothes have never deserted her. The main difference between the June of today and the June of forty years ago is that her hair is now gray. She's never once dyed it and tells me, "Gray hair is gray hair, and I'm proud of it." She remains as beautiful as ever.

She married my father, who was nine years older than her, and they spent the early years of their marriage in New York City. There my father could afford to romance her with plays, restaurants, and a summer home in Lake Peekskill. When I was born in 1944, she became a full-time mom, and she excelled at that, too. She sewed dresses, knitted sweaters, made creative Halloween outfits, led the Brownie troop, taught in my Sunday school, attended PTA meetings, and supported my brother and me in all our activities.

When my father's business started to fail, Mom needed to go to work, but her lack of a college degree made finding employment difficult. She held various jobs as she tried to find better-paying work, including positions as a salesclerk at Sears and in a toy store and doing office work in a research institute. To make ends meet, she sold real estate on the weekends. When Mom sold a house, the new owners often invited her to their new home. Mom would bring them a cake that she baked, and she would often become friends with her clients. When Dad stopped working, she was offered a full-time position selling real estate, but she feared that the commissions she would earn would not be enough to support our family. We all encouraged her to give it a chance, and she did.

My mother worked late into the evenings and on weekends, and she flourished in her new career as a real estate salesperson. People loved her, and she loved them. She truly enjoyed seeing the gratitude on their faces when they purchased their dream homes.

Her eyes light up when she's around other people; working in sales was so natural to her. When she became office manager of the real estate company, she worked even more hours because she had a lot of detailed paperwork to do, a task she wasn't particularly fond of.

Nevertheless, she never missed a second of being a great mother to my brother and me. During the workweek, she prepared dinner early in the morning and refrigerated it, so when I came home from school, I could just pop it into the oven. Our family, like most other families, ate dinner together every night. Mom made our school lunches, and to this day I've never had a better egg-salad sandwich than the ones she packed in little brown bags. Our house always looked immaculate, too.

She was the original superwoman.

The secret to Mom's success was her positive attitude. Unlike my father, she cheerfully plunged ahead to solve life's problems.

From her I learned that being able to rise above adversity can make the difference between success or failure.

Mom was always honest, hardworking, and sincere. She would make a perfect sales manager.

Mom still worked long hours, and I thought she and my father had fallen into a rut in Peekskill. My parents were not making any changes to their lives or experiencing anything new or fun. I thought starting a new life in Boulder could be their salvation, just as my mother becoming the sales manager for Blue Mountain Arts would be my salvation.

"Mom, you know our orders are increasing daily." I barreled ahead with my own sales pitch, crossing my fingers that she would see the wisdom of my idea. "Why don't you and Dad come to Boulder for two months and just try it? Dad can continue to sell our cards and posters, and you can hire and be in charge of salespeople. We'll rent you an apartment. If you don't like it here, or if you don't think you can make a living at this, you can go back. I know you'll love Colorado, and you'll make way more money than you're making now. Just try it."

But I knew the real way to get to my mom was through her heart. "I really need you," I told her truthfully. That did it.

Two weeks later, my parents came to Boulder. Mom's first order of business was to work out an arrangement with Madco. With just one phone call and a follow-up letter, she and Mike Drukman worked out a territorial agreement. And for thirty years, Madco remained one of our top sales organizations, while Mom continued her close friendship with Mike and his wife, Bobbie.

My mother became known and respected as the best sales manager in an industry where there are very few women in that important position.

After realizing how effective my mother was as sales manager of Blue Mountain Arts, we learned an important lesson that we would try to implement over and over again: It is essential to have the right person in the right job, a person whose strengths match up to the requirements of the job.

My mother retired from her position as sales manager in 1997 when she was eighty years old, but she continues to be a director of Blue Mountain Arts. People still refer to my mom as "larger than life"; she is as much a part of Blue Mountain Arts as Steve and I are.

All this, in addition to being the best mother in the world.

Since I have a mother
whose many interests
keep her excited and occupied
Since I have a mother
who interacts with so many people
that she has a real feeling for the world
Since I have a mother
who is always strong
through any period of suffering
Since I have a mother
who is a complete person
I always have a model
to look up to
and that has made it easier
for me to develop into
an independent woman

The most important attributes in the art of managing employees are that the managers be fair, honest, and direct with the people who work for them.

chapter eleven

Mistakes

I go downtown to work
I'm not sure who my
friends are
and who are not
I'm not sure whom to
trust
and whom not to
I'm not sure of anything in this world
anymore
Back home in the mountains
I'm sure of the huge boulders
in front of the blue sky
I am sure of the tall spruce trees
outlining the rocky mountains
I am sure of the birds and the marmots
and the grasshoppers
and I'm sure of
you

When our company consisted of over forty employees, we realized that we needed several people to manage the employees. Being in charge of them was becoming very time consuming for us, and we wanted to focus on designing products. We seemed to have a knack for hiring competent, hardworking, nice employees, but we had a hard time finding the right managers.

Managers need more than good skills; they have to be leaders, they have to be fair, and they have to be honest. We hadn't been able to figure out if prospective managers had these characteristics. And even when we thought that we had found good managers, we were unsure how to manage them. So we did whatever we thought was best at the moment, eventually learning, but not before making some harmful mistakes that hurt us.

We advertised for several management positions and received many applications. One person stood out from everyone else. This person had been a high-school valedictorian and had majored in math in college. I immediately checked the references that were provided on the resume. I spoke with an employee at this person's previous company, and though the woman I spoke to sounded apprehensive, she didn't elaborate. It seemed to me as if she were jealous, so I discounted her comments and wondered why I ever bothered to check references since I rarely listened to them anyway. By the end of the week, I had hired this person and a couple of other managers.

Although most of our employees were mellow, organic, young people in their early twenties, we thought our new managers, who were a bit more seasoned, would get along well with them despite their differences.

The next week was exciting. Waldenbooks ordered another ten thousand copies of *Come Into the Mountains, Dear Friend*, and salespeople from many states in the country called to ask if they could represent Blue Mountain Arts. I couldn't help but smile as I remembered all the salespeople who had rejected our products because they thought poetry wouldn't sell.

Within a couple of months, our new managers revamped many of the systems that initially had been set up. Blue Mountain Arts was becoming quite efficient, and the employees seemed to be in awe of the managers' accomplishments.

But soon I began noticing strained smiles on the faces of many of the employees. I also noticed that no one had come into my office to chat lately, despite the fact that we had all been friends. When I finally asked one of our employees what was wrong, she asked me furiously why I was so against the employees. She said that her manager had told her and the other employees in the department that I had issued directives and was responsible for several hard-nosed decisions and rules that were extremely unfair. This was a complete surprise to me. I had no idea what she was talking about and I told her so. No wonder everyone was mad at me.

I confronted the manager. "Never use my name on any decision you make for your employees," I said. "These people look up to you. They believe you and expect you to be honest."

Against my better judgment, and because I didn't have time to correctly analyze the situation, I decided to give the manager another chance.

I had so many things to do. My mom and I were busy preparing for an upcoming sales meeting. I had to write and give a speech on how Blue Mountain Arts had started and also plan an agenda for the meeting.

The day before the sales meeting, one of our employees asked me to go to lunch with her. I arrived at a health-food restaurant in Boulder at noon and saw her sitting at a large table with a group of Blue Mountain employees.

"Well, this is a surprise!" I said. "I thought we were just going to lunch with each other."

"I did, too, but the other people insisted on coming."

I suddenly felt nervous. Was I going to hear new stories I would have to defend in front of all these people? I dreaded the confrontation that was sure to come, but if they were going to yell at me, they might as well do it now.

"Well, what do you all want?"

To my surprise, they stated that they were fed up and couldn't work for this manager anymore. I was relieved that this wasn't an attack against me, but puzzled. "What's the problem?"

The employees gave a detailed description of their problems. They told me that they had placed so much faith and trust in their manager, but little by little, it had been uprooted. They realized that what they had been told about Steve and me made no sense. They said that their manager even tried to turn them against one another by telling them things they'd purportedly said about each other.

"It was like there was some kind of spell over us," one of the employees said.

I went back to the office, mollified that the employees had opened up to me, but hurt and disappointed that they'd believed the manager's tales about us in the first place. I had considered our employees to be friends—people I respected, who respected me, and with whom I had a nice relationship.

At just about that same time, we received a letter from another employee in a different department telling us that the staff in that department had lost respect for their new manager. They were completely demoralized and could no longer work for this person. The letter said that the manager came to work late, didn't keep appointments, and was clearly having personal problems. The letter also stated that they were disappointed in Steve and me for not observing this.

We were especially taken aback by this situation because this manager had been a personal friend and confidant of ours. We knew that she had a lot of talent but was on a downward personal spiral. It wasn't fair for this person to be in charge of any employees until her problems were sorted out.

We had recently hired a third manager who had a very impressive resume, but was soon criticizing other departments for "completely slacking off" and not working hard enough. This manager verbally threatened another one of our managers and jokingly alluded to doing physical harm.

"What did we get ourselves into?" we wondered. We couldn't hire strangers and we couldn't hire friends to become Blue Mountain managers.

Although none of these experiences seem that important in themselves, together they have had a lasting effect on me personally. I was totally confused about friendships and how to act with employees.

I became extremely guarded with everyone except my closest and oldest friends. My strong guard became my personality. Where I used to be social and accessible, I became reticent, closed, and less likely to open up.

We were artists, not business people, but we owned a business. I had to remind myself of that regularly. If we wanted to, I suppose we could have kept Blue Mountain Arts small, with only Steve and me as employees. But we wanted to increase our audience in order to spread our messages and create a life's work from our poems and paintings. And we constantly had new ideas that we looked forward to implementing. To do this, we had to build and expand our company. Besides, growing Blue Mountain Arts as a business was challenging in so many different areas, and most of them were a lot of fun. We just needed to learn how to choose the right people and manage them, and I knew that eventually we would. I just wished we didn't always have to learn important lessons the hard way.

These events contributed to our eventual understanding that the most important attributes in the art of managing employees are that the managers be fair, honest, and direct with the people who work for them.

Striking a Balance

Though I want
people to read what I write
and I like
being known (this is what I always wanted)
and I enjoy
having an all-consuming career
I also need
privacy and solitude
and I want
to have normal relationships with people
But all this
doesn't go together
So I won't compromise my
personal life one bit
to help my career
because if I did
I'd be shutting out of my life
the things I love most

chapter twelve

Someone Else to Love

We traveled almost continuously, going from trade show to trade show in Los Angeles, New York, Chicago, Atlanta, and Dallas. The Los Angeles Gift Show was held at the L.A. Convention Center except there wasn't enough space at the convention center for all the companies to display their products. To accommodate all the exhibitors, newer companies that didn't have seniority were given space to display their products in the Biltmore Hotel Ballroom. When the ballroom filled up, brand-new companies were relegated to hotel rooms at the Biltmore. Of course, the buyers and storeowners attending the show went first to the convention center; some went to the ballroom; but only the die-hard, duty-bound buyers and storeowners visited the hotel rooms.

Naturally, Blue Mountain Arts was in a hotel room.

Although the chances of storeowners actually leaving the convention area to come to our room were slim, Steve and I were optimistic. We also looked at it as a way to save money. We presented our products during the day, and even though there were no beds, at night we slept under the display tables in our double sleeping bag.

The traveling, setting up and dismantling of our display booth, and more traveling were zapping my energy. Toward the end of our sales trip, I grew more and more exhausted. At one point, I had to stay in bed while Steve went to the show.

Once I got back to Boulder, I napped every afternoon. I thought I was sick with mono or at least the flu, but when I went to the doctor, he gave me considerably different news: I was pregnant!

Not completely ready for this, I started a journal to record my feelings about being pregnant, which later became a book called *Someone Else to Love.*

On May 12, 1975, I gave birth to a long, thin baby boy. Jared Polis Schutz was eight healthy pounds, with delicate, light skin; soft, red cheeks; and bubbly, ocean-blue eyes. I held him in my arms, Steve by my side, relishing the miracle of the birth of our child.

Steve and I realized we had brought an enormous responsibility upon ourselves, and we also realized that we wanted to be with our baby all the time. Fortunately, we had the flexibility to bring him to work with us, so we moved his crib into our office and brought him to work with us every day. He spent his youngest years embraced in the loving atmosphere of Blue Mountain Arts.

The Blue Mountain employees grew accustomed to, and soon enjoyed, the unconventional arrangement. Bob Gall, who eventually became president of Blue Mountain Arts, was an accountant assigned to close the books for Blue Mountain Arts in 1976. He recalls coming to our office to be interviewed by Steve and me and wondering why the "woman listening intently to every word I said was holding a baby in her arms." Apparently this didn't bother him too much, because he joined Blue Mountain Arts soon afterwards. Cliff Scott, who eventually became director of Art & Editorial, spent his first afternoon at Blue Mountain Arts in the break room where we all were celebrating Jared's first birthday.

We took our baby boy everywhere with us. In the mountains, he sat in a little backpack on Steve's back; when we went to trade shows, he was there in his baby seat, wearing a nametag and reveling in the attention from all the people who visited our booth. And when we attended meetings, he was in either Steve's or my arms. He was part of the Blue Mountain family.

chapter thirteen

Fragility of Life

In March 1976, we invited my parents to go on a four-day vacation with us in California. My dad looked so healthy. He wore a brown sweater vest over a crisply-ironed, tan shirt, and he was well shaven, with his thinning hair combed back. His laughter was infectious. We had recently given him an award for Blue Mountain Arts Salesman of the Year, and the achievement pleased him immensely. Everyone at Blue Mountain congratulated him on his success. He was finally on top again, and he enthusiastically discussed the stores he sold posters to and his plans to sell more.

"So, Dad, what are you going to do with all that money you've earned?" I asked.

"Since I've been selling Blue Mountain Arts, I've had a secret savings account," he said, eyes twinkling. "Bet you can't guess how much is in it."

He didn't wait for my answer. "Twenty-five thousand dollars! I haven't helped Mom pay any bills because I'm going to surprise her!"

I leaned over and kissed his cheek. The weekend was happy and memorable; my parents played with their grandson on the beach, and they looked truly happy. I never wanted this vacation to end.

My parents returned to Boulder three days later, while Steve and I stayed behind for one more night in California.

At two o'clock in the morning, a phone call interrupted my sleep. It was my parents' apartment manager with the news that my father had passed away.

"This isn't possible," I thought. "He was here a few hours ago. He played with our baby on the beach. He was smiling. Impossible."

I didn't know what to do. I was in California; my mother was in Colorado. I hung up the phone and sat on the bed stunned. My dad was happy for the first time in many years; why did it have to end for him?

I cried all night long, trying to catch the thoughts that whizzed through my mind. What were my last words to him? I'd never get to say anything else to him, ever. I'd never lost anyone close to me. My mind blurred, and I felt detached from my body. I couldn't figure out anything. I could barely grasp the reality that my father was not alive and that I'd never speak with him again or see his dimples.

We took an early morning flight to Denver, and my tears splashed on Jared's face. He felt like my only lifeline to reality, and I rested my head on Steve's shoulder.

Once I got to my mom's apartment, we faced the task of planning the funeral. The chilly attitude of the funeral-home staff horrified me. They kept giving me prices and asking me to prepay. How could they discuss money matters when my father had just died? Fortunately, my brother Robbie arrived in Boulder and took over the gruesome details.

I switched on the radio and was appalled to hear a Cincinnati Reds baseball game. Didn't they know that my Dad, their biggest fan, had just died? How could they play a game when David Polis had just passed away?

Nothing made sense to me. As I wandered around Boulder, stricken with grief, I realized no one seemed to care that my dad had died. Stores were open. Movies played. Restaurants were packed full of smiling diners, and people laughed and joked wherever I went. "How could life go on as if nothing had happened?" I thought.

We closed Blue Mountain Arts for several days and moved in with my mother for three and a half months. Robbie and his family moved to Boulder, and we became closer than ever.

Awakened to the fragility of life, after my father's death, Steve and I started to think about what was important for us to do with our lives.

Steve and I wondered how we'd ever conduct business as usual. After all, my father had been the primary motivator for us to grow the business. We realized that though his involvement had been short, his work, encouragement, and ideas had been crucial to the direction of Blue Mountain Arts' infant years. The company had given him a new, positive outlook on life, and he'd devoted his last years to making it a success. Though we would forever mourn his passing, at least we knew that he had recently been happy and filled with faith in the future of his family and pride in himself.

Steve and I knew that if we stopped now, all my dad's hopes would have been for naught. We would forge ahead with Blue Mountain Arts. We knew that Dad would've wanted us to continue to make his Blue Mountain dream a reality.

It is important to periodically reflect on and examine your priorities and your vision to see if you need to make changes to what you are doing.

* * *

People have similar needs and emotions, regardless of what they say, where they live, what language they speak, or what they look like.

chapter fourteen

Publicity and Fame

After my father passed away, Steve and I realized that our priorities had changed dramatically. Raising and loving our son, Jared, would be our most important commitment, followed by our devotion to Blue Mountain Arts. We needed to assess the many time-consuming aspects of our work and figure out a way to have more time for our family life.

That summer, we found ourselves tackling an unexpected side-effect of our cards and posters being so popular: publicity and fame. Dealing with a public image was an entirely new challenge.

We had recently published *Someone Else to Love.* I thought no one would like the book because it didn't describe being pregnant as a positive, earthy, glowing experience. To my great surprise, hundreds of women wrote to me, telling me that they had been afraid to admit to having the same negative feelings during pregnancy that I had written about, and my poems helped them feel less guilty.

After receiving these letters, I wanted more women to read the book, but I knew most people had never heard of it. Like other authors, Steve and I would need to do a publicity tour.

We'd done some publicity stints in the past, mostly book signings and interviews with local newspapers, but for *Someone Else to Love,* we decided to do a full-blown, two-month publicity tour. Steve was always a private, very self-contained person, but he knew how much I wanted to do this. In addition to exposing *Someone Else to Love* to more people, the glamour of television and newspapers intrigued me, and it seemed that publicity tours were a necessary part of making a book known to the public. We didn't have any media training, so we just decided to be ourselves, wearing what we usually wore, saying what we believed in, and holding our son.

One of our first stops was XETV, a San Diego television station based in Tijuana, Mexico where we were to be interviewed. As we waited in the velvet-flocked lobby of the old El Cortez Hotel in downtown San Diego for a driver to take us to Tijuana, Steve noticed a stout man standing by the door wearing thick, black glasses that rested on his little nose. He ran a hand across his shiny, bald pate and clutched a two-foot long, plastic bug to his chest.

"What's that bug for?" Steve asked.

"I'm going to Tijuana to be on TV to talk about bugs and insecticides," the man said.

"It's horrible how we overuse insecticides, don't you think?" Steve asked. "The damage to the environment and our health is so much worse than any damage caused by the bugs." Steve spoke for a generation of organic agricultural advocates whose bible was *Diet for a Small Planet.*

"I disagree completely," the man said, waving the bug at us. "We should use insecticides wherever we find bugs. Insecticides are safe if you follow the directions on the labels."

"Where do you work?" Steve asked.

"I'm a professor speaking on behalf of an association of insecticide manufacturers."

I choked back laughter. Steve and I, who had built a career extolling the virtues of nature, would be on the same program as a man who looked like the very type of bug he wanted to destroy. We weren't prepared for sharing the stage with an absurd bug-man. We just hoped the people watching the program wouldn't believe everything he said.

Fortunately, the show went well. The questions weren't too difficult, and the cameraman superimposed our posters in the background as I read from the book. To this day, of all the television programs Steve and I have ever been on, the camerawork on this one was by far the most creative.

Our first radio appearance on the *Sally Jesse Raphael Show* didn't go nearly as well. The host—a substitute for Sally Jesse—asked Steve point-blank, "What kind of a girl is Susan?"

I laughed. Here we were, sitting in a little booth with big microphones in front of us, feeling very artificial but trying hard to act natural, and the host asks Steve the one question I knew he couldn't answer. Steve is not a person who speaks with descriptive adjectives.

"She's nice," he said.

"Is that all?"

Steve hesitated. "No," he said. "She's great!"

The host saw he wasn't going to get a better answer than that from Steve, so he asked me a battery of questions, most of which I responded to with one- or two-word answers. By the end of the show, we practically ran out of the studio in embarrassment. I remembered my miserable failure on that first radio program during the 1970 National Stationery Show and realized that radio was definitely not my medium.

Steve, Jared, and I traveled to do publicity wherever we had trade shows, so in addition to speaking with reporters, we spent four days of every week, from nine to five, selling our cards and books at various trade shows.

Finally, we returned to Colorado and did phone interviews with magazines, such as *Fortune*, *Mother's Manual*, *The Saturday Evening Post*, and *New Woman*.

We should have been delighted with the publicity, and we would have been had we been allowed to discuss the feelings and emotions in our messages. However, the reporters were only interested in our business story and the success of Blue Mountain Arts, which we were proud of, but they weren't the sole focus of our lives. While we celebrated the beauty of love and nature, the media seemed only to celebrate business and material wealth.

We were completely candid with reporters, but many of them couldn't believe that Steve and I spent all our time together. We tried to explain our lifestyle and what was important to us. We told them how we worked toward the same personal and career goals, supporting each other at all times, and how we constantly bounced our ideas off each other, knowing we had a trusted partner who would give us honest feedback. We told the reporters that we loved being with each other.

Some of them tried to poke holes in our relationship. Others tried to find a dark side to our marriage, but we just didn't have one. I know it may have sounded unbelievable to them—or even to anyone reading this book—but it's the truth. We just don't have a dark, sad, or stormy aspect to our relationship, and I'm very thankful for this.

The articles and headlines were extremely positive and usually accurate, but they rarely mentioned our poetry, art, and ideas or our helping people communicate their feelings to one another.

The *San Francisco Examiner* was one of the few papers that portrayed us in a balanced, introspective manner and focused on us, not just our business:

ALL THEIR LIFE IS TOGETHER

The calculated gamble paid off, not only in terms of dollars, but in terms of a happily unorthodox, total togetherness life style in which the Schutzes seem to have found quietude and certainty.

Somebody said, "There is no place to go because you are the place." It could easily have been these bright, young personalities so blithely sure of themselves and of each other....

Stephen, incidentally, is secretary-treasurer of Blue Mountain Arts; Susan, with her drift of fine, pale brown hair and bee-stung upper lip, is president—a state of affairs she brushes aside as of significance "only when we are dealing with men who might otherwise think I'm a secretary and ask to speak to my husband."...Stephen has an Omar Sharif look; the day we met, he was splendid in a buffalo hide jacket....

"I associated pregnancy with mysticism and fear; however when I was pregnant, fear and misery dominated the nine months.... And now, when I look at my son, I can't remember being miserable at all," [Susan stated].

Boulder [is a place] where the Schutzes live idyllically in a house in the foothills with the Rockies at their backs.... [What is] the secret of successful togetherness? "We are both creating. And we are one hundred percent honest with each other." Meeting them, one is inclined to believe these 31-year-old self-made successes who work hard to produce something people like, may well live happily ever after.

It was an interview we did on a Philadelphia television show that was the catalyst that caused us to start to think about what we were doing. The program had gone exceptionally well; we talked about *Someone Else to Love* and our feelings about being parents, and I read a poem to my son. We had been hoping for so long to have just this kind of opportunity on television, and for the first time, we did.

As we left the television station, someone approached me and asked, "Are you really a millionaire?"

"What?" I asked, shocked. "Where did you hear that?"

"I just saw you on TV."

"That never came up," I said.

"It was printed on the bottom of the TV screen. You know, when you read to your little boy? It said, 'Housewife Turned Millionaire.'"

"I'm not a housewife, and I'm not a millionaire!" I said.

We'd had enough of this publicity tour, so we went back to the mountains.

A week later, Steve, Jared, and I sat in the fresh, crisp air and gazed at the city that lay peacefully below us. We watched marmots play in the mountains above our house and reveled in the beauty of our surroundings.

The ringing of the phone shattered the silence. Nancy Trent, the woman who had organized our publicity tour, said *People* magazine wanted to write a feature story on us and spend three days with us in Boulder.

"You can't refuse *People*," she said. "It's one of the most well-read magazines in the country!"

Steve and I discussed the pros and cons of this. Most authors would do anything to be in *People*, but we wondered whether the reporter would concentrate on our book and poetry and art, or write a sensational story about a business couple.

I thought back to when I was a fourteen-year-old apprentice in a summer stock theater in Mahopac, New York, where I had dreamed of becoming a famous actress or author and having stories written about me. Now here I was, eighteen years later, with the opportunity to have this dream come true. Nancy was right. We couldn't turn it down.

Several days later, a reporter and photographer spent three days with Steve, our son, and me. They followed us everywhere; we drove our motorcycle to one of the highest points in the mountains where Steve and I often sat on a rock writing poems and drawing illustrations, and they took a magnificent photo of us with the Rocky Mountains below. The reporter told us he was a huge fan of ours, and he put us both at ease.

Three weeks later, a four-page story with photographs of Steve and me appeared in *People* magazine. It was the same business story as all the other magazines with absolutely no mention of our messages.

But the event that made me really reexamine my own desire for fame occurred when we were attending a John Denver concert. While John Denver sang "Rocky Mountain High," Steve and I held hands, admiring the magnificent surroundings of natural, red-sandstone formations in the Red Rocks Amphitheater near Denver. The wind blew slightly. Steve and I kissed, feeling so good to be alive and in love in such a beautiful place. The moment was mystical.

"Isn't that Susan Polis Schutz?" I heard a woman say, shattering the moment. "Let's ask her." They poked my arm and asked.

"Yes," I said.

They giggled, and one of them said she saw us in *People*. Though the girl was sweet, and I felt honored to be recognized, the rest of the concert was not enjoyable. I couldn't be spontaneous with the music and feelings that the night had evoked earlier. I wondered if people were looking at me. Did I look like they thought I should? Would I say what they thought I should say?

I also realized that once a person becomes a public figure, people no longer react to her or him normally. People may seem afraid or in awe of the person, listening to every word he or she says as though it's gospel truth, expecting the celebrity to be perfect. If this were to happen to us, our lives would no longer be honest, real, spontaneous, or free.

"But that's what fame is all about," Steve said. "You always wanted to be famous."

"I know," I said, "but I'm not so sure now."

I didn't want to lose touch with who I was! I didn't want to lose touch with reality. And I definitely didn't want to bring up our son in a made-up world.

I realized how important it is to periodically reflect on and examine your priorities and your vision to see if you need to make changes to what you are doing.

My priorities and visions had changed. My love for my husband and son had become the most important part of my life. My old dream of fame now seemed superficial.

Steve and I needed time to think about future publicity. We took Jared and went to a California beach.

We walked along the shore, holding hands and enjoying the day. Steve carried Jared under one arm. We listened to the waves rush onto the sand.

Then suddenly, a woman ran up to us.

"Oh, I just saw the great article about you in *People*! Your story is so inspiring. Can I have your autograph?"

Steve and I looked at each other, signed the piece of paper, and continued on. There I was, with an old scarf on my head, carefree and peaceful with my family, just trying to relax and live my life.

Though we had witnessed only a tiny glimpse of what fame would be like, I had seen enough to know that I didn't want what came along with fame: a complete lack of privacy.

Perhaps if we hadn't been parents we wouldn't have minded it so much, but we realized that living in the spotlight wouldn't fit in with our family life.

In the coming years, we learned that our desire for privacy was not unique. As we published the poetry and lyrics of famous singers and actors, we observed some of their lives firsthand.

We became friends with Leonard Nimoy, the famous *Star Trek* actor, writer, and director, when we published his poetry books. One day, the three of us were hiking along a ridge in the foothills west of Boulder, overlooking a magnificent panoramic view of the Continental

Divide. In places and moments like this, it seemed as if we were the only people on earth; we relished the beauty and silence.

"Are you Leonard Nimoy?" someone shouted into the silence. "Are you Mr. Spock?"

Leonard turned around quietly and nodded his head.

The fan ran over and asked for his autograph, and Leonard graciously signed the paper. The fan had meant no harm, but our peaceful moment had ended so abruptly that we couldn't recapture the serenity.

Leonard told Steve and me that the best kind of fame is to have your name known and respected but not your face.

Steve and I agreed. Leonard Nimoy, as we learned, is a wise man.

In late 1976, our confusion about publicity crystallized into a firm decision. I had liked the attention of talking to reporters. It was exciting, though ultimately unfulfilling. We decided to balance our private and public lives as simply as possible: We would only let magazines and newspapers reprint our poems and artwork and not seek out personal publicity or grant interviews.

* * *

At the same time, though, we had committed to one more book tour to publicize our first international book.

By 1977, we had created several books of poetry and art, and countless posters and greeting cards. So when Ole Christensen, owner of Athena International in England, a greeting card and poster publisher as well as a large chain of retail stores, asked to print and distribute our cards and posters in Great Britain, we were thrilled. Christensen's skill for discovering new artists brought fresh works to England through his own galleries and a sales force that also sold to stores throughout Europe. We thought he would be the perfect publisher for our work.

A week later, the contract arrived with wording that was perfectly acceptable to us.

With the advance we received for the British editions, we purchased a beautiful, round, leather couch for our living room. Over twenty-seven years later, when we sit in this room, we still remember how we paid for our couch and our excitement over being published internationally.

When we signed the contract, Christensen asked us to come to England for a publicity tour, which would begin the moment stores had our cards and posters. He would pay for our entire trip. Moreover, we wouldn't just be tourists; he made it sound as though we would be honored guests. I had never been to Europe, and though we had vowed not to give any more interviews, we had to honor our commitment and it was a great opportunity to travel for free to another country.

We landed at Heathrow Airport on February 1, 1978. Christensen made good on his promise, and to our delight, a limousine picked us up at the airport and drove us to The Dorchester, one of the most elegant hotels in London.

Though we wanted to eat in the stately room where we had heard that the Queen had tea, we had to go to sleep. We were supposed to be at the BBC radio station at five the next morning to appear on a program, and London time was seven hours ahead of Colorado time. We only got a few hours of sleep, and the next morning we were happy that our first London publicity event was not on television. I had huge bags under my eyes, and the interviewer hardly talked to us.

The next day, our appearance on a popular television show confirmed my belief in our mission. The famous host, a muscular former athlete with blond, curly hair, sunburned skin, and blue eyes introduced us to the audience.

I read a long poem to Steve, and the burly host looked me in the eyes. "Do you really feel that way toward your husband?"

"Of course I do," I said. "I wouldn't have written the poem if I didn't."

He chuckled. "I can't imagine anyone having those feelings. They're so…trite."

"Love is the deepest emotion someone can have," I protested. "Have you ever been in love?"

His rugged face actually blushed. He wasn't ready for an argument.

"Yes, I have," he admitted. "But I wouldn't describe it in words like yours," he continued. "No, I just wouldn't describe it at all. It's not that important."

I told him that love is basic to human happiness for everyone, regardless of who you are or what you do.

"Only people who are not in touch with their real selves claim they don't have emotions, and they're the unhappy people in the world," I declared on live television.

We went back and forth for the rest of the show, with me defending the world's most important emotion. Right before the show was about to end, his voice softened.

"I have a confession to make," he said. "I have a drawer full of poems I've written. I've never shown them to anyone. I didn't want to seem emotional."

I extended my hand to him and noticed the camera focusing on our hands as the program came to an end.

It's so difficult for people, particularly men, to admit to having sensitive feelings, and they find it almost impossible to speak about them. I've found that the people who are the most vocal in denouncing emotional expression are often the ones who have been hurt the most and who need to be reached out to the most.

The talk show host reaffirmed my belief that all people have similar needs and emotions, regardless of what they say, where they live, what language they speak, or what they look like. Over the years this has been proven, again and again.

Our goal, once more, became clear. People needed to be free to communicate their emotions. If Steve and I could help individuals get in touch with, appreciate, and speak about their emotions, perhaps the world would become a more caring place.

Nothing ever goes exactly as you plan it, and nothing is ever as easy as it may seem. But if your dream is worthwhile and it's something you truly seek, the challenges, adjustments, and hassles will be worthwhile—as long as you don't compromise what's truly important.

chapter fifteen

Finding the Right Balance

I wish there was one grand artistic depot where the artist need only hand in his artwork. As things stand now, one must be half a businessman, and I don't know if I can endure this.
~Ludwig van Beethoven

By the end of 1978, Steve and I had partially prioritized the important aspects of our lives.

Fortunately, we were able to hire people to help take care of many of our household chores. Although women have become more equal to men in the last fifty years, many men still relegate most domestic work to women, even if the women have jobs outside the home. I wonder how these women, or single women, manage to do everything. It surely leaves them no time for their own needs.

But we owned a publishing business, which required us to work many more hours than a normal job. Most of our days were filled with the details of running Blue Mountain Arts, and though our company revolved around creativity, Steve and I had little time to be creative. The more people we reached, the more complex our company became. Managing it was stealing away our spontaneity and time. We had worked hard to achieve balance in our lives, and we now needed to figure out a way to maintain it.

We didn't like managing. In fact, our mistakes showed us we weren't particularly good at it. We didn't want the business to dominate our lives, and we also didn't want to force our own creativity if it just wasn't there. We didn't want to feel pressured to create something that wasn't from our hearts.

So we hired Roger Ben Wilson, who'd been doing freelance work for us almost since we started Blue Mountain Arts, to form an art and editorial staff to create and illustrate cards on a regular basis. Roger hired gifted, devoted artists, editors, and writers, such as Cliff Scott, who would later become director of Art & Editorial; Douglas Pagels, who would become one of Blue Mountain's most popular and prolific writers; Faith Gowan, an artist who was the art director for many years; and Jody Kauflin, an artist who recently became our art director. Many of the people Roger hired still work for Blue Mountain Arts.

The Art & Editorial department's atmosphere was loose and free, designed to cultivate artistic freedom; we even moved this creative group into a different building from the shipping, accounting, and order departments. Roger was bright and inventive, and his vision helped position Blue Mountain Arts' Art & Editorial department at the forefront of the industry. Under Roger's supervision, Blue Mountain Arts expanded into music (my ardent hobby). He hired a producer, gathered musicians, including my friend Myrna, and we rented an engineering studio. We recorded my lyrics with melodies written by my brother, my band members, and me, and made a record album. The other band members and I sang or spoke the words to each song.

Since I love music so much, this project was a fulfilling adventure, one that was a lot of fun to do. Steve and I knew that we had to get back to spending more of our time doing creative projects like this. But we wouldn't be able to accomplish this until we figured out how to make Blue Mountain Arts less burdensome.

We thought about various ways to cut down our management time. We had recently increased the number of Blue Mountain Arts books, and we thought if we could find a New York publisher to publish and distribute our books, it would lighten Blue Mountain's load. If the arrangement worked out, perhaps in the future, the publisher could publish all our books and even our cards. We wouldn't need to expand our own company, and we could return to writing and drawing.

I called several publishers and set up an appointment with one of the most respected publishing houses in New York City, which we thought would be the most appropriate publisher for our books.

I tried not to get too excited; after all, we were just investigating this idea, and Steve seemed cautious about the plan. But the world of publishing fascinated me. I'd read at least one book a week since I was a child, and I'd always wanted to be a writer or editor in New York City. Just going to the office of this publishing house would be a thrill.

A week later, we walked into the sumptuous offices of this famous publisher, and I was so impressed.

I approached the young receptionist.

"Oh, I know who you are!" she said. "You write poetry and live in Colorado." She looked at Steve. "And you illustrate all of Susan's poems. I have so many of your cards! Let me take you to Mr. Jacobson's office. That's a beautiful shirt, Stephen. You look like a cowboy." She smiled flirtatiously at Steve.

As she knocked on Mr. Jacobson's door, a deep voice called out. "Come in, Dear."

I must've looked startled, because the receptionist laughed and said, "Oh, don't worry. He calls all the females in the company 'Dear.'"

Mr. Jacobson was a short, balding man in his mid-fifties. His metal glasses and tailored, gray, pinstripe suit contributed to an air of importance. He complimented us and gestured to the man and woman sitting to his left on large, soft, leather chairs, saying they had been key to the success of many bestselling books. He introduced Milton Ames, the company sales manager, and Molly Edson, the editor-in-chief.

"Milton knows exactly what's happening in the business," he said. "He's in charge of the most aggressive sales force in the book industry— he knows what sells and why. Molly's our editor-in-chief. She knows what women want in the way of books. Molly will be of great value at this meeting. Well, now that we've all met, let's proceed.

"I admire what you've done in publishing. Now, perhaps you can explain what we can do for and with each other."

Steve cleared his throat and glanced at me. "Our business has grown larger than our wildest dreams, and we're spending more time managing the company than creating poems and drawings, which is what we really love to do. Since our books sell so well, we think we have something of value for a New York publisher. If you were to publish our books, we could get back to creating."

Milton Ames stood and tugged at his blue polyester jacket. He asked me how many copies of *Come Into the Mountains, Dear Friend* had sold, and I told him about fifty thousand copies.

Mr. Jacobson stood up and loosened his tie. "That is an impressive number for a poetry book," he said, shaking his head. "I didn't know so many women buy poetry books."

Steve and I knew that just as many men bought our books, but neither of us chose to say anything.

"Well, what do you want in a deal?" Mr. Jacobson asked, still standing.

Steve stood up and cleared his throat again. "We'd like you to publish one of our books as a test. If it sells as well as we predict, and you're happy, then we could work out a future arrangement for more books and maybe other products. We'd like a reasonable advance so we know you'll support our book with as much effort as possible."

I smiled at Steve. He was so capable in these situations. No one ever intimidated him. Steve's strength and intelligence were impressive, and he always got to the point of things so quickly.

"I think it would be silly to publish just one book," Mr. Ames said. "We should do four books at first."

"But what if you're not happy with the sales, or we're not happy with your methods?" I objected. "It seems safer for you to publish one book first, and then go with the others when we're both happy with the results."

"I think Milton's right," Mr. Jacobson said. "We'd like to go full-steam ahead, and four is better than one. I'm sure we can agree on the size of the advance. I'd like to go ahead with this project. Milton will be in charge of marketing and selling your books, Molly will be your editor, and I have another appointment to go to now. I think a fifty-thousand-dollar advance would be fair, don't you?"

Fifty thousand dollars! We were shocked. That was an enormous amount of money. We barely contained our excitement as Mr. Jacobson shook our hands and sent us to a conference room with Mr. Ames and Ms. Edson.

The conference room, like everything else in the building, awed me. Framed covers of bestselling books and photographs of famous contemporary authors hung on the walls. I imagined our book covers on the wall next to them.

Ms. Edson interrupted my daydream.

"Milton, I think the size of the books should be smaller."

I glanced at Steve. Change the size? What for?

"Molly, the book sells so well as it is," Steve said. "Why change it?"

"Women carry small purses," she said. "They can't fit your book into their purses. It's a deciding factor in whether or not a woman will purchase a book."

Steve blinked, momentarily befuddled by her bizarre logic. "That's ridiculous," I blurted out in my usual, tactless style.

"Really, Susan, believe me, you're losing customers by keeping the book the size it is," Ms. Edson said.

"I would change the color of the books," Mr. Ames said. "I think your use of several colors of ink is brilliant, but the colors are too dull."

"Women like bright colors," Ms. Edson added.

"How do you know what women like?" I asked.

Ms. Edson straightened her rumpled skirt and answered, "I've been in publishing for ten years, and after that long, you learn that if you want to sell books, you do certain things. I have several other ideas."

Steve jumped in. "But our books already sell well. That's why Mr. Jacobson wants to publish our book."

"You mean books," Mr. Ames corrected him.

Ms. Edson plunged ahead. "For the artwork, Steve, you should use acrylic paint rather than airbrush. Your look is too soft and pastel-ly. When you brighten up the colors, acrylic will pick up the color better."

Steve pursed his lips. Ms. Edson's suggestions simply didn't make sense to us. Ms. Edson ticked off several more silly ideas.

Steve and I felt the same ire growing in each of us. I was afraid of saying something I'd regret. I wanted the meeting to end.

Steve read my mind. "I think Sue and I need to leave now. We have to catch a plane. We'll continue this conversation by telephone."

Ms. Edson and Mr. Ames blinked, surprised by the sudden end to what they thought was a productive meeting. They said that they would call us to go over our publishing venture.

We walked to our hotel, working out the stiffness that had developed from sitting for so long. Steve took my hand.

"What do you think?"

"I am afraid of Mr. Jacobson, I can't stand Milton, and I detest Molly," I blurted. "Can you believe the crazy idea she said about purses? What do you think?"

"From the minute I met Mr. Jacobson and his sales manager, I knew we'd get bull," he said. "Sue, your poems sell because they say what's in the hearts of millions of people. It has nothing to do with book size or color. They don't have the slightest idea what we're doing. Do you know what would happen if we published our book with them?"

"The first thing they'd do is change our book to their standards, and we don't want to do that," I said, frustrated. "Our books would sell okay, but in two years Molly would tell Milton—who would tell Mr. Jacobson—that poetry doesn't sell anymore."

Why were Steve and I so angry at a few tame and mildly offensive suggestions? I guess we just didn't want to give up any creative control.

We thought we were right, but I was still disappointed. For a moment I wondered if we were just too darn independent and head-strong to listen to their viewpoints. After all, they were an old, large publishing company.

We walked along Fifth Avenue, holding hands tightly, breathing in the warm, autumn air in silence.

Steve smiled. "Do you know how lucky we are that we don't have to kowtow to New York publishers or anyone else for that matter?"

Pigeons flew over our heads, and we stood silently for a moment, watching the people hustling across the street, to and from work. We realized how much we loved the freedom Blue Mountain Arts offered us, and we didn't want to give up any of it.

Being avid romantics, we always expected things to be beautiful, perfect, and ideal. Our relationship and family conformed to our standards, but nothing else came close. If we wanted to live our lives according to our own plan, we'd have to work hard to make the best of every situation.

Nothing ever goes exactly as you plan it, and nothing is ever as easy as it may seem. But if your dream is worthwhile and it's something you truly seek, the challenges, adjustments, and hassles will be worthwhile— as long as you don't compromise what's truly important.

When a problem occurs, don't try to distance yourself from it or assume it will just go away. You MUST face it head on and solve it.

* * *

A company's management style must be consistent with the company's philosophy and history.

* * *

A manager must guide employees to do their best and encourage them to respect one another.

chapter sixteen

Learning from Our Mistakes

We saved our creative integrity by not publishing our books with a New York publisher, but we hadn't solved the initial problem: the overwhelming demands of running Blue Mountain Arts.

We motorcycled to a scenic overlook in Boulder where we could see the outskirts of Denver twenty-five miles away. We loved this beautiful spot, but we never had time to go there.

"All we seem to do is manage people and systems—eighteen hours a day," I complained.

I gripped Steve's waist, leaning my cheek against his back, and watched a hawk circle in the distance.

We had devoted so much time to building our company and watching it grow. Now we were at the beck and call of our company twenty-four hours a day. We had no free time, and our creative energy waned with each passing day. There had to be a way to solve this problem.

We discussed our predicament and then made an important decision. We would try to hire one person who could be in charge of Blue Mountain Arts.

With this person running the company, Steve and I could begin to relive our reasons for starting our terrific business.

That's why we decided to hire Mr. Charles Lausch to be the CEO of Blue Mountain Arts.

Mr. Lausch was a handsome man who looked and acted nothing like most of the employees at Blue Mountain Arts. At sixty years old, his graying black hair was as impeccably styled as his three-piece suit.

Elegant, older, and authoritative, he was everything we weren't, and everything we thought Blue Mountain Arts might need.

We already had a good business relationship with Mr. Lausch. He'd been the manager of a chain of stores that had been selling our posters since our company's inception, and he always encouraged us in our artistic and business endeavors. During his interview, he nodded, smiled, and said everything to convince us that he was the right man to head up Blue Mountain Arts.

"I'm proud of you two," he said. "You've grown from making one poster to creating a full-blown publishing house. Not many people can do that."

Mr. Lausch was a father figure to me, and I could tell that he thought of me as a daughter. Turning over the management of Blue Mountain Arts to someone would be frightening, to say the least, but our fears were diminished by our trust in Mr. Lausch.

We talked with Mr. Lausch for about an hour, and then we asked him if he had any interest in managing Blue Mountain Arts. He affectionately touched our shoulders and said that he would love to. We were relieved and told him that we would work out the details and call him. He said that whatever we worked out would be fine with him.

The next day, Mr. Lausch visited us and immediately signed our half-page contract. We shook hands, and then just as he was getting up to leave, he turned and said, "One thing, though...I believe it'd be best for the company if I have complete authority over the employees. I'm afraid I'd be undermined if they speak with you, so I think they should come only to me."

It sounded like a reasonable plan to us. After all, Mr. Lausch, not Steve or I, would now be in charge of the entire company. We both worried that our employees might ignore the CEO and come to us anyway because we'd become friends with so many of them. We knew the initial adjustment period could be rough, so we decided that a clean break would be the easiest and most effective transition for our employees.

A week later, we introduced Mr. Lausch to the company employees and explained we would be leaving on a trip soon. After working so many eighteen-hour days, we desperately needed time off—real time off. Mr. Lausch made a few comments to the crowd.

"I'm honored to be your CEO, and my door will be open to anyone who wants to speak to me," he said, smiling at the light applause. "I do, however, think that we should dress a bit neater around the office," he added.

Our employees—mostly clad in T-shirts, jeans, or shorts—shuffled a bit.

"Your work is a reflection of your appearance, and if you look sloppy, your work could be sloppy," he said. "Thank you so much, and as I said, my door is always open."

With that, Steve, Jared, and I took off for Northern California.

Maybe it's the way the eucalyptus, pine, and humid sea air blend together in a uniquely Northern California smell; maybe it's the miles of woodland, perfect for hiking and biking; or maybe it's the open-minded joy of the people and the knowledge that no matter who you are, there's a place for you, but over the next several months, we were able to rediscover our life together. We wrote, drew, visited customers, and celebrated our first nonworking, real vacation soaking up the Northern California atmosphere.

Then Sally Ann called.

Sally Ann worked in the Blue Mountain Arts order department, and she'd always been our friend. Now she sounded panicked.

"Susan, Mr. Lausch won't talk to us at all! He doesn't know our names, and he won't let us wear shorts to work. He's not fair.

"Susan," she said, agitated, "it can't work this way. It's not the same place anymore."

Steve called Mr. Lausch.

"Who called you?" he asked. "What did she say?"

"Charles, you've got to treat people fairly," Steve said. "We've always talked to anyone who needed us, and you said you'd do the same. The employees expect that of you."

"Stephen, this is a business, not a day camp. You can't be friends with employees and expect them to respect you. I made decisions they didn't like, and now they're trying to reverse them."

"What decisions?"

"Oh, I did away with the volleyball court and the garden. They're just trying to prove they can get them back by running to you."

"You got rid of the garden?"

"Reverse my decisions now, and they'll never listen to me again. You'll be back to being bothered every day with business decisions."

He brought up a sobering point. We didn't want to go back to eighteen-hour days again. On the other hand, getting rid of the volleyball court was one thing, but the garden? This garden of organic herbs and vegetables was planted and nurtured by the employees during their lunch breaks and after work. What could be accomplished by getting rid of this garden?

"Now are you going to back me or not?"

He'd been in business longer than we had. He had a business mind, and we were just two artists trying to run what had become a bona fide publishing house.

"Well?"

Against some serious misgivings, we decided to back him.

A month later, we returned to Boulder to see how our company had fared in our absence. As we approached our building for the first time, I gripped Steve's hand. A crowd stood out front, and they didn't look happy.

"What's going on?"

Steve slowed down. "It looks like...Oh, Sue, they're protesting."

Sure enough, on our first day back to work, we nearly walked into a full-blown protest march...against us. All those years we had spent protesting, marching, and holding signs—often against unfair labor practices—and now our own employees were picketing us!

"Susan and Stephen Don't Follow Their Own Messages!"

"Down with Management!"

"We Want Our Garden Back!"

"Blue Mountain Arts Let Us Down!"

We were shocked and completely dumbfounded. We weren't about to face this crowd without knowing the facts. In a burst of cowardice, we turned and ran, but not before I saw one more sign: "Hire Sally Ann Back!"

Hire her back? What on earth were they talking about?

Later that night I called one of our employees.

"Mr. Lausch is out of control," she said. "He fired Sally Ann for no reason. We're fed up with him, and we're fed up with you. We aren't being treated fairly. Where've you been all this time? You totally abandoned us!"

It turned out that Mr. Lausch had come from a military background, and he was used to managing employees in a militaristic style, a style that was wrong for Boulder in the 1970's, and particularly wrong for Blue Mountain Arts, which personified the "make love, not war" philosophy. Not surprisingly, after years of working with our laid-back managerial style—one in which we talked to everyone in an open and frank manner—our employees didn't take to being treated like infantry. Steve and I tried to encourage the best work from people, knowing that creativity starts with freedom; Mr. Lausch demanded the best work from people, believing that hierarchy and rules lead to respectful and more productive workers.

In the next few days, we learned of the changes Mr. Lausch had made to Blue Mountain Arts. He'd hired three middle managers—all of whom wore gray suits—to take charge of the employees. The middlemen reported to Mr. Lausch, and only they had direct access to him. Contrary to his open-door promise, he kept his door shut. Since he wouldn't talk to the warehouse workers, they couldn't tell him about what they thought was unfair. To make matters worse, labor relations had sunk so low that our warehouse employees staged a nonunion wildcat strike, and Mr. Lausch fired the striking workers. Then he replaced them, saying, "Good riddance to the troublemakers. Now we can get back to work."

A little while later, the new warehouse workers complained of not being treated fairly, and again Mr. Lausch ignored them. This time, though, the employees contacted the Garment Workers Union and unionized the Blue Mountain warehouse.

"Susan, when you and Steve ran the place, we were all equal," one employee told me. "We were part of a family, and we all had the same goal. We had fun. Now no one cares about us, and we have no one to talk to. He took away our garden. He fired all the old employees. You never came to our defense. We had no choice but to unionize. We had to be heard. If you had stayed, none of this would have happened."

We'd betrayed our employees. Blue Mountain Arts was built first by Steve and me, then by my parents, then our friends, and now a huge family of people was responsible for its success.

We learned that when a problem occurs, distancing yourself from it will not make it go away. You must face it head on and solve it.

Our cards and books continued selling, but the internal structure of our company crumbled: costs skyrocketed, office employees picketed us, the warehouse unionized, and no one was happy.

Steve and I were devastated. What a mess we'd created!

We took a walk in the Boulder foothills where the only distractions might be an animal in the brush or a fallen log in the path. We've always solved our problems by talking them through, and the mountains offer the perfect backdrop for self-examination.

The truth was, we genuinely liked Mr. Lausch. But that didn't necessarily mean he was the right man to be in charge of our business. In fact, he couldn't have been more wrong.

Once we realized this, we acted quickly to correct the situation. Steve—gallant husband that he is—volunteered to break the news to Mr. Lausch. I couldn't bring myself to do this. In his meeting with Steve, Mr. Lausch acted every bit the professional businessman. He still didn't understand why we sided with the employees, and though he knew that things weren't going well, he truly didn't understand why. He listened to Steve, cleared out his desk, and left Blue Mountain Arts forever.

When we hired Mr. Lausch, I thought maybe Blue Mountain Arts needed a touch of professionalism, a touch of "class," to make it into a smoothly running, efficient company. But Blue Mountain Arts is not, and never has been, a machine. It's a labor of love and creativity, and neither of those things can flourish in an authoritarian atmosphere.

Steve and I learned many valuable lessons from this unpleasant experience, the most important of which was: A company's management style must be consistent with the company's philosophy and history.

Our company needed a leader who understood its values and employees and who was willing to grow and change as the company grew and changed.

In a successful work relationship, a manager must guide employees to do their best and encourage them to respect one another.

Our belief that the most important assets of a good manager are fairness and honesty was reinforced.

In addition, we've always felt that "troublemakers"—Mr. Lausch's word for the warehouse strikers—usually have a reason for making "trouble." I believe most people don't like to complain. If they're complaining, especially if they're willing to put their jobs on the line to do it, their reasons are—nine times out of ten—legitimate. At the very least, they should be heard and their problems should be addressed.

Most importantly, we realized that Blue Mountain Arts is our child, and just because our child had grown up didn't mean we could abandon it. Since we were responsible for our business, we had to be directly and personally involved in it. For a while, we had lost sight of that principle. When the pressure got to be too much for us, we should have faced the problem head on and solved it. Instead, we ran away, closed our eyes to what we did not want to see, and the problem didn't go away—it only worsened.

We vowed never to let Blue Mountain Arts down again. Though we were not sure what to do next, with this experience behind us, we certainly knew what not to do. And we also knew that we'd be working very long days again.

I became the president of Blue Mountain Arts once again, only because I found that otherwise people would always look to Steve, not me, for answers. They didn't believe that a woman could have business or product knowledge. My title made them listen to what I had to say. In reality, Steve and I were co-presidents.

We still thought that finding a CEO was the solution to our business problems. We were on the right track but with the wrong person, so we decided to look for another CEO. This time, however, we would try a different method.

I called up a well-known headhunting firm and told them what we needed. I asked that they send me resumes of qualified candidates for the CEO position. They sent us several that we did not like, but one seemed interesting, and we decided to interview that person. The headhunter told me that Mr. Wedge was the perfect candidate.

Several days later, Mr. Wedge came to our offices. He was about fifty-five years old, with a charming personality and a British accent. We immediately liked him. He told us about his impressive background: He had graduated from a top university in England and then was a squadron commander in the Royal Air Force during World War II. We told him all about our company, and he seemed to have well-thought-out and carefully-spoken ideas.

After about two hours, Mr. Wedge left, and our first instinct was to hire him.

Nevertheless, we had learned our lesson from previous hiring mistakes and promised ourselves that before hiring anyone, we would always check the applicant's references and listen carefully to what was said.

Steve didn't believe everything Mr. Wedge had told us about his being a hero in the Royal Air Force because so few pilots survived the war. We contacted the RAF, and they had never heard of Mr. Wedge! I then decided to call the university to find out if Mr. Wedge had really gone there. Within minutes I was speaking to the right person, who told me she had the names of every graduate at her fingertips, and there was no Mr. Wedge. In fact, she told me that he had never matriculated there at all. Unbelievable!

Neither of us ever imagined that Mr. Wedge had made up his resume. The headhunter apparently had not even investigated his background.

Though we were upset, we were thrilled that we had learned from our past mistakes and that we hadn't blundered into what might have been an even bigger one.

After our experiences with Mr. Lausch and Mr. Wedge, we grew up a little. Though we still had no idea what we would do about our business problems, we still had confidence that we would figure out an answer soon.

A good manager should concentrate on the most important part of the business. He or she should "look outward, rather than inward" and focus on what the company is supposed to accomplish.

* * *

An important task of a successful business is to help society by improving the quality of life.

* * *

Develop a common vision and direction for the organization, and stick with it.

These three lessons are adopted from *Management: Tasks, Responsibilities, Practices* by Peter F. Drucker.

chapter seventeen

The Calm Before the Storm

After Blue Mountain Arts bounced back from its short-lived military regime, Steve and I found ourselves right back where we had started. We'd tried the idea of having our books published by a New York publisher, we'd hired a CEO who didn't work out, and we'd almost hired another one who could have been a disaster. None of our plans had solved our problems. Maybe we were a little wiser, but we were still working eighteen hours a day.

On July 10, 1980, we had a beautiful baby daughter. In the hospital, I watched my little, ethereal baby sleeping in her bassinet and realized that we stood at a crossroads, personally and professionally. We loved our company, but our family remained the most important aspect of our lives. Something had to give: We would have to spend either less time with our children or less time at Blue Mountain Arts.

Five years earlier, we'd decided that our first priority was, and always would be, parenthood. So making the choice to spend less time at work was easy. Carrying it out, however, was not.

By 1980, Blue Mountain Arts had grown to over one hundred employees and two hundred sales reps. Our company was starting to be well known, both nationally and internationally, for developing the concept of the non-occasion greeting card and for helping people to convey their feelings. We consistently had to create more books and cards to keep our reputation intact.

If we really wanted Blue Mountain Arts to continue growing, we had to develop a more organized, systematic management style. No longer could we run the company by the seat of our pants, always making—and learning from—our mistakes. Nor could we keep inventing ways of doing things and then wait to find out if they succeeded or failed (a "let's-see-if-it-works" management style).

We realized that we needed to learn about management. We could take a course, but we didn't like the idea of going back to school. Instead, we went to the business section of a bookstore and discovered a book called *Management: Tasks, Responsibilities, Practices* by Peter F. Drucker, a well-known management consultant and professor.

Steve carefully read this eight-hundred-plus-page book, which, in addition to teaching us about what is important in running a business, gave us the self-assurance that many of the "common sense" decisions we had made were right.

We were pleasantly surprised to discover that some of the same lessons that we had learned by trial and error were detailed in this book. For example: We had thought that we were bad managers because we shied away from day-to-day management and instead focused on creative work and visiting retail stores. But this is exactly what Drucker advised. He said that a good manager should concentrate on the most important part of the business. He or she should "look outward, rather than inward" and focus on what the company is supposed to accomplish.

We were relieved to see that he also reinforced our discovery that an effective manager places people in positions where their strengths are productive and their weaknesses irrelevant.

The most pleasant surprise was Drucker's advice that an important task of a successful business is to help society by improving the quality of life.

Steve and I had started Blue Mountain Arts with the goal of helping society and the individual. Now Drucker not only validated our goal, he also made us realize that it wasn't just simple idealism on our part, but a very important aspect of management.

We learned from Drucker to develop a common vision and direction for the organization, and stick with it.

We asked ourselves, "What is our vision and direction?"

After several hours, Steve and I came up with a mission statement. This statement, written in 1980, has been followed exactly without any changes for over twenty-four years:

The purpose of Blue Mountain Arts is to publish quality works that help people communicate...We shall continue to publish unique paper items that have a visual and emotional identity with each other, thereby reinforcing our company image. It is important to stay within our look, but our look can grow...We shall continue to publish items that have a strong demand without the need for advertising so that the energies and resources of our company can be directed toward developing creative ideas and sales...We shall not compete with the major card companies by offering a broad range of products, but rather strive to develop a niche for ourselves by concentrating in a few specialized items that are successful...At all times we will serve customers to the best of our ability, and we will always uphold the customer as being extremely important.

Now that we had defined our philosophy, we examined the structure of the company. Extracting ourselves from the day-to-day business of Blue Mountain Arts meant that we would have to reorganize our company—no easy feat.

Blue Mountain consisted of three departments: Operations, which included order fulfillment and shipping; Sales; and Art & Editorial. After our failure to hire one person to be in charge of the entire company, we thought it would be better to get strong leaders to direct each area. And we realized that Steve and I would have to be in charge of these directors.

We appointed Bob Gall, who had worked for Blue Mountain Arts since 1977, to become director of Operations. Bob, with light, ruddy skin and wavy, red hair, had been the head of the Blue Mountain accounting and purchasing departments. His understanding of the inner workings of the company—not to mention his easygoing disposition—made him well liked and respected by the employees. His sincerity, honesty, and fairness would be a great asset, especially since he'd be in charge of most of the employees.

Cliff Scott, a six-foot-four, slim, incredibly good artist and designer, was promoted to director of Art & Editorial. Cliff had worked for an advertising agency in Chicago before coming to work at Blue Mountain Arts in 1976. He says he took one look at Boulder and never wanted to go back to Chicago.

We appointed my mother, June Polis, to be director of national and international sales. She had been with us since we started Blue Mountain Arts and had been our sales manager since 1974. Now she would also be in charge of the Boulder sales support employees, in addition to all of Blue Mountain Arts' two hundred sales representatives.

The mistakes Steve and I made in our management choices taught us that if we had the talent in our company, it was far better to promote from within, rather than to hire outsiders. From our perspective, we knew our directors' strengths, and we wouldn't spend any time guessing whether or not they would be effective. From the rest of the Blue Mountain Arts employees' perspective, they wouldn't be faced with having to develop trust in a new leader, and they would know Steve and I recognized and rewarded adept work and leadership.

We knew that we would have to stay involved with our company for this plan to work, but we would now only have three managers and our Colorado assistant, Shirlee Goetz, reporting to us.

Finally, Steve and I reached the long-term planning stage. We read our mission statement to our new directors and discussed Blue Mountain Arts' potential and goals, and how the mission related to organization, sales, and creativity. We emphasized that the directors had to be in constant communication with each other. As leaders, they would need to direct their areas, but also work together to bring cohesiveness to Blue Mountain Arts.

Steve and I would no longer have to worry about the day-to-day minutiae of running a growing company, but we would guide the directors, offer leadership, and ensure that Blue Mountain Arts would continue to prosper in the future.

Most importantly, Steve and I would have time to be with our children and each other, and also to get back to being creative.

This time we got it right! The proof of this is that after almost three decades, the same directors continue to be in charge of Blue Mountain Arts.

You have to find a way to balance your work, private life, and everything else that is important to you.

chapter eighteen

AireBrush Feelings

Steve and I had made major adjustments to accommodate our family's needs: We avoided personal publicity, we reorganized the company, and we quietly moved to a new home in a different city in order to preserve our family's quality of life and privacy.

Steve and I now felt at ease with our roles in Blue Mountain Arts. We kept in close contact with the three Blue Mountain directors via phone and fax, and we finally had time to devote to our own family and creativity.

Every day, we learned more about how much our greeting cards and books affected people. A couple wrote us to say that they'd planned on getting a divorce, but when they read one of my poems, they reunited. An elderly man who'd given his late wife our cards thanked us for all the joy they had brought her. Stories like these were so uplifting.

Greeting cards convey a sentiment. Blue Mountain publishes what the writer feels and that's why the poetry on our cards is so specific and personal.

I write poems to Steve, my children, and my family about our relationships and what love means to me. I also write about being a woman and my general philosophy. Many people tell me that I am able to write what they feel but cannot say. In fact, I write to express my own feelings because I have difficulty talking about them.

Why do I write?
I write because
I see something
or touch something
or smell something
or feel something
that I cannot understand
until I try to describe it
in written
words

Steve and I wanted to design a new, beautiful, original way of presenting the poetry on our greeting cards. We wanted to create something that would make people more aware of our cards and that would have a look that would be immediately recognizable as Blue Mountain Arts. It would be soft, elegant, and unique. That was our premise when we started to create the line of cards that would come to represent Blue Mountain Arts.

Steve and I like to browse in art stores, and we love paper. Every card line we've ever designed has started with the ideal paper; whether it was parchment, deckle-edged, or our handmade flower-petal paper, the paper creates the foundation for the look of the card.

We visited a local art store and as we wandered through the paper section, I found the loveliest paper I'd ever seen: a light blue, heavily-textured, watercolor paper with a dark blue deckle, or rough edge. We bought several sheets and dashed home.

Steve experimented with his airbrush, trying different colors and styles. I suggested we try soft pastels in the background, with darker colors for the lettering and illustrations.

The hand-lettered poem stood out against the soft colors, and each image illustrated the free-verse, personal messages. It was always so much fun when Steve and I excitedly went back and forth with our ideas. Once again, our imaginations blended together to form a new concept. We worked on this for a couple of months, and finally we were happy with our new creation.

Cliff Scott, the Art & Editorial director, led his team of artists in designing graphics for the rest of the card line and also engineered beautiful displays to hold the cards. This was the typical way we created all our card lines. Steve and I would conceive the vision for the cards, and then Cliff and his artists would enhance and illustrate finished samples for our approval. Patti Wayant—Blue Mountain Arts' talented, meticulous editorial director, who has been with us for over twenty-five years and is responsible for putting together all the poetry for our books and cards (other than mine)—and her editors, including Gary Morris, who has been with the company for over twenty-three years, would choose poetry for each card.

Cliff called the manufacturer of the paper and asked if they'd make special, colored deckles on white paper for us.

Six months later, the paper arrived. Our first test run was lovely, but the illustrations looked drab.

We thought back to when we silk-screened the posters; we often used fluorescent inks to liven up the colors, so we decided to do this again.

"You're nuts," the printer said. "I've never heard of that. It'll glow in the dark!"

"We did it before," Steve said. "It'll be fine."

"Whatever," the printer responded, "I'll do it. But it's not a good idea and it really won't work."

Maybe not, I thought, but at least we would try to get the results we wanted.

So many people—from teachers to parents to printers—say, "Follow the directions" or "Do things the way they've always been done" or "What are you, crazy?" or "What's the matter with you? Why do you try to do things your way?" Adults who hear these kinds of admonishments can choose to ignore them or be convinced that the naysayers are right. Children, however, may just suppress their creativity. If children are forced to conform long enough, their ideas will eventually be stifled and diminish to nothing.

The fluorescent ink did indeed liven up the colors, and once the printer perfected the exact mix of regular and fluorescent inks, the new cards looked vivid and radiant.

After eight months of conceptualizing these cards, we were thrilled with their distinct look. They stood out from all other cards and, even at a distance, were easily recognizable as Blue Mountain Arts. We didn't realize at the time how important creating a look would be.

The paper, the words, the fold, the illustrations, the colors—each element contributed to our look. The only thing missing was a name. After scrapping many ideas, we decided on AireBrush Feelings, a name that used both the medium and the message.

After printing over five hundred different cards and monitoring their sales, in the summer of 1981 we launched the thirty-six best AireBrush Feelings cards. Mark Oberman, one of our very best sales representatives, who has been with us since 1974, called to tell us that the cards were "flying" out of his stores.

They took off like we'd never imagined. Nancy Trent, who'd arranged our book tour in 1977, was again flooded with requests for publicity, but she kindly turned them all down.

"*Good Morning America* called!" she said one day. "They want you to talk about and read your poetry with the AireBrush cards in the background."

"I don't know, Nancy," I said. "We don't do interviews anymore, and I'm not good at reading my poetry."

"But this will only be about your poetry. They won't ask you anything unless it's about the poetry or art," she said, rushing ahead. "You can't turn this down!"

After a few days of badgering, I gave in and agreed. I practiced reciting my poems and actually began looking forward to the program. If I could talk about my poetry, I was sure I'd be happy.

The day before the show, my daughter got sick. I called Nancy.

"Nancy, my daughter is sick. I have to cancel."

Nancy sucked in air. "Are you crazy? I can't cancel *Good Morning America*! Get on the plane now!"

"She has a fever," I said, "and an earache. I can't leave her."

"Then you call *Good Morning America*," she said, and slammed down the phone. I winced. I'd never heard the normally effervescent publicity specialist get angry. I was her worst nightmare.

I called *Good Morning America*, bracing for the worst, and later wrote down the dialogue.

"I'm terribly sorry,
I can't be on your show.
My daughter has an earache."
"You what?"
"I can't be on your show.
My daughter has an earache."
"Are you crazy?
No one cancels this show."
"I'm really sorry but she can't fly now."
"Well, why can't you?"
"Because I can't leave her.
I'm really sorry. You'll have no
trouble replacing me."
"You're damn right. I can list a thousand people
who will come on with three minutes' notice.
I'll always remember this.
Your daughter has an earache,
so you can't be on my TV show.
This is a first."

Despite the lack of publicity—and canceling my appearance on *Good Morning America*—AireBrush Feelings became the number-one-selling card line in America according to studies conducted by trade magazines.

Storeowners were surprised that our new card line sold faster than any they'd ever carried. Some of them had thought Blue Mountain Arts was just a fad. Now they realized we were here to stay.

Blue Mountain Arts was on top of the world. Steve and I had our creative freedom back and, most importantly, a new addition to our family. We had a baby son on October 6, 1983.

Our third child seemed like an angel, the most perfect child of love. We now lived and worked in our own little enchanted world.

We finally had struck an equilibrium between creativity and management, work and family, and our public and personal lives in a way that satisfied and fulfilled us. We worked while our children were at school, stopped when they came home so we could be with them, and started work again, if we needed to, when they went to sleep. We'd been fortunate in so many ways: with people who liked our work, with employees who liked what they did, and with children who loved us. And, of course, we had each other and our friends.

Little did we know that those groups would become our primary support and biggest source of strength during one of the most difficult times in our lives. The balance we'd worked so long to create was about to topple with a resounding crash.

Choose your professional advisors very carefully. They should understand and appreciate your concerns and values.

* * *

Set aside emergency funds to help you survive unexpected hard times.

chapter nineteen

What Are You Getting Yourself Into?

After finding the Hallmark cards that I had confused with our own Blue Mountain cards in the shopping center store in 1986, I immediately knew that Hallmark could destroy Blue Mountain Arts. At first I was distraught, but Steve's positive attitude helped me regain my confidence and the will to fight this giant.

"Steve, there is no way we can go up against Hallmark," I said the next morning at breakfast.

"Yes we can," he said, his eyes steely. Even though Hallmark was an enormous corporation that probably had an entire team of lawyers to do their bidding, we knew that we were right. "They published the cards," Steve reminded me.

We had a lot of work to do. Most importantly, we had to find and hire a competent, knowledgeable lawyer in the copyright and trademark fields. Unfortunately, we were starting from scratch, so we spent the next two weeks asking for recommendations, and then Steve interviewed twelve lawyers by telephone.

Six of these lawyers didn't have a keen understanding of the relevant, specific laws, so we knew we couldn't use them. Two lawyers, who happened to be professors as well, told us that we didn't stand a chance with this lawsuit. We eliminated them. Steve spent another week on the phone, asking the other four lawyers detailed questions about the precise laws and what they thought of the look-alike cards. Steve asked the best prospects to write a short explanation of their opinion, which is called a brief.

We met with one lawyer who sounded as if he had a good feeling for what we were trying to do, but when he tried to explain the law to us, I couldn't understand a word he said. I asked him why the law was so incomprehensible. I held up one of our cards and one of Hallmark's and said, "We created this card. Hallmark created this one, which in my opinion looks exactly like ours. It's pretty simple. I don't want to hear a technical, scientific explanation." We decided not to use this lawyer either.

We realized that it is essential to choose your professional advisors very carefully and that they must understand and appreciate your concerns and values.

The last written brief we looked at made an immediate impression on us, and we thought we may have found the lawyer we'd been looking for. His brief was clear and concise, with a practical, down-to-earth tone. We made an appointment to meet with its author, Harry Melkonian, at the Buchalter, Nemer, Fields & Younger law offices in Los Angeles.

Mr. Buchalter, a distinguished, elderly man with a gray mustache on his deeply-lined face, greeted us from behind a massive desk in front of a window that looked out on an incredible view of Los Angeles.

"This is Harry Melkonian," Mr. Buchalter said, pointing to a younger man with thick glasses and thin black hair combed to the side. Harry Melkonian did not look like a lawyer at all, but more like a computer hacker. "I personally trained him. He's a fine young lawyer."

Mr. Buchalter leaned forward and dove in.

"What is the volume of Blue Mountain Arts?" he asked. "How long have you been in business? Do you make a profit? Let me see your cards."

He read each card. He turned them over. He opened them up. He felt the paper.

"Now, let's see the Hallmark cards."

I gave him a few, and for the first time since we'd been in the room, he became animated. "My God! They look just like yours!"

For the next half-hour, we discussed the intricate parts of the law, while Mr. Buchalter and Mr. Melkonian flavored their complicated conversation with earthy comments about copying.

"Isn't there a law that says it's illegal to do what they've done?" I asked.

"I'm sorry, Susan," Mr. Melkonian said. "The law's complicated, even though this appears to be a clear case."

Mr. Buchalter sat back in his chair and set his piercing gaze on me.

"Let me tell you what will happen if you pursue this. If you fight a company like Hallmark, you will lose all your privacy. You'll be inundated with so much paperwork that you won't have time for anything else. They can break you. You will not be able to create. Your business will suffer. Life will become difficult."

Difficult times were not new for us. We'd fought the odds without even realizing what we were doing. Steve and I realized that there would always be obstacles to overcome, and we'd just have to barge through them.

And now, everything we'd fought for was on the line. We couldn't stop fighting just because of this obstacle's size.

"I think that these cards look just like our cards," Steve said. "We're not just fighting for ourselves; we're fighting for the rights of all artists to create and protect what they create."

"You may be right," Mr. Buchalter said. His gaze softened when he realized the depth of our commitment. "I think you are. But are you prepared to fight a giant? Do you have the money to fight Hallmark?"

He paused for a moment, and then spoke in a deep, resonant voice that shook me: "Do you have any idea what you are getting yourself into?"

We thought about his questions. I'd worked and earned money all my life, starting in the third grade when I wrote and sold a neighborhood newspaper. In junior high, I mowed lawns and sold refreshments at entertainment events. During high school, I worked in retail stores, and in college, I was a waitress, cleaned hotel rooms, corrected students' homework, and graded tests. Steve and I both paid for our college educations. Even with our scholarships and the money we earned working part-time, when we graduated in 1966, we had student loans totaling twenty-thousand dollars, which would be the equivalent of over one-hundred-thousand dollars in 2004. We had no money when we left for our trip in the pickup truck. Our only assets were our posters, and to eat or pay for gas, we had to sell those posters.

When Blue Mountain Arts became successful, we never wanted material things beyond necessities, and since I'd always lived in fear of debt, we had saved as much money as we could for a rainy day. That rainy day was now, and fortunately we had the resources to fight Hallmark. Our frugality had paid off.

Setting aside emergency funds would help us survive unexpected hard times.

During the next couple of years, I would hear in my mind, over and over again, Mr. Buchalter's deep voice warning us, "Do you have any idea what you are getting yourself into?"

We didn't—not really. There was no way I could have guessed what we were in for, no matter what Mr. Buchalter told me. But even if I had, nothing would have stopped us.

"If I were younger, this would be a case I would want to try myself, but I don't have the energy anymore, and Harry is capable of doing this," said Mr. Buchalter. Right then and there, we hired Harry Melkonian to represent Blue Mountain Arts against Hallmark. We would not let Hallmark beat us.

People are responsible for their actions, regardless of what they say.

chapter twenty

Card Wars

"It's almost like having someone kick sand in your face and laugh, knowing they're bigger than you," cried greeting card artist Sandra Boynton who believed that a new group of Hallmark's cards emulated her designs. "If you sit there and take it, you lose, but if you stand up and fight them, you're going to get bruised."

Steve and I were sympathetic to Sandra's plight. The $3.2 billion greeting card industry was rife with accusations of unfair play. As word of Hallmark's actions got out, more and more small greeting card creators spoke up, asserting that their card designs were also being copied. It seemed to us that the entire alternative card industry was in jeopardy.

Alternative cards, first published in the early 1970's, departed from the traditional rhyming verse, specific-occasion, or one-line-joke studio cards. It was around this time that Steve and I had popularized the "non-occasion" poetry card.

Our cards addressed feelings and emotions rather than celebrating events. Alternative card makers weren't as interested in market share and profits as our predecessors were, so most of us were able to be more innovative. We only needed an audience big enough to support our costs, which were much smaller than those of the "big three" greeting card companies: Hallmark, American Greetings, and Gibson. Most alternative companies had a unique, identifiable look, and they exhibited much creative freedom.

From our viewpoint, it appeared that in an attempt to regain their lost market share, Hallmark released card lines mimicking the alternative cards, confusing consumers, and infuriating the alternative card company artists. Hallmark's "Personal Touch" cards were, to our eyes, exactly like Blue Mountain's AireBrush Feelings and WaterColor

Feelings cards; Hallmark's "Shoebox Greetings" brought to mind Recycled Paper Company's cards that featured the works of Sandra Boynton. Hallmark's drawings of cats, flying hippos, cows, and other characters looked similar to the ones Sandra had made famous. The recycled paper was similar, too, and the size of the characters in proportion to the white space on the card was the same. Even the signature on the cards seemed to resemble Sandra's. She signed all her cards on the right side, beneath the character, with a large "B" in "Boynton." Hallmark's cards were signed "Bowers," with what looked to us like a strikingly similar script and large letter "B."

Another group of Hallmark's soft, watercolor cards featured paintings with short verses that resembled Flavia Weedn's surrealistic cards published by Roserich Designs. Flavia had been designing cards since the early 1970's. She was devastated and believed that these cards looked a lot like hers, but the words didn't say anything meaningful. In an interview, she said that it made her feel as if she had been erased. "It is a very emotional thing with me. It's like they're sticking a knife into my heart and twisting it."

We realized the artists weren't the only ones under attack.

Storeowners stepped forward with shocking stories. A Hallmark card store employee watched, stunned, as a Hallmark company salesman pulled Blue Mountain Arts cards off the shelves, paid for them, threw them in a dumpster, and replaced them with Personal Touch cards. More and more storeowners called in with episodes of Hallmark removing our cards from stores; the phones constantly rang at the office and at our home. Unhappy storeowners called us. Angry sales representatives called us. Scared manufacturers called each other. Headlines screamed of a greeting card war.

As much as I longed to ignore the phone calls, we couldn't. We tried to keep track of the stories as best we could, and we soon came to believe that the strong-arm tactics were part of a much larger plan of Hallmark's to eliminate its competition.

We heard from storeowners and store managers who told us stories about Hallmark offering them a ten-percent discount and special credits if they would sell only Hallmark cards. They sadly told us that Hallmark had tried to pay them to get rid of everyone else's cards.

Owners were afraid that if they sold other companies' merchandise they could lose their businesses. They worried that if they didn't comply, Hallmark would stop selling them Hallmark products altogether. Storeowners were very upset because their livelihood was at stake.

What Hallmark seemed to forget was that they weren't dealing with mindless automatons. They were dealing with independent storeowners who chose to open their own businesses so they'd answer to no one but themselves, these storeowners treasured their independence. They wanted to continue to carry Hallmark cards as their main item, but they didn't expect or want anyone, including their main supplier, to dictate how they ran their businesses. These small business owners were free spirits in a free country. And they, too, started fighting back.

When Hallmark tried to stop three stores in Denver from carrying Hallmark cards because they also carried other companies' cards, the stores sued Hallmark, charging violation of federal antitrust laws.

Nevertheless, we lost our place in a number of stores because Hallmark told the frightened owners to get rid of Blue Mountain Arts cards.

Even stores that didn't carry Hallmark cards joined the fight. Diane Pell, owner of a card and gift shop near the Hallmark facilities in Kansas City, grew furious with the Hallmark artists who came to her store and methodically purchased dozens of cards at a time, never with envelopes.

"It's for research," they told her.

"It's for lifting ideas," she said back, and placed a sign in her window: "HALLMARK RESEARCHERS ARE NOT APPRECIATED IN THIS STORE."

"They came in with notebooks and pads and copied ideas down," said Rick Keyes, owner of another store in Kansas City. "One of them bought seventy-two cards in one visit."

Harry Melkonian, our new lawyer, advised us to give Hallmark the benefit of the doubt by writing a letter explaining our grievances.

On May 16, 1986, Steve wrote a letter to Mr. Hughes, the co-chairman of Hallmark who had visited us earlier. In it, he detailed a number of Hallmark's actions that we believed to be unfair trade practices. We deeply hoped that Mr. Hughes didn't know of Hallmark's tactics and that he'd condemn them, correct them, apologize, and encourage everything to return to normal.

On June 5, 1986, we received a letter, not from Mr. Hughes, but from Mr. I. W. Hockaday, the new President and Chief Executive Officer of Hallmark.

> It is not Hallmark's policy to plagiarize the designs or editorial materials of competitors...You and I are not copyright experts... Have your intellectual property attorneys identify the specific instances where they think actionable infringements have occurred; present them to us and if we agree, we will discontinue the offending item...
>
> Hallmark does not have a policy of making discounts available to dealers who become exclusive Hallmark outlets...
>
> It is not Hallmark's policy to buy up dealer's inventories of competitive cards in return for the dealer taking on the Hallmark line...

The letter continued on with Mr. Hockaday denying that the storeowners were in danger of losing their leases or that Hallmark's cards had, in any way, copied ours.

Steve and I were outraged. So many stores around the country had told us about Hallmark's tactics. The eighty Personal Touch and hundreds of Shoebox Greetings cards looked so much like ours and Sandra Boynton's cards that even we couldn't tell them apart. Fans wrote us in confusion, asking which cards were really ours!

Mr. Hockaday repeated that it wasn't Hallmark's "policy." It may not have been Hallmark's "policy" to do these things, but it seemed to us that they sure as heck were doing them. I firmly believe people are responsible for their actions, regardless of what they say.

We asked Harry Melkonian to respond to Mr. Hockaday's letter. Perhaps with an attorney behind us, we thought, Hallmark would see we meant business and rethink and mend their ways.

In his letter, Harry Melkonian explained why we believed the Personal Touch series copied Blue Mountain Arts and why it constituted unfair competition. He asked them to stop publishing and distributing the offending cards.

As we awaited Mr. Hockaday's response, stores continued calling us. Hallmark's Shoebox Greetings and Personal Touch distribution increased daily.

Not only did I have to look at imitations of our cards in stores, but also every time I turned on the television. Hallmark's advertisements made me sick. Their "Hallmark Hall of Fame" television specials showed family-oriented, uplifting plays and helped encourage Hallmark's image of a thoughtful, sensitive company who cared enough to send the very best.

I was overcome with helplessness. If Hallmark continued distributing Personal Touch cards and forced stores not to carry Blue Mountain Arts, eventually Blue Mountain Arts—and other alternative card companies—would die out. Most of the stores that the alternative card companies sold their cards to were independent Hallmark stores. If these stores stopped selling our cards, it would be almost impossible for the alternative card companies to make up for the lost business.

At least we weren't alone, I reasoned. California Dreamers, Inc., publishers of photographic greeting cards, sent a DECLARATION OF INDEPENDENCE to stores that carried Hallmark cards:

> We are not afraid of your free choices; we are afraid that your choices may no longer be free!

Recycled Paper Products placed an advertisement in trade magazines that defied Hallmark's wholesome image, touting THE HALLMARK HALL OF SHAME and outlining Hallmark's improprieties.

Flavia Weedn of Roserich Designs also ran clever ads in the trade magazines.

I hated waiting for Hallmark's response to Harry's letter. I wanted to stand up and act against this awful situation, but my hands remained tied to legal intricacies. Roserich Designs claimed that its sales declined rapidly in the wake of Hallmark's behavior, and they issued a statement: They were suing Hallmark for unfair competition. According to the lawsuit, Hallmark offered products deceptively and confusingly similar to Roserich cards, bought and discarded Roserich inventory, and offered discounts on the condition that retailers wouldn't carry Roserich.

I kept calling Harry to find out if we had received an answer from Mr. Hockaday. On June 26, ten days after we sent our letter, we received a brief letter from Charles J. Egan, Vice President and General Counsel of Hallmark. The letter to Hockaday had been referred to him, and he "was in the process of looking into our infringement claims," but he'd be going on vacation and wouldn't be back until mid-July.

"In the interim, I would appreciate it if you could cite to me specific examples of Hallmark Personal Touch cards that you believe infringe on Blue Mountain cards," he concluded.

I threw up my hands in disgust. It seemed to me that either Hallmark was completely obtuse or completely deceptive. We talked with Harry again about how we felt that Hallmark was copying our entire line, not just one or two cards. He told us that by focusing on one or two designs, Hallmark deliberately avoided the issue, and sending Egan specific examples would never resolve the problem. We needed to prove that Hallmark's actions violated the law. The only way to do that would be to sue Hallmark.

"It'll take all your time," Harry reminded us. "It'll be expensive, invasive, and it'll take an enormous toll on your personal lives and your company."

Steve and I went home to speak with our children about suing the largest and most well-known company in our industry.

Our eldest son, Jared, was eleven years old, our daughter was six, and our baby was two. We sat down with them and explained, in detail, what Hallmark had done to other card companies and us. We told them what Harry had said.

"It'll take a lot of our time," Steve repeated. "So much time that we might not be able to pick you up from school. We won't be able to stop work to be with you when you come home. We'll have to work at night and during the day. We'll have to spend a lot of money on legal fees."

A lump stuck in my throat. I felt that not only was Hallmark potentially taking away our company, but they also threatened the sanctity of my family life. I looked at each of my children and sighed.

"Do you think we should become involved in a legal battle with Hallmark?"

My daughter and oldest son looked at Hallmark's cards and became furious because they could not tell which cards were ours and which were Hallmark's.

"Yes!" they yelled.

"We'll help you in any way we can," Jared offered.

Tears sprang to my daughter's eyes. "But what if you lose?" she asked.

"We know we're right," Steve said. "We just don't know if we can prove that Hallmark did something illegal."

"We'll all work hard and do the best we can, and if we lose, it'll be better than doing nothing at all," I said. "At least we'll know we tried."

"I don't like this," she said.

"Neither do we," Steve and I said in unison.

"I don't need any more toys," she said, shrugging.

"If you win, you'll help save other companies and artists, too," Jared added. "You have to fight this. It's not fair or honest."

His statement reminded me of a discussion Steve and I had had many years earlier with a friend, John Boswell, a successful literary agent and author in New York. We had described the honesty and integrity of the greeting card and book publishing industries.

"You guys are living in an ivory tower," he said. "It's a dog-eat-dog world out there."

We shook our heads and told John he was wrong. Not the greeting card or book industries, we said. They're very honest.

Now I hugged my kids, resolved to fight Hallmark, and called John.

"You were right," I said. "It is a dog-eat-dog world after all."

chapter twenty-one

Friends

Step to the music you hear.
~Henry David Thoreau

Many storeowners, salespeople, employees, and industry people called or wrote us saying how much they liked doing business with Blue Mountain Arts and how angry they were at Hallmark. They told us details of Hallmark's latest tactics. The storeowners and salespeople trusted us, and we trusted them. We knew how important our customers were, and everyone at Blue Mountain Arts went out of their way to treat them fairly. Nevertheless, Steve and I had no idea how strongly the industry had felt about us, and we were overwhelmed by its response.

Since the children started school, Steve and I had stopped going to trade shows, but my mother and other Blue Mountain employees went to every one. Mom had developed so many personal relationships among the storeowners and salespeople that they went straight to her with any problems, knowing she'd solve them in a moment.

And now, when we were struggling, the storeowners went to bat for us. Steve and I wanted to thank them, along with our friends and family, so we planned a Blue Mountain Arts party at the Museum of Modern Art for the first night of the 1986 National Stationery Show in New York City. It would be a celebration of our fifteen years of "caring and striving for excellence."

During that difficult time, the night of our party stands out as a beacon of love and support.

My mother, resplendent in a soft, purple leather suit that offset her shining, gray hair, set the tone for the party with a short, warm, introductory speech and then pointed to her grandchildren and introduced them to the audience.

Dressed in a multicolored suede jacket with a blouse and slacks, I talked about the first fifteen years of Blue Mountain Arts' history, and Steve, handsome in his suit with a brown leather jacket highlighted with bands of handmade, Southwestern rugs, spoke about our future—the next fifteen years.

Many storeowners and representatives remembered us from our trips in 1971, and they were delighted to see how far we'd come since living in a truck. Some of them came to the podium reminiscing about how Steve and I had sold them our hand-silk-screened posters.

Blue Mountain Arts' directors, Bob Gall and Cliff Scott, each spoke about how their departments strove for excellence. They were followed by Cathy Catanzano, the innovative manager of Order Fulfillment, and Mindi McDermott, manager of what has been called "the best Customer Service Department of any company." Rachel Billingsley, Blue Mountain's accurate manager of Accounting, was scheduled to speak, but she gave birth to a baby boy on that day. Each of these people has continued to work for Blue Mountain Arts for close to thirty years.

Then storeowners, buyers, artists, and salespeople spoke about everything from the history of the industry to the universality of our message to the longevity of our relationships.

In a speech entitled "Support of Retailers' Freedom of Choice," David Hill, our local Boulder attorney, spoke briefly about how retailers must be free to choose what they want to do in their own stores. A wave of whispers cascaded through the audience. Many had been wondering when we'd address this issue. I longed to stand up and announce a plan of action, but I knew I couldn't act in haste or be unprofessional. We had to take all the proper steps and give Hallmark every opportunity to make things right.

Mike Drukman—the Madco representative my mother had hired twelve years earlier—gave a speech that dazzled me.

I have been a representative for Blue Mountain Arts for over a decade, which in our industry is like two or three lifetimes...I think of Blue Mountain Arts as if it were a play. And I am thoroughly convinced that fate played a role in the casting of the Blue Mountain Arts play. How else would we have the creations of one of the world's greatest love affairs between a female freelance writer who writes poetry in her spare time and a male physicist who enjoys painting in his spare time? Susan and Stephen definitely dance to the beat of a different drummer. They step to the music they hear, and that beat has provided millions of people worldwide with the ability to express themselves better than they ever dreamed possible.

As he finished his speech, for the first time I realized that Steve's and my dreams just might have come true. Mike was validating exactly what Steve and I originally said we wanted to do. When Steve and I were dating each other in 1968, our favorite quote was the one Mike referred to, and Steve and I had promised to follow Thoreau's philosophy. This was absolutely amazing.

Mike closed his speech by making a joke:

Blue Mountain Arts has just had the ultimate tribute paid to them. Hallmark, who advertises "When You Care Enough to Send the Very Best," has announced to the world that they cared enough to copy the very best.

The audience cheered and laughed.

My mother then announced that she had a surprise for the audience. "Susan's going to recite several poems, accompanied by music," she said. "This is the first time she's ever done this live in front of a large group of people."

I have a deep, emotional response to certain music, so I had wanted sensitive flute and piano music to accompany my poetry reading. I had found a flautist, Leonard Goulis, whose notes were passionate, and a masterful musician, Richard James, who played piano and keyboards. I chose two melodies, "Daydreams," a song that Jane Olivor beautifully sang, and a tune that I had composed and Richard arranged. I tried to incorporate the rhythm and feeling of the music with my words, and we had practiced intensely for days prior to the party.

First, I read a love poem to Steve, and then just as I was about to read the poem that I had written to our daughter, the lights were turned off. Our daughter, wearing a pink and white pinafore dress, walked on stage and sat on a wooden stool. The lights were turned back on and I smiled at her awkwardness; she always preferred climbing trees to playing with dolls, and she almost never wore a dress. She straddled the stool and swung her legs back and forth, tugging and pulling the lace at the bottom of her dress.

My day always becomes wonderful
when I see your
pretty face smiling so sweetly
There is such warmth and intelligence
radiating from you
It seems that every day
you grow smarter and more beautiful
and every day
I am more proud of you
As you go through different stages of life
you should be aware that there will be many times
when you will feel scared and confused
but with your strength and values
you will always end up wiser
and you will have grown from your experiences
understanding more about people and life
I have already gone through
these stages
So if you need advice or someone to talk to
to make sense out of it all
I hope that you will talk to me
as I am continually cheering for your happiness
my sweet daughter
and I love you

As I finished the last line, I looked at our little daughter, sitting there so real, so guileless, so unaffected, and I was overcome with love for her. I explain my feelings the best way I know how to in poems, but as I had written to Steve, words can never fully express the depth of my love for him and our children. Now, in front of all these people, I spontaneously walked over to our daughter and kissed her small cheek. She looked embarrassed and surprised, but pleased by my unexpected show of affection.

Suddenly I realized that the theater was silent. Did I mumble? I wondered. Maybe they hadn't heard a word I'd said.

Then, without warning, a roar of applause swept over us; the men and women in the audience had been regaining their composure. My mother approached the podium, tears streaming down her face, and thanked everyone for coming to our party.

I proceeded to the garden for dinner and saw dozens of people with teary eyes. The poetry reading had truly moved them.

One burly storeowner approached me, "I have a daughter who went away to college this year," he choked out. "Your poem reminded me how much I miss her."

Hundreds of people, many of whom had been crying, hugged and complimented Steve and me. Though I had been told that people identified with my words, I never observed them actually letting down their guards and exposing their sensitivity, love, and understanding beneath tears.

I felt so touched and fortunate to be a part of all this.

A number of people came to me and said that I should write a book about Steve's and my story. They said that it was inspiring to see a man and woman who loved each other, who loved their family, and who had built a business on love. "Your story could help a lot of people."

Since I'd kept a journal about our relationship and how we first started Blue Mountain Arts, I thought that maybe I would write a book. It would be a long-term project, and I would not consider having it published while our children lived at home. If our story could encourage people to reach for their dreams, it would be worthwhile.

For the first time, I entertained positive thoughts about our situation with Hallmark. The verbal and spiritual support and the love that permeated the Museum of Modern Art that night would give us the strength and endurance we needed to overcome any adversity. And we would need it. Two months later we announced our lawsuit against Hallmark.

chapter twenty-two

Blue Mountain Arts v. Hallmark Details

After anxiously and impatiently waiting to speak out against what we felt Hallmark was doing to us and other alternative greeting card companies, we finally filed our lawsuit on July 8, 1986.

Although it seemed as if we were accusing Hallmark of simple violations, the legal aspects were quite complex.

It is hard to comprehend the enormous amount of work, preparation, tactics, and research that occurred during our court case, so I thought it would be interesting to recount many of the details.

Our case against Hallmark Cards, Inc., contained three categories of claims:

1. Violation of the federal law that protects the trademark of a product (called the "Lanham Act"),
2. Activities that represented "unfair competition," and
3. Copyright infringement.

We requested an immediate court order to stop Hallmark from shipping their Personal Touch cards until a jury trial decided on the card line's fate. This kind of court order, called a "preliminary injunction," is very hard to get, but we had to try for it, because if Hallmark indefinitely delayed the jury trial date—a realistic scenario— we could be out of business long before we ever got to court. We had to stop them as soon as possible.

The federal law that protects trademarks contains a provision that makes it illegal, under certain conditions, for someone to imitate the appearance of another company's product for the purpose of passing off his or her imitation as the authentic product.

In order to apply this provision of the law, one must prove that the original product has a recognizable look and that customers are confused by the imitation product.

Our recognizable look consisted of a combination of "unique and distinctive features." In other words, our look wasn't just one thing. We didn't consistently use one illustration, one poem, or one color scheme. It was the whole package that Hallmark copied: a combination of features that Steve and I had meticulously designed, which, together, presented the distinct, recognizable look of a Blue Mountain Arts card.

In a nutshell, that was our first "complaint."

Our second "complaint" described the unfair competition practices of selling deceptively similar cards, and our third "complaint" described the elements of Hallmark's Personal Touch cards that infringed on Blue Mountain Arts' copyrights. Our motion for the preliminary injunction requested that they stop selling and manufacturing the "copycat cards" and "stop engaging in unfair competitive activities."

Now, finally, we could stand up and fight.

On August 18, Hallmark denied any wrongdoing by issuing the following statement:

> Hallmark did not copy Blue Mountain Arts card lines, and did not infringe on any right of Blue Mountain Arts…and denies each and every allegation.

Hallmark stated that our cards were not unique, that they did not have a "look," and that there was no "substantial similarity between the Hallmark cards and the Blue Mountain Arts cards."

We expected that much. What we didn't expect was for Hallmark to deny that Blue Mountain Arts greeting cards existed at all:

> We deny that Blue Mountain has in fact developed any reputation…We request that the complaint be dismissed and Hallmark be awarded its costs and attorney's fees and such other further relief as the court deems proper.

Rage flooded my mind. Steve and I knew we were in for a long, hurtful battle.

The day we filed our lawsuit, the press discovered it.

The *Wall Street Journal* came out with one of the first articles—a half-page story with the headline:

HALLMARK IS IN DAVID-AND-GOLIATH BATTLE,
ALTERNATIVE CARD FIRMS FIGHT FOR SPACE, IDEAS

The article exposed the sweeping problems in the greeting card industry. The story ended with a statement from Patty Moore, Hallmark's manager of product information: "The cards reflect current design trends," she said, "but each card's design and message are Hallmark originals."

Although Steve and I had made a conscious decision six years earlier not to grant personal interviews, we couldn't abide by that policy now. We were not only fighting for the life of Blue Mountain Arts, but we also were fighting for the rights of other small publishers and artists. Artists must be able to protect their creations and sell them anywhere they want to. We had taken on this battle, and with it came a responsibility to inform the public. If we didn't speak out and answer reporters' questions, it might seem as if we had something to hide. We couldn't let the Hallmark spokespeople's ridiculous statements go unanswered!

It seemed as though every news article included Hallmark's maddening clichés: "We are not trying to eliminate the competition, but we will do things necessary to ensure we remain the number-one greeting card company..."; "Hallmark is merely responding to the way people want to communicate..."; "Are we aware of what our competition is producing? You bet we are..."; and "The new products and programs reflect our intention to stay number one."

Steve was never comfortable talking to the media, so I granted our first interview in years to Mary Beth Nibley, a reporter for the Associated Press.

A full-page article, with a photograph of Steve and me, appeared in over one hundred newspapers. Nibley wrote:

> Some card merchants think there's no question that Hallmark got tired of watching more and more space in the 22,000 U.S. stores that carry Hallmark merchandise get taken by tiny competitors.
>
> "It's fairly common knowledge that the major card companies, especially Hallmark, have decided to go after the alternative card market," said Bonnie Sellers, marketing director for Renaissance Greeting Cards, in Fanford, Maine....
>
> Industry insiders generally consider Ms. Schutz a pioneer in the high-emotion card business.

In addition to almost daily interviews, Steve, Blue Mountain Arts, and I were inundated with enough paperwork to fill several large rooms. Hallmark could ask us to give them memos that could potentially help their case. In fact they asked for a copy of almost every report, memo, and greeting card we'd ever produced. Blue Mountain Arts' employees worked full-time for months photocopying all the requested papers, eventually filling up over fifty boxes. Harry Melkonian warned us that this was a common tactic large companies used to get smaller companies to buckle during a lawsuit. Luckily, since the beginning of Blue Mountain Arts, we had kept meticulous records, and this was one of the main reasons that we were able to proceed with the case.

We soon learned the other tricks, tactics, and overwhelming details of a lawsuit: interrogatories; depositions; document requests; opposition to document requests; motions; counter-motions; long, rambling briefs; and counter-briefs. I could go on ad infinitum.

My first personal experience with the Hallmark lawyers set the tone for the rest of the trial. We had to arrange a date for my Denver deposition, where I'd answer all their questions and provide information for the preliminary injunction hearing in Federal Court.

Hallmark's lawyers asked Harry when I'd like to have my deposition taken, and Harry turned the question over to me.

Believing that the Hallmark lawyers would cooperate with my

wishes if I were honest and flexible with them, I told them, "Anytime is fine. But the absolute latest I can do it is September eighth. My children start school on the tenth, and I have to be home the day before."

We had a family tradition of celebrating the last day of summer vacation with our children. Since school represented work and summer represented freedom, we all had one last carefree fling. Then we'd spend the evening watching a rented movie while the children arranged their new binders. Early the next morning, we'd drive the children to their first day of school in our vintage 1957 convertible, which somehow managed to sputter and chug its way along the highway year after year. Finally, we'd attend a back-to-school coffee for the parents and sneak extra muffins to our children in their classes.

Family traditions like these may sound trivial to some, but they were so much a part of us that they had come to represent the security and joy of our family life. The children expected and looked forward to these rituals.

I explained this to Harry, and he assured me the deposition would occur well before school started.

A week went by, and Hallmark's lawyers still hadn't spoken to Harry about my deposition. Harry called them, and after many more phone calls, they finally responded that the only day they would take my deposition was September ninth, the day before school started. That meant I had to be in Denver, and I couldn't possibly join my family at home on the last day of summer vacation. The Hallmark lawyers said they could not change the date. I told Harry that I wouldn't go to my deposition. He told me that I had no choice, and he once again tried to change the date to no avail.

Rather than leave me out of our family tradition, Steve and the children came to Colorado with me. We agreed that they would leave in time to get home before school started, and hopefully I'd be on the plane with them.

At 7:30 A.M. on September ninth, with a mile-high attitude, I drove into Denver, the Mile High City. I've always been forthright in answering people's questions and that, combined with my fury for having to be in

Denver that day, worried Harry. He was as anxious to get my deposition over with as I was. During the drive to Denver, Harry explained the details of a deposition.

"A deposition is a sworn statement, under oath, that can be used in a court of law in which a witness or party is questioned by one or more of the lawyers in the lawsuit," he said. "It is a means of discovering the facts before the trial as perceived by the witnesses. A deposition can be used to impeach the witness's testimony at trial if the trial testimony differs from the deposition. It can refresh the recollection of a witness who's forgotten the facts at trial and can be used where a witness can't attend the trial. Then the deposition may be read to the judge or jury as if the witness were present."

I hadn't realized the importance of my deposition until I listened to Harry's comprehensive definition. Consequently, I entered the building in Denver with more apprehension than anger and with the hope that I wouldn't say something wrong.

In a small room, with Harry at my side, I faced Andrea Williams, the Hallmark lawyer. I had been afraid of meeting her and was surprised by her frailty. I'd pictured a stern, strong, large woman, but instead, she was petite, thin, and small-boned, with short, red hair and a chilly air of detachment. She fired away.

"What is your name?

"What is your educational background?

"How did you start Blue Mountain Arts?"

I was sure her questions led somewhere, but I didn't know where.

"Do you consider one letter with one poem a manuscript?

"How many poetry manuscripts does Blue Mountain Arts receive in a year?"

I quoted her a number, shaking my head and wondering who on earth cared about our definition of a manuscript. What did these questions have to do with anything? I worried that she would get me to say something ambiguous or stupid that she'd bring up in court later. I felt as if she was just keeping me here to waste time and make me so mad that I'd say something that would help her case. If so, she accomplished her task. I was mad. I began giving short, curt answers.

"Do you spend more of your time now writing books and other kinds of work rather than the cards?"

"Generally the books are made of the poetry cards that we've published," I answered.

"It's a collection of poems?"

"Yeah."

I decided to give her an example. I told her that most of the poems that I had written to my daughter, including those that had appeared on our cards, were incorporated into my latest book, *To My Daughter, with Love, on the Important Things in Life*.

"Is there someone on the staff that goes back and identifies the poems?"

"No, I go back."

"But to identify them, someone has to go back over the years and pull together all the mother-daughter poems, correct? Did you do that or did someone else do that?"

My patience slipped away.

"My daughter has only been alive for six years, so it wasn't very hard to select the poems. And I just started writing most of the poems to her in the last few years."

Ms. Williams smiled. "The first four years are terrible."

I stared at her. I was not in the mood to talk about motherhood with this woman.

"I asked your husband this," she said. "I just want to confirm that you haven't conducted any seminars or focus groups with consumers to see what it is about your poetry that makes them buy the cards."

"No. Definitely not."

"And have you or your company conducted any kind of survey like that?"

"Definitely not."

Hallmark had conducted customer surveys to find out why people liked our cards and my poetry, and I realized Ms. Williams was hoping to discover that Blue Mountain Arts had also directed customer surveys.

The fallacy in this logic was that we had never polled people. We tested cards in the marketplace by printing and sending cards to a small number of stores to see which designs people liked well enough to buy. We allowed customers to make choices about whether or not they wanted a card we designed; we didn't design cards according to surveys, as Hallmark apparently did. We had never asked or surveyed people about what we should create. We let our hearts guide us.

After three hours, Ms. Williams finally asked her last question.

"One of the things you say is that Hallmark has over $1.2 billion in sales per year, is that right?"

"I've read that, so I said it," I replied.

"That's all I have for now."

My deposition was over! I ran to the ladies' room and washed my face, confused by the events of the day. Had I said anything that Ms. Williams could turn around to Hallmark's advantage? I really didn't know! "This isn't about justice," I thought bitterly. "It's about leading people on and manipulation." Was the system really weighed so heavily in favor of the powerful? Would their power and size crush the smaller, weaker side? I loathed everything I'd witnessed so far. Did any of this have anything to do with right or wrong?

Then I thought of Steve and the children and ran for a telephone.

"United Airlines, how may I help you?" a woman answered.

I gave her my flight information. "I'm running late. Will my plane leave on time? If I get there ten minutes before departure can you let me on?"

"I'm sorry, Ma'am, it is leaving on time, and once we close the door, we cannot allow anyone on. You'll have to get here earlier if you want to make the plane."

I ran from the telephone booth, hailed a taxi, and told the driver to speed to the airport. I would not miss my children's first day of school.

I got to the airport and dashed to the United terminal. They were closing the door to the jetway.

"Please, please let me get on the plane!" I pleaded to the attendant.

"I'm sorry, but—"

"My family's on that plane, and if I don't get on I'll be left in Denver until tomorrow morning, and it's my children's first day of school, and I have to get on that plane! Please let me on!" I begged.

She regarded me for a moment, deciding whether I was a desperate mother or a bona fide lunatic. Apparently she decided on the former, because she opened the door and accompanied me to the airplane.

Everyone on the plane looked at me, surprised and a little irritated; they thought they'd be leaving, and here was this harried woman running to the back of the plane. I looked around for my family.

"Mom!" our children shouted at once, and they ran into the aisle with Steve to greet me. The five of us embraced in the aisle, laughing and acting like long-lost relatives. A few passengers even clapped, most likely thinking that I hadn't seen my family in months.

I fell into my seat. I was frazzled, but I didn't want to spoil the moment with my family. After my miserable day, I felt secure and happy just to be with the family I loved so dearly. They stabilized and uplifted me like nothing else could.

Several days later, I received a frantic call from Cliff Scott. Unnamed callers who claimed to be Hallmark employees were promising "information" in exchange for compensation. Bob Gall also received a similar call from a supposedly ex-Hallmark employee who said that she had "titillating information" for us. Harry had told us that high-profile cases often bring "crazy people out of the woodwork." But he also warned us that there is always the chance that this might be a tactic or trick. Who would have known this, and what would have happened if we hadn't known, I nervously wondered.

I wanted to crawl into a cave and hibernate until the hearing; I wanted to get away from the lawyers, depositions, and everything else related to the case. I didn't know the law well enough to know what could jeopardize our case, and I lived in fear that I'd say or do the wrong thing.

Every day, Steve and I understood more about what Mr. Buchalter meant when he asked us: "Do you have any idea what you are getting yourself into?"

Nature is the most peaceful environment for clarifying your thoughts and putting things into perspective.

chapter twenty-three

The Hearing Is On, the Hearing Is Off

"Susan, Harry's on the phone."

"Can I call him back? I'm preparing for a TV interview. The crew is setting up cameras right now."

"He says it's very important."

Weary, irritated, and anxious about the hearing, I left the television crew setting up in the employee children's playroom at Blue Mountain Arts. We were two days away from the October 22, 1986 court hearing, and Steve and I hadn't slept in forty-eight hours. In that time, we'd read and gathered last-minute information for our lawyers, carried two boxes and two briefcases of files on a plane to Denver, and been informed that we would be greeted by a Denver news crew in our Boulder offices.

"Susan!" Harry said when I picked up the phone. His voice sounded odd.

"What's wrong?"

"I have very bad news."

I asked myself what more could possibly go wrong. Was Hallmark going to block another document from evidence? Were they going to ask for more records and documents from our company's history?

"What is it?" I asked Harry wearily.

"The hearing may be delayed…The hearing may be off, Susan."

My mind blanked. The hearing may be off?

"The Hallmark attorneys filed a motion called a 'recusal,' asking the judge to remove himself from the case because the judge's son, a law student, has clerked at Dave Hill's Boulder law firm."

"But didn't Dave tell them about that a long time ago? Didn't the Hallmark lawyers say it was all right?" Panic crept into my voice. "Why did they change their minds?"

"Well, they claim they knew about the son working there in the past, but they didn't know he'd continued to work there."

Fury blurred my vision. I gripped the phone. Why hadn't Dave told his firm the judge's son couldn't work there until the case was over? How could this happen with the hearing only two days away?

I took a deep breath and exhaled. "What happens now?"

"Tomorrow at noon the judge will call us into his office to tell us that he might remove himself from the case. I'm leaving Denver right now to come to your office. Wait for me there."

I couldn't speak. I could barely think.

"I'm so sorry, Susan," Harry said. "I'm upset about this, too."

The phone rang the moment I hung up.

"Susan? This is Dave Hill." He sounded terrible.

"Dave, how could you let the judge's son work for you again?"

"I didn't know he was still working for us."

My last bit of control slipped away. "How could you do this? What about all the witnesses? What about all the preparation? This isn't fair!"

I slammed the phone down, trembling, but I had to keep myself together; I had an interview in a few minutes.

I smoothed my shirt with my hands, combed my hair, went into the children's room, and prepared for the television appearance. I had to be professional and composed; if anyone guessed something was wrong, I might either blurt out the whole story or burst into tears. I did not want to do either of those things on camera.

Once the cameras were turned off, though, I waved a quick thank-you to the newscasters, told Steve I needed to talk to him, ran to our office, and locked the door.

"The hearing's off!" I shouted, finally breaking down. I gave into the tears that had threatened for the last hour, realized I had a painful headache that was rapidly becoming a migraine, and felt dizzy all at the same time. I couldn't bear to have this lawsuit go on any longer. It would mean that months would pass before a new judge would hear the case. It would mean that we'd have to spend more time on our case, more money for lawyers, more time thinking, planning, and gathering information. It would mean that we'd continue to have no time for ourselves and little time for our children. And, of course, we'd still be unable to write or create. I couldn't stand another day of this. I was ready to give up.

"You know, we could use the time well, Sue," Steve said after getting over his initial shock. "We really need more time to perfect our case."

We looked at each other, me with a red, weak face, him with a concerned, weary expression.

"But then again, I just want it to be over, too," he amended.

Someone knocked on the door.

"Who is it?" Steve asked, grasping my hand.

"It's Harry," came a voice.

"He can't see me like this," I said. "You go."

Steve went outside to greet Harry and came back several minutes later.

"There's a chance that the judge might not remove himself from the hearing, so we have to proceed as if it is on," Steve said.

"I can't meet with Harry now," I told Steve. "I just can't deal with any more of this. What about the witnesses who are flying to Colorado tonight?"

Steve told our long-time Colorado assistant, Shirlee Goetz, who has recently retired after working for us for twenty-six years, to call all the witnesses and cancel their trips to Colorado, and he suggested that I go home and rest. I nodded mutely. Shirlee volunteered to drive me home because she noticed that I was not in any condition to drive. As we approached my driveway, she kindly told me that things would turn out all right. I hopped out of the car and ran right to my bed. I felt sick, both physically and mentally.

After a nap, I called Steve who, without the benefit of any sleep, had continued to work with Harry.

"Let's take the children into the mountains and pick aspen leaves tomorrow," Steve said.

"Yeah," I said. "The leaves are gold now. The kids will love that."

"Since the hearing will be canceled, we'll just have a vacation with the children. I mean, it could have been a lot worse. We could've lost."

"I know, but I really don't know if I have any energy or fight left in me," I said.

When we woke the next day, we smelled the Colorado air and took an invigorating hike in the mountains with our children.

Nature is the most peaceful environment for clarifying your thoughts and putting things into perspective.

"To hell with Hallmark."

"We can't let them continue to ruin our lives," Steve added.

Steve went to work for a few hours, and because I couldn't face people yet, I stayed home with the children.

At one o'clock, the phone rang. I didn't want to answer it and risk ruining my time with the kids, but in light of the previous day's events, I had to.

"Yes?"

It was Harry. To everyone's surprise, the judge had decided not to remove himself from the court hearing. He said that the Hallmark lawyers knew about the situation, and had admitted there was no impropriety, so there was no precedent set for removing himself, even if Hallmark said he should. I'd never heard Harry so excited.

"So what does all that mean?"

"Susan, the hearing is back on. You'd better get down here right away. We have a lot to do."

My other phone line rang. It was Dave Hill, trumpeting the same news.

I hung up both lines, wondering if I'd just dreamed everything about yesterday and today. My anxieties rushed back at the new turn of events. How could we get ready? I had lost a whole day. How could we get our witnesses to Colorado from Indiana, New York City, and Boston in time for the trial? How could I meet with our lawyers about the trial? I'd spent the morning collecting aspen leaves with the children, the court far from my mind, and now I had to refocus.

I had to get into the right frame of mind. I sat back a moment and thought about what Hallmark had done to us, how their actions tore us to pieces, and I quickly renewed my determination.

I went to the office and began calling everyone we had called the day before. My mother, brother, and, especially, our witnesses would have to know that the hearing was back on. I started with Mike Drukman in Boston, who would have the most difficulty getting to Denver on time.

"Is Mike there?" I asked Bobbie, Mike's demure wife, explaining what had happened.

"Oh, my goodness, he's at a Red Sox game," she said. "I'll get the message to him though, don't worry!"

Within an hour, Mike, who'd been enjoying a World Series game between the New York Mets and the Boston Red Sox in Fenway Park from somewhere behind first base, felt a tap on his shoulder. He turned to see a policeman.

"Mike Drukman?"

"Yes…"

"I have a message for you. You need to leave this baseball game immediately and go directly to the airport to catch the last flight to Denver. The Blue Mountain Arts hearing is back on, and they need you."

Mike dashed out of the park and made it to Logan Airport just in time. In fact, against all odds, every one of our witnesses made it in time for the hearing. With about fourteen hours to go, I was tired and frightened. I just wanted the ordeal to be over, but the night had just begun for Steve, Harry, and me.

Twenty-four hours before the hearing—right around the time when we knew there would actually be a hearing—Harry received three boxes of memos and documents from Hallmark. The documents contained references to Blue Mountain Arts, Steve, or me, and they were supposed to have arrived weeks earlier. True to form, Hallmark waited until the last minute; we assumed they hoped to delay the hearing or that our lawyers wouldn't have time to read all the memos.

Since Steve and I couldn't read the confidential memos, Harry had to read every document himself. We'd be privy to the confidential information only if Harry decided to enter it into the hearing the next day.

Among the thousands of papers, a very fatigued Harry discovered some revealing and disturbing memos written by Hallmark executives. He also realized Hallmark possessed every single product catalog we'd ever produced, all filed in boxes with "Hallmark" stamped on them. Not only had they studied and dissected us, but they also had managed to get our catalogs, which were only sent to stores and reps, certainly not to competitors.

Steve and I stayed up all night reading pages of our depositions and fan mail. Steve highlighted the parts of the depositions we wished to keep confidential (like the dollar volume of our card lines); he had to go through thousands of pages of depositions by five in the morning.

My job was to reread our fan mail and highlight quotations Harry could read in court. The benefits of this task were twofold: We'd counter Hallmark's argument that no one had heard of us, and on a personal level, I'd regain confidence from reading the warm, thoughtful letters.

We weren't inconsequential. We did affect people, no matter how much Hallmark tried to prove otherwise.

By four in the morning, we felt like throwing in the towel. Hallmark was so far ahead of us we'd never be able to catch up.

We delivered the fan-letter quotes and confidential markings to Harry at five o'clock, went home, showered, and dressed in our court clothes: a navy suit for Steve and a pink wool suit for me.

As I dressed, the phone rang. My stomach sank. Calls at seven in the morning could never be good.

"Sue, I have some bad news," Harry said.

"Don't tell me the hearing is off again!"

"No, it's on, don't worry," he said. Then he told me that we couldn't use the fan mail quotes I had highlighted because it was hearsay. He also wanted me to tell Steve that Hallmark said nothing in the depositions could be confidential, including the sections Steve had highlighted.

I yelled at Harry for not knowing this before we stayed up all night reading depositions and fan letters. I couldn't think straight, and the hearing was just two hours away.

We'd waited so long for this day, but at that moment Steve and I both felt despondent. Usually when I feel miserable, Steve's strength and support boost my spirits and I do the same for him. On that morning, though, we were both miserable, and I thought nothing could bring us out of it.

We woke the children and told them to get dressed. My daughter approached me.

"Mommy, I'm afraid you're going to lose," she said, teary eyed.

I buried her small blonde head in my arms and chest and held her close to me. Steve and I looked at each other, and our eyes met with love. In comforting our daughter, I had found a well of strength I didn't know I had. At the moment when Steve and I could no longer cheer up each other, our children did it for us.

"Honey, don't worry," I said. And now, with our children by our sides, we were ready to go to court.

chapter twenty-four

Batting .800

I paused outside the courtroom and shifted the weight of my toddler and his canvas baby bag in my arms. My head pounded despite the Excedrin I'd taken, and my eyes ached. I felt ready to take on Hallmark, but I just wanted the day to be over.

All five of us walked through the big, wooden doors of the courtroom, which actually was a lecture hall at the University of Colorado in Boulder. It looked exactly as I'd imagined it would: a large, cold room with high ceilings and wood paneling. My mother, always early, had saved seats for us up front. My brother, Robbie, my sister-in-law, Rae, and their two children sat behind us. Since they had moved to Boulder, our families were extremely close, and having them there was comforting.

I settled the kids in and looked around. Spectators filled the room. The press was there in droves, and I recognized many storeowners and greeting-card company owners, as well as at least twenty Blue Mountain Arts employees. Dozens of people I didn't recognize sat on the benches that lined the back wall.

I looked forward at the attorneys' tables and panicked. Hallmark had a large cadre of lawyers sitting around their table. "Susan, no matter how many lawyers they have, they can only speak one at a time," Harry said when he saw the look on my face.

Our side was led by Harry, our honest, down-to-earth attorney, so competent at understanding and explaining complicated issues. His enormous flexibility allowed him to shift with the direction of whatever legality was presented to him. And he was as angry at Hallmark as we were.

Assisting Harry was Ricardo Gomez, a young, caring lawyer whose specialty was organizing all the different aspects of our case, researching legal cases, and developing briefs. I'll always remember the concern in his voice the first time we had dinner: "Are you okay?" he asked us. "I mean, are you able to cope with everything Hallmark's doing to you? Can you survive all this pressure and misery?" He displayed the same concern he would have given a family member, and tears shone in his eyes as he hugged me.

Also in the courtroom helping us were lawyers from Harry's firm, Rick Brookwell and Jim Hicks, who was also an excellent writer, and Steve Briggs from Dave Hill's firm.

Due to time constraints, our hearing could only take one day, and both sides were under a time limitation.

The judge entered the room. His gray and white hair and moustache added to his distinguished bearing. Judge Carrigan looked like a fair, honest man. I relaxed a little. I kissed my baby son and held him tightly.

Judge Carrigan called Dave Hill to the podium and spoke to him for a few minutes. Dave approached me.

"Susan, the judge said there's no jury, so you don't need to have your children here," Dave whispered.

"What's that supposed to mean?"

"You don't have to put on a show for the jury to demonstrate you're a good mother since there's no jury."

"Tell the judge that I take my children everywhere and that they're staying with me!"

Did Judge Carrigan think I was a phony? I loved my children, and I wanted them to be with us. That's why I brought them to court. Anger pierced my exhaustion. If the judge thought I was that insincere, how would he ever believe my testimony? The trial hadn't even begun, and I already felt as if we'd lost.

The Judge asked Harry to make his opening statement. Harry stood, ran his fingers through his hair, and spoke in his quiet, determined manner.

> We are asking for a preliminary injunction in order to preserve our ability to survive. Blue Mountain Arts has been marked for destruction by the unquestioned giant of the American card

industry, Hallmark, unless a preliminary injunction is issued...

What makes this case different is that we do not claim today...that Hallmark has copied a particular Blue Mountain Arts card. Rather, we seek to establish something that is far more insidious: that Hallmark so copied our style that they have issued approximately ninety cards that look as if they came from the Blue Mountain Arts plant. We intend to show that Hallmark cards are inherently confusing and have, in fact, confused the public.

Harry explained that we weren't talking about any one individual card or item, but rather the aggregate of physical features that constitute Blue Mountain's recognizable look (our "trade dress").

You can spot a Blue Mountain Arts card a mile away, until today, because today we have this stack of Hallmark cards, which we submit visually are identical to our own...

He said that the visual look of a Blue Mountain Arts card was as much a trademark as the big, blue letters of IBM were, that my poems had appeared in millions of poetry books, and that Steve had designed these cards with features that provided a unique look.

Harry told the court that we needed to prove, in addition to the basic standards for a preliminary injunction, that our customers and the greeting card industry confused the cards and that Blue Mountain's recognizable look did exist.

We also had to address the more esoteric issue of "functionality," since "functional" features are not protected. Harry argued that a creative person can design an infinite number of variations on a product, such as a greeting card, and the aggregate of all the parts is not functional, even if the individual parts are functional by themselves.

"It's fine for competitors to publish inspirational poetry cards," Harry informed the court, "as long as they're not confused with ours."

He explained that he'd show the court a number of inspirational cards currently on the market that looked nothing like Blue Mountain Arts cards. Only the Hallmark line looked like ours, and that was the only line we were contesting.

Harry sat down as Andrea Williams stood to give her opening statement.

"Blue Mountain Arts is trying to use the Lanham Act to protect their products and say that Hallmark cannot make a product that effectively competes," she said. "Hallmark can make a second-rate product that doesn't get the job done and the consumer won't buy, but cannot meet them head on."

I gritted my teeth.

"The case turns on a legal issue," she went on. "The question is: What is trade dress and does Blue Mountain Arts have one?" She dissected each card to show that every card didn't have the exact same features.

My heart went out to our first witness, our soft-spoken director of Art & Editorial, Cliff Scott. Next to Steve, he hates making speeches more than anyone I know, and the judge kept asking him to speak louder. Cliff identified the features of the cards and explained how Steve and I guided him to keep the same physical attributes on every card.

The spotlight on the witness stand creates enormous pressure; you wonder constantly what the lawyer's getting at, even with the simplest of questions. One wrong step could be disastrous. There's no black or white, right or wrong in the law, as much as one would hope for it. To complicate matters, the lawyers are always objecting, bantering, arguing, and doing any number of things to throw off your composure.

Judge Carrigan called Steve next. Like Cliff, he spoke softly.

"How did you choose the features for the cards?" Harry asked Steve.

"We wanted our cards to be unique from any other card on the market, so that our customers would recognize them...

"We do not vary the features of our cards, because if we did this too much, the customers might not recognize our look. We wanted to maintain a consistent look over a long period of time so we'd establish that look very strongly in the mind of the consumers."

Steve has always been so good at explaining difficult concepts in simple terms. I remembered how he had tutored me in a physics course I took when I was a senior in college. I couldn't understand a word of what my professor said, but when Steve explained it to me it was easy to understand.

Harry and Steve went back and forth, interrupted occasionally by Ms. Williams' objections. Every objection felt like another nail in our coffin, and I held my breath each time the word "objection" was shouted until the judge ordered "overruled" or "sustained." How did lawyers get used to this? And didn't being overruled so many times embarrass Ms. Williams? I glanced at Jared who was scribbling on a piece of paper.

"Are there other ways to make cards with long, inspirational poems?" Harry asked.

"Of course," Steve said. He explained the ways he could personally design a handmade-looking card with inspirational poems and a nature drawing. "I could sit here and describe another thousand or five thousand ways."

Harry sat down. Ms. Williams approached the bench and handed Steve a pack of Hallmark's Personal Touch cards.

"Do these have the Blue Mountain Arts look?" she asked.

"Yes."

"Is this confusingly similar to the Blue Mountain Arts look?" she asked again. "And this one?"

For fifteen minutes, she handed Steve one card after another and asked the same question: Is this confusingly similar?

After dozens of detailed questions about our cards, displays, my poetry, and his art, Steve examined each Personal Touch card right on the stand. He selected eight cards that were either "non-offending or only had some possibility of offending." He showed an acceptable Hallmark poetry card that didn't look like a Blue Mountain card, proving that we didn't care if Hallmark competed with us.

At last, he stepped down. When he approached our bench, Steve's face was drenched in sweat. His nervousness hadn't kept him from standing firm on the important questions. I dreaded my turn on the stand.

Judge Carrigan called my name. As I approached the stand, I thought about how I liked having an audience under normal circumstances. Now, though, I agonized: What if I spoke too soon? I rarely deliberate about what I'm going to say, and controlling my tendency to speak quickly and spontaneously would be difficult.

"Are you Susan Polis Schutz?" the judge asked.

"Yes," I said, chuckling to myself. I hoped the other questions would be as easy.

Harry asked me to tell about the meeting we'd had with Mr. Hughes, Hallmark's co-chairman of the Board.

I opened my mouth to answer, but Judge Carrigan interrupted.

"Do you have a first name for him or is it just Mr. Hughes? Is that all you know?"

I thought for a moment. I didn't know his first name.

"No, just Mr. Hughes."

"Mr. Hughes called us to ask for a meeting," I continued. "I'd heard from some retailers that Hallmark was going to come out with a line of poetry cards that looked like ours."

Ms. Williams, Harry, and the judge suddenly got caught up in some kind of conflict about hearsay, settling only when the judge said he wouldn't take into account the truth of any statement made by a person who was not a witness in this courtroom and subject to cross-examination. Both lawyers looked satisfied that the objection had been settled.

On the other hand, I felt hopelessly lost. Hearsay always confused me. I was a witness, and though I was telling the truth about someone, the judge had ruled that it was still hearsay unless the other person was present in the courtroom to corroborate my story. But Mr. Hughes was not there, and I'd been asked about him. Still, based on the judge's ruling, I was at least allowed to tell what happened at the meeting.

I finished describing our meeting with Mr. Hughes and then answered a series of questions about poetry, fans, stores, trade shows, and how we designed our AireBrush and WaterColor Feelings cards.

Harry asked if I had ever confused a Hallmark card with one of my cards.

"I went into a store in California and thought Hallmark's cards were ours," I said.

"And what did you do right after you saw that the card was a Hallmark card?"

"Exactly?"

"Yes."

I swallowed and embarrassedly said, "I ran out crying."

"Your Honor, pass for cross-examination."

Ms. Williams approached me and asked about the artwork and poetry on our cards. I didn't like answering her questions; I couldn't shake the idea that every question had an ulterior motive.

"When Mr. Hughes visited you, he didn't threaten you in any way, did he?"

"Threaten me? With what?"

"With anything."

"Of course not. He was very nice."

"Did you reveal any Blue Mountain Arts' secrets to Mr. Hughes?"

"We have no secrets!" I strongly blurted out.

"Damn it," I thought, flustered. I let my anger get ahead of me again. My comment had nothing to do with anything relevant, but by yelling, I made it seem important. I imagined the headline: SUSAN POLIS SCHUTZ SAYS SHE HAS NO SECRETS!

"I have no other questions."

I blinked. I felt like running away. Did I say something that helped her case? I had absolutely no idea! She'd cut off my testimony rather abruptly, but judging from the look on her face, I think she did it on purpose. Neither she, nor Harry, nor I knew what I would say before I said it. My blunt style made me a loose cannon for everyone.

I took a deep breath as Harry approached the witness stand. At least I didn't have anything to fear from him.

"Have you ever mailed brochures to people other than retailers?"

"We have a list of about fifteen thousand fans that receive our mailings," I said.

Harry dismissed me, and I cheered him on. His question was a smart one. Hallmark had claimed we didn't promote our cards to customers— an important part of owning a look—and Ms. Williams tried to imply that we only promoted them to stores. But in addition to mailing our brochures to stores, we also had a small newsletter we sent to fans. Once again, I hoped the simple truth would win out.

Harry called the next witness, Dr. Abraham Wolf, who presented a survey demonstrating the obvious fact that Blue Mountain Arts' customers confused Hallmark's imitation cards with ours. One of Hallmark's attorneys, Mr. Low, cross-examined Dr. Wolf, pointing out that out of the six hundred people who were surveyed, only ten had previously purchased Blue Mountain Arts cards.

Mr. Low spent another twenty minutes poking holes in Dr. Wolf's survey, downsizing us further and further into oblivion.

Harry turned around the argument in the end, but I was seething at what had been said by Hallmark's lawyers.

I breathed a sigh of relief when Judge Carrigan announced that court would be in recess until 1:30 P.M.

We took the children to lunch. I had no idea how well we'd done, but I didn't look forward to returning to the Hallmark lawyers. As I stood in line for a sandwich, I bumped into Mr. Hatch, the owner of the store where we'd sold our first posters fifteen years earlier. He patted us on the back and said that he'd had a lot of fights with Hallmark over the years and that he despised many of the things they had done. "But," he concluded, "I am sorry to say that your lawyers just aren't in the same league as Hallmark's lawyers."

Just what we wanted to hear! We were dejected, but we still had faith in Harry. He was honest and decent, and his was the league we wanted to play in.

I changed my son's diaper in the bathroom and placed cold towels on my face. My eyes ached. I gazed at myself in the mirror—at my swollen eyes, my pale face—and could hardly see or think about the morning's events.

"I think the morning went well," Harry said when I rejoined my family. "We only have an hour after lunch, though, and I'm afraid there won't be enough time to put all our witnesses on the stand. I'm only going to use our paid, expert witnesses."

This upset me because Steve and I felt strongly that industry professionals were much more important as witnesses than paid experts. The way I saw it, paid experts, though they knew what they were talking about, were virtually useless; one expert would be paid to prove the defendant's point, and another to prove the prosecution's point. They negated each other. So why bother?

"You have to put in Mike Drukman," I said strongly, "or Jeff Willsey. Both men have been in the business for years, and they are not being paid to testify."

We had to illustrate the widespread effect of Hallmark's actions. Only industry insiders, not paid experts, could do that.

For the first ten minutes of our last hour, Harry and the judge clarified documents and exhibits while I worried over whether Harry would call only our experts to the stand.

I smiled at Harry and pointed to Mike Drukman and Jeff Willsey.

"Your Honor, for its next witness the plaintiff would like to call Mr. Jeffrey Willsey."

I was so relieved. One of Harry's best characteristics is his humility; he never lets his ego get in the way of good judgment or listening to what his clients suggest.

Steve and I didn't know Jeff, but since 1976 he'd been the president of Sunrise Publications, a greeting card company, and he'd been on the board of the National Greeting Card Association. He looked handsome and debonair, and I hoped he spoke as well as he dressed.

"Is Blue Mountain Arts your competitor?" Harry asked.

"Yes, Sir," Jeff said.

"Does Blue Mountain Arts have a distinctive look?"

"Yes, Sir."

"What's the significance of that look?"

"The importance of a distinctive look becomes more important the smaller you are, and it becomes doubly important if you're limited to one or two looks within your company. In fact, I'd say it's so important that it's a question of actual survival. Without looks, without niches, visual niches, with this market, small companies have no hope of competing with companies that have powerful distribution."

I smiled. Jeff did speak as well as he looked.

"If you, as a card publisher, were to make an inspirational poetry card, would you make it in the style of Blue Mountain Arts?"

Jeff answered, "No, because in my opinion, as a manager of a company, I view Blue Mountain Arts as owning that look."

Harry called Mike Drukman to the stand.

Harry introduced Mike to the court, saying he'd been a sales representative in the greeting card industry continuously since 1958 and was now the president of Madco, a sales organization in New England. He'd represented Blue Mountain Arts since 1974 in addition to dozens of other card companies. Ms. Williams objected to his qualifications as a lay witness.

Here was a man who'd been in the industry for so many years, who was intimately familiar with Blue Mountain Arts and at least twelve other card lines, and he was not an expert? Yet someone who was paid to give an opinion and who had no direct contact with greeting card companies was a qualified expert? I rolled my eyes.

"How many different greeting card lines have you observed over the last thirty years?" Harry asked Mike.

"It's been twenty-eight years…I certainly observed every line that has achieved any sales prominence in the industry over that period of time."

Ms. Williams objected.

"I'm not clear what he's qualified for or that the question is within whatever that area of expertise might be," she said.

"He's in the business. He has been in it for over twenty years and he has seen all these cards…any line that's achieved any prominence, he's seen," the judge explained. I gently touched Steve's shoulder.

"Objection overruled," said the judge. "Counsel may repeat the question."

Harry asked him again: "Is Blue Mountain Arts at all recognizable when you look at its AireBrush Feelings and WaterColor Feelings lines?"

"It has the most recognizable look of any lines that I have ever seen."

"Have you seen Hallmark Personal Touch cards?"

He had.

Did he find them to be similar to Blue Mountain Arts AireBrush and WaterColor cards?

"Objection, Your Honor," Ms. Williams said again. I sighed. Would this ever be over?

"This is one of the issues in this case, and I don't see that this witness, however long he has been in the business, is in a position to answer whether the consuming public might be confused by the cards."

"Overruled."

"I have found the Hallmark cards to be confusing with Blue Mountain Arts cards," Mike answered. Harry sat down and Ms. Williams stood up for cross-examination.

"Your testimony is that every Personal Touch card has the Blue Mountain Arts look, whatever that might be, is that right?"

"No."

"You mean some of the Personal Touch cards don't look similar to the Blue Mountain Arts cards?"

"The overall look is confusing."

Mike stepped down. Our side of the case was over.

I thought we presented our side well. In simple terms, Harry and our witnesses defined the Blue Mountain Arts look and its prominence in the industry. They showed that Hallmark's Personal Touch cards looked like our cards and that people confused them, and we demonstrated how we actively promote our cards.

Ms. Williams stood. "Here we go again," I thought.

"I'd like to make a motion that the preliminary injunction be denied at this time, because the plaintiff has woefully failed to establish some of the key elements in its burden," she said. She continued to say that we had not established that our AireBrush or WaterColor cards had a look or trade dress, nor had we proven that the consuming public associated that look with Blue Mountain Arts. She went on to imply that not only did we not have a look, but if we did, then no one else could make poetry cards.

"I don't know where to start identifying what they didn't prove," Ms. Williams continued. "What is 'look'?"

In a five-minute speech, Ms. Williams relegated our company, our cards, and Steve and me to total oblivion. I pinched myself to make sure I still existed.

"Thank you," Judge Carrigan said. "The motion is denied."

Perhaps he saw the truth; at least he wanted to hear more about the case. But I still wondered whether he truly understood the magnitude of what Hallmark was trying to do to small greeting card companies.

As we collected our papers from the table, Jared ran up to me excitedly. "Blue Mountain Arts was great! Your batting average is eight hundred." He showed me the slip of paper he'd been writing on, a scoreboard of *Blue Mountain Arts v. Hallmark*. He observed that the judge had overruled Hallmark's objections many more times than he had overruled Blue Mountain Arts' objections. "That means you're more honest. I think you won!" He always had a unique and creative way of analyzing things.

I kissed Jared and hoped he was right.

Listen carefully to what people say. Just because they are able to express something in a persuading manner doesn't necessarily mean that it is right. It is not the choice of words, but the meaning of words that matters.

* * *

The most complicated concepts can be explained in simple, easy-to-understand words.

* * *

It is a valuable attribute to have "thick skin" so hurtful remarks don't adversely affect you.

chapter twenty-five

A Frog Is a Frog

I settled into my seat after a brief recess. My quick lunch had done little to calm my nervous stomach. I don't think I've ever felt as drained as I did that afternoon in the courtroom. We'd spent the morning building our case, watching it get torn apart by Hallmark's clever lawyers, and then seeing how Harry managed to put the pieces back together. Our side was finished, and now it was Hallmark's afternoon in court. I knew that their witnesses would sound great regardless of their insincerity, and at the rate they were going, I wouldn't have been surprised if Hallmark claimed that Personal Touch had a look that *we* had copied.

The afternoon found me alternately depressed and elated with the twists and turns of the case.

With each witness, my hope faded. Hallmark presented a survey that tried to show that Blue Mountain Arts did not have a recognizable look and was completely unknown. I felt defeated. How would the judge know the real facts? Harry argued that their survey was invalid, but it had even me believing that we didn't exist.

A few turnarounds by Harry brightened up the afternoon. One credible expert witness, a professor of art history who looked like Donna Reed, said that there were similarities in Hallmark's cards and ours. But since her expertise was artistic style and technique, she proceeded to dissect the differences in the artwork. "I don't think it was a matter of copying," Professor Scott said. "It's likely that some artist who produced the Personal Touch cards was inspired by some of the cards that they saw in the Blue Mountain Arts group."

As I felt my ire rise again, our white knight came charging forward in the form of Harry Melkonian.

"As a professor with your background, when you look at a work of art, you're looking at it with somewhat different eyes than, say, someone like myself, aren't you?"

"Yes," Professor Scott said.

"That's why you're an expert?"

"Yes."

"So when you categorize things, it may not be the same way that I, as a layman, would categorize things, correct?"

"Yes."

"Take a kind of silly example," Harry said. "You know what a frog is?"

"Yes."

"If I brought in a dozen frogs that I caught out here somewhere in warmer weather and put them on a table, and I asked you to categorize them, you could very well say it's a bunch of frogs."

"Right," Professor Scott said.

"You'd say, 'and they all look the same to me'?"

"Uh-huh."

"If I brought in a comparative zoologist, an expert in invertebrate anatomy or vertebrates, whatever they are, and he took the stand, and I asked, 'Would you categorize those?' he might come up with Latin names half a mile long for each one, all completely different, right?"

"Yes."

"So perception and ability to categorize is very much a factor of education, schooling, and experiences?"

"Yes."

"When it comes to art, yours is a very special one?"

"Yes…"

Harry wasn't fancy. He didn't use big words. He didn't look like a movie star. But he got to the essence of everything in a direct, simple, honest way. In five minutes, he'd unraveled her entire testimony by showing that she looked at the cards through an expert's eye and did not look at them as a regular person would. She only focused on the art, not the entire card. Professor Scott had dissected each card's artistic style. Card buyers don't do that.

Harry had managed to redirect the court's attention to the real issue. He said that an ordinary person looks at a card as a whole. He gave a brilliant analogy when he said, "A frog is a frog is a frog."

I learned from Harry that complicated concepts can be explained in simple, easy-to-understand words.

I could never be a lawyer; I'd never be able to think so fast and come up with counter arguments to prove what was right. Jared tapped me on the back in congratulations, and Steve and I grasped each other's hands.

Again and again, the creator of Personal Touch, the artistic director, and even the vice president of the line said that if they didn't make their poetry cards like ours, they couldn't make cards at all. And they gave scientific reasons for why they "had" to make greeting cards that looked just like ours. All of them, in one way or another, implied that Blue Mountain Arts was neither original, nor popular, nor at all significant in the world of greeting cards. And they all denied copying.

A Hallmark attorney asked a witness, "As the person who initiated this project that resulted in the Personal Touch line that's at issue, did you direct anyone to create a 'me-too' product or to create a product that imitated the Blue Mountain Arts line?"

"Absolutely not," he said.

I couldn't believe he said this. We thought we had proof that Hallmark had knowingly copied us. One Hallmark document that was introduced into evidence actually purported to describe what made the Blue Mountain Arts cards unique. But the rest of that document devastated me.

Two pages of a handwritten memo by Hallmark attempted to dissect and apparently explain how to copy the way I write. The Hallmark document said:

> Think like a young person and write what you feel, not obligatory things...Speak to the children of the '60's...
>
> 1. Just find a quiet place and then vividly create a mental image of who you want to address...
> 2. Don't try to rhyme...
> 3. Take on simple feelings.
> 4. Think of the person you are sending the card to and see what comes to mind...Don't worry about being sentimental...
>
> Consumers talk again and again of [her] work being "warm and serious, sentimental and personal"...The length of her writing expresses caring. Specificity is an asset, not a liability...In expressing her life, people feel that way but didn't know it until they read her work.
>
> FORMULAS
> 1. Using "I"
> 2. Conversation letter-like, but casual
> 3. Use "of" and "okay"
>
> THE PLOT OF A BLUE MOUNTAIN ARTS CARD
> 1. Intro
> 2. Set-up
> 3. Explanation
> 4. The "make it right" (i.e., forgive me)
> 5. Relationship
> 6. Work must be lifelike, poetic conversation

Steve and I have always created from our hearts, and the only thing I know about my poems is that they represent my most honest feelings, which I need to express in writing. My poetry does not have a formula, a plot, or a plan.

I felt so cheapened, so invaded by their callous dissection that for the next two years, whenever I tried to write poetry, I'd see that document in front of my eyes, and I just couldn't write. I even lost my desire to write.

It is a valuable attribute to have "thick skin" so hurtful remarks don't adversely affect you. Unfortunately, I have very thin skin.

Another Hallmark employee testified at the hearing that Hallmark knew it "was getting beaten rather severely by the Blue Mountain line in the stores that carried" Blue Mountain Arts, and that Hallmark had even brought in focus groups to decipher why our cards were popular.

A Hallmark design manager came up with scientific, technical, and aesthetic reasons for using every feature of our cards. He rationalized why using the Blue Mountain Arts' features was the only way to make a greeting card. He said the high-quality, watercolor, textured paper was chosen because he wanted to make it feel as if it were a real painting, and if they had not chosen this paper, there would have been a "texture problem." The deckle edge was chosen "so there was not a mechanical cut on the edge. It's a feathery edge so it was used for aesthetics." He never gave a reason for choosing all our features in combination with one another. I thought how easy it would have been if he had just told (what we saw as) the truth and said, "Yeah, we copied Blue Mountain Arts."

Instead, he implied that the only features consumers liked and wanted on a greeting card were the exact ones Blue Mountain Arts cards had. How did he know this? By having Hallmark employees watch interviews with customers through one-way mirrors. This was starting to sound like a spy novel.

Harry asked this man one more question. "In lecturing to your artists, have you ever shown them Blue Mountain Arts cards?"

"Yes I have," he replied.

"Nothing further, Your Honor."

In the last minutes of the hearing, both sides read more exhibits into the record. The time for closing statements had come.

Harry rose.

"One of the key issues that should be made here is...Hallmark makes eleven thousand cards. Blue Mountain Arts makes a handful of cards. A couple hundred...If those lines are being copied at the present time, harm to Blue Mountain is clear and manifest. And the irreparability is clear. The balancing of hardships is clear...

"We submit that by any kind of balancing test, Blue Mountain Arts must come out as the prevailing party."

"That's got nothing to do with it," Judge Carrigan interrupted. "Justice is blind. We have a blindfolded goddess. I can't consider things like that. I can only consider the facts and the law."

I knew the judge was right. It didn't matter how big either company was; it only mattered who was right.

Harry explained that it was perfectly fine if Hallmark used some of the same features that we had used on our cards, such as a deckle edge or uncoated embossed paper. But they could not use the aggregate of all the Blue Mountain Arts card features so as to confuse our customers. He went on to deconstruct their expert's survey.

"And [Hallmark's survey] has nothing to do with this case. They went out and surveyed people who don't even buy our cards." He explained that people who weren't aware of our cards couldn't possibly be confused by the Hallmark copies, so they weren't part of the relevant population.

I silently cheered him on. That was why they'd found such a tiny percent of people who knew us. Harry proved that we existed after all!

"We surveyed the relevant population, and the evidence showed that those people were substantially confused," Harry continued. "For Hallmark's own documents—which they strived mightily to explain away, and I don't think they did—recognized Blue Mountain's unique appearance. They recognized that Blue Mountain had a loyal customer base."

> The case is really simple...Hallmark...put out a line of cards that Ms. Davis said was not doing well, was a failure. Hallmark went out and spent all kinds of money on studies on this and that, to find out why people bought Blue Mountain cards. The art director shows Blue Mountain cards to his artist staff, and what comes out is a card—we submit, by common sense—that looks like a Blue Mountain card.

Harry summarized the essence of our lawsuit:

> The Court has to sit down and look at the cards. It can take
> the survey data. It can take the testimony of witnesses who say
> they're confused. But the Court must look at the material and
> ask, "Is this confusing? Why was it done this way?" If Blue
> Mountain loses its niche, it could very well cease to exist, once
> displaced from a store with Hallmark's marketing power. The
> documents I read express Hallmark's desire to try to displace Blue
> Mountain from the stores using this Personal Touch line...It's
> trying to get us out.

Judge Carrigan told Harry his time was up and invited the defense's
closing arguments.

Ms. Williams stood up. "The first point I want to make is there has
been no evidence of harm to any of the plaintiffs put on today. They
know what their sales are. The Personal Touch cards have been on the
market since April 1, 1986, and there has not been one iota of evidence
that they have lost any sales or accounts."

Frustration surged through me again. We had lost so many
customers and she had been told that.

"The second point I want to make is a summary of what we've been
talking about: the trade dress must be separate from the product."

Ms. Williams held up a huge blown-up image of a card with several
layers of transparencies of artwork. She said:

> Blue Mountain is claiming that it makes cards that have long,
> sentimental poetry on two flaps of the three-fold sides. All right,
> that's part of the trade dress. Let's take it away. [She lifted the
> transparency.] What do we have? We have a piece of artwork. They
> are claiming the artwork, soft-color background, foreground with
> a contrasting scene. Take that away, what do we have? [She lifted
> the next transparency.] A piece of paper. They are claiming the
> paper, no printing on this side, the deckle edge. There's nothing
> left if you give them what they claim.

In other words, what she was saying was that the only way to make cards was the way we designed ours.

"Hallmark knew about Blue Mountain. They were competing with Blue Mountain. But they did not copy it," Ms. Williams said. She then sat down again.

After listening to the Hallmark lawyers and witnesses, I learned how important it is to listen carefully to what people say. Just because they are able to express something in a persuading manner doesn't necessarily mean it's right. It is not the choice of words, but the meaning of words that matters.

Judge Carrigan thanked the lawyers for presenting their cases as well as they could under the circumstances, and once again he proved to be more than fair. He said he would have preferred that the hearing be three or four days, but the federal court schedule just couldn't allow that kind of time. He said:

> It seems to me that in these circumstances that counsel are likely to think of all kinds of things on their way home that they could have said in the few remaining minutes of their closing. I used to do that all the time, all those wonderful arguments that you never get to make. And for that reason if you wish you can submit any additional brief in the nature of closing arguments, not over ten pages long per side, by Monday at 4:00 P.M. This will mitigate some of the seeming harshness of this procedure that's been forced upon us by the judge shortage.

Steve and I stood, dazed, and left the building with our children. The moment we stepped outside, we were overrun by reporters and photographers. The cameras flashed in my eyes, and I suddenly realized our day in court was over.

I covered our children's faces as we ran to our Suburban to race to the mountains. It was finally finished!

My relief, though, could not assuage the fear that Blue Mountain Arts might be finished as well.

It is vital to protect yourself and stand up for what you believe in, no matter what or who the opposition is; however, filing a lawsuit should be the last resort to accomplish this.

chapter twenty-six

The Ruling

The case was out of our hands now. I had no idea if we'd won or lost, but we had done the best job we could. We had spent an enormous amount of our time, thoughts, finances, and emotions defending our principles. There was nothing else we could do.

For the first time in months, I allowed myself to relax. Worrying wouldn't change the outcome of the case. Steve and I decided that we would be with our children, concentrating entirely on them and their activities until Judge Carrigan announced our fate. It could take one day or many months; we had no way of knowing.

We flew back home, and for the next few days, while the children were in school, I spent the days sleeping. After my long "nap," I recovered my strength, and our situation seemed better as I became more rested. Our lawyers kept calling us, but since we'd decided to escape from that world, we didn't return their calls. They begged us to wear pagers; they felt we had to know the results of the court order the moment it was filed. Everyone was afraid we wouldn't be found at the important moment, and they would have been right.

"We'll wear the pagers," I told Harry at last, "but only if you promise not to contact us about anything other than the judge's decision!"

"Okay, okay," Harry said, laughing. He gave our pager numbers to an attorney who worked near the Federal Courthouse in Denver; he'd be the first to know, and he'd page Harry, Dave Hill, and us.

For the next three weeks, we picked up our children from school, and each day we went to a different park or play area. We rediscovered the beauty and importance of family life and appreciated, once again, what a source of stability and true love children can be. We reveled in our brief resting period.

But every once in a while, a chill crawled up my spine, and when I slept, nightmares intruded. In one nightmare, Steve and I had been silk-screening our posters when a Hallmark employee appeared and ripped them into shreds. I'd envision Steve and myself walking in the mountains, hand-in-hand, and I would see people from Hallmark walking past us with matches in their hands, ready to set fire to the trees. I thought I was relaxing, but inside I was still a wreck: anxious, disillusioned, and scared.

On November 20, 1986, as Steve and I were ice-skating with our children at a local rink, a sound coming from my pocket cut through the music blasting from the speakers. I froze and nearly fell as I stumbled to the wall. Our children hugged us. My eyes met Steve's.

Our pagers were beeping.

Still wearing our skates, the five of us hobbled to the only pay phone, where several people waited in line.

"I can't make the call," I told Steve. "You do it."

The line inched forward with agonizing slowness until, finally, Steve got to the phone.

"This is Steve Schutz."

I watched his face closely for a sign of the verdict. His eyes widened a moment…and then he grinned wildly, thanked the man on the other end, and slammed down the phone.

"We won! We won!"

We jumped up and down in our skates. Steve was told that the judge had written the preliminary injunction in enough detail that it could stand up on appeal, and they were faxing us the twenty-five-page order. We removed our skates as quickly as possible and went home.

Our daughter wrapped her arms around me, tears flowing down her little face, and my oldest son shouted that the American judicial system was great. Our youngest son had no idea what was going on, but he laughed and clapped with us.

Our pagers beeped again. Dave Hill called. Harry Melkonian called. Rick Gomez called. All with the same astounding two words: "We won!"

Our lawyers told us that the Associated Press and United Press

Me at three years old, 1947.

*Me at six years old
with my brother, Robbie,
three years old, 1950.*

*Me sleigh riding
with my dad and friends,
Peekskill, NY, 1951.*

Me and Steve,
New York City, 1968.

Playing the recorder for some of the students
in my Harlem class, 1968.

*Steve took this picture as we handed out literature at a
"grape boycott" rally to support underprivileged farm workers, 1968.*

*Steve took this picture of me holding a sign at an anti-war march
in New York City, 1969.*

*Our wedding day,
Peekskill, NY,
April 13, 1969.*

*Steve and me
in front of the
Princeton house
in the woods,
1968.*

On the way to Woodstock in our painted Oldsmobile, 1969.

In front of the Boulder foothills, 1970.

Cross-country skiing across the Continental Divide, 1970.

Steve's handmade pouch and my pocketbook made by Boulder artist, Gid, that we wore every day, 1970.

The National Stationery Show in New York City, 1970.

Our Boulder basement living quarters and silk-screen factory, 1971.

Our Boulder transportation, early 1970's.

Me and Steve on our favorite rock near the top of the Boulder Flatirons, 1976. Appeared in People *magazine.*

You've met Susan Polis Schutz. Now meet her mother, June Polis.

JUNE POLIS

This mother used to help her daughter sell scout cookies. Now she helps her market the fastest-selling line of greeting and gift products in the industry. In fact, she's national sales manager of Blue Mountain Arts, Inc.

To hear her tell it, she's not surprised that her daughter is the best-selling poet in the country. Or that Blue Mountain Arts has sold over 25 million notecards and ½ million books, not to mention record-breaking sales in calendars and prints. She doesn't even act surprised that because of the demand for Blue Mountain

Arts' products in over 7,500 outlets, she's had to hire 85 sales representatives to help care for them all.

But then . . . mothers are like that.

For information write us on your letterhead today to:

SEPTEMBER, 1976

An advertisement that appeared in Gifts & Decorative Accessories *magazine, September, 1976.*

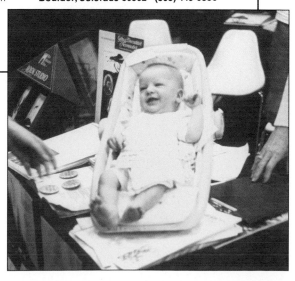

Jared greeting people at the Chicago Gift Show, 1976.

Mom with Jared, our first baby, in Boulder, 1975.

Our darling daughter, 1980.

Our angel, 1983.

Appeared in Associated Press syndicated newspaper story, 1983.

*Appeared in many
newspapers and
magazines, 1984.*

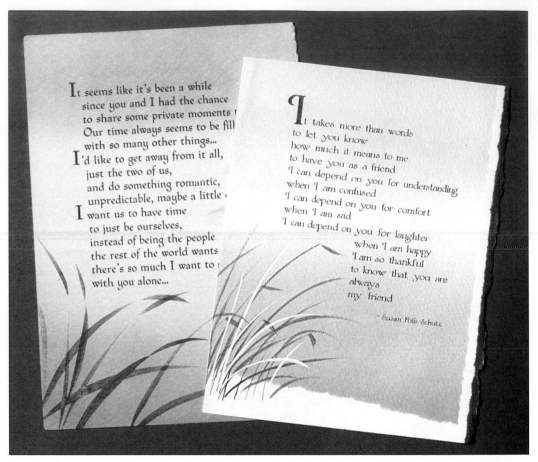

It seems like it's been a while
since you and I had the chance
to share some private moments [
Our time always seems to be fill
with so many other things...
I'd like to get away from it all,
just the two of us,
and do something romantic,
unpredictable, maybe a little (
I want us to have time
to just be ourselves,
instead of being the people
the rest of the world wants
there's so much I want to :
with you alone...

It takes more than words
to let you know
how much it means to me
to have you as a friend
I can depend on you for understanding
when I am confused
I can depend on you for comfort
when I am sad
I can depend on you for laughter
when I am happy
I am so thankful
to know that you are
always
my friend

~ Susan Polis Schutz

Hallmark "copy" on left; Blue Mountain Arts card on right, 1986.

Photo by Laura Galinson.

Steve was on the stand during the preliminary hearing for
Blue Mountain Arts v. Hallmark. *My family is sitting behind me, 1986.*
Appeared in the Boulder Daily Camera.

This picture appeared in hundreds of newspapers in the United States. Associated Press *and* Rocky Mountain News *headlines read:* **"Card Designers Hail Court Ruling"** *and* **"Hallmark Cards 'Personal Touch' Ruled Copy-Cats,"** 1986.

Photo by Laura Galinson.

20/20 filmed me singing with children of employees in the Blue Mountain Arts playroom, 1987.

"20/20 filming... Stephen and Susan Schutz are filmed by cameraman Ken Sanborn and soundman Jack Gray of the ABC television program, 20/20 on Wednesday near U.S. 36 south of Boulder. They will be featured on the show February 12." Boulder Daily Camera. *Our truck is in the background, 1987.*

Working in the mountains. As seen in Scripps-Howard Newspapers, 1988.

The first bluemountain.com homepage, September, 1996.

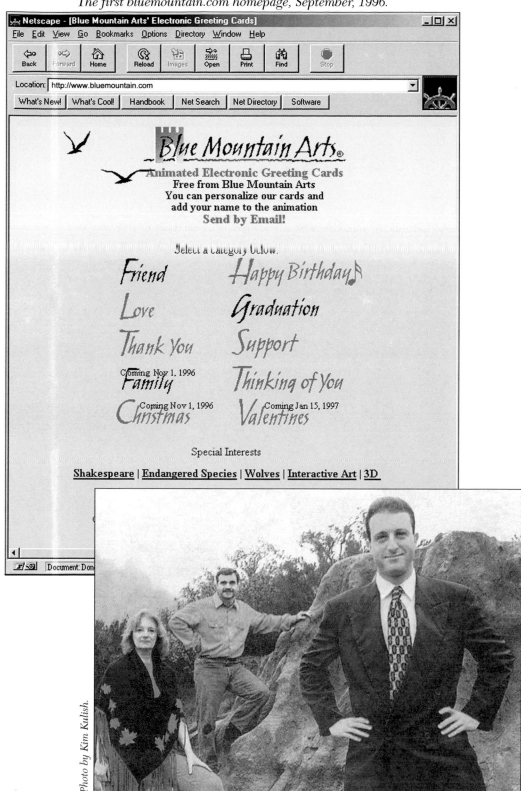

Me, Steve, and Jared.
As seen in the New York Times, *January 23, 1999.*

Blue Mountain Arts employees, Boulder, 2002.

Blue Mountain Arts products on display at the
National Stationery Show in New York City, 2003.
From left to right: Bob Gall, Hank Steinbuck, and Rae and Robbie Polis.

International wanted to talk with us, so they advised that we read the judge's decision and call back the reporters immediately. Otherwise, they'd run the story with comments only from Hallmark.

Judge Carrigan, in addition to all the other cases he had to finish, in only four weeks had written a complete, comprehensive, and thoughtful document.

"Personal Touch was created with the intent of displacing Blue Mountain," his decision read.

He quoted a Hallmark internal memo that said, "The retailers think that Hallmark missed the mark on their attempt at alternative greeting cards...Hallmark can either steal ideas from the other alternative greeting card companies or be innovative."

Judge Carrigan issued his first conclusion: "Hallmark did not choose the latter; it chose to imitate instead of innovate."

The court order explained the details of the plaintiff's burden of proof in a trade dress infringement claim. Little by little, and step by step, he demonstrated that the look of our cards is distinct and recognizable; he also demonstrated the ridiculousness of Hallmark's claim that Blue Mountain's way of making emotional cards was the only way to make such cards. He pointed out a number of emotional cards on the market that did not copy the look of Blue Mountain Arts and quoted Hallmark's internal memos that said we had a distinct look.

Judge Carrigan wrote: "It is apparent from these memoranda that Hallmark not only believed Blue Mountain cards have an inherently distinctive look, but that their look is easily recognizable and attributable to a source that has generated a loyal customer following."

Then, much to my surprise and delight, Judge Carrigan wrote about Professor Scott, "whose credentials and experience as an art connoisseur were impressive," he wrote, but "the average consumer cannot detect differences in minute stylistic details among or between the competing cards...there is a likelihood of consumer confusion. Neither Professor Scott's testimony nor that of any other defense witness dissuades me from making such a finding."

Judge Carrigan mentioned how one of the Hallmark product

managers was given the responsibility to make the Personal Touch line successful, and under her leadership, Hallmark had purchased two hundred Blue Mountain Arts cards for the purpose of analyzing the look. "At one point, Hallmark even posed to a panel of card dealers the following question: 'How do you feel about Hallmark copying Recyled Paper, Blue Mountain Arts, and California Dreamers?'"

Judge Carrigan offered his opinion on the way Hallmark's Personal Touch cards looked when placed next to Blue Mountain Arts' AireBrush cards and concluded that the "enlargements were virtually identical; so nearly identical as to preclude a finding of coincidence."

After explaining a number of similar copying cases and laying out a few more Hallmark memos, he wrote:

> I find and conclude that there is substantial evidence to support a finding that Hallmark copied Blue Mountain's cards for the purpose of benefiting from and "cashing in" on Blue Mountain's already established reputation and goodwill...
>
> I find and conclude on a preliminary basis that the AireBrush and WaterColor Feelings cards possess an established and secondary meaning that is being diluted by Hallmark's intentional copying...
>
> I preliminarily find and conclude, for purposes of preliminary relief, that the Hallmark Personal Touch cards are so substantially similar to the plaintiff's trade dress that there exists a likelihood of confusion in the minds of the consuming public...

Judge Carrigan ended the statement by enjoining and restraining Hallmark from "producing, manufacturing, advertising, promoting, offering for sale, selling or distributing...eighty-three Personal Touch greeting cards pending a future trial...If Hallmark is allowed to further dilute the Blue Mountain Arts look prior to a trial on the merits, Blue Mountain Arts will be ruined and any success it might gain through trial would be a Pyrrhic victory."

Though Hallmark had been on trial, Steve and I found that we, too, had been on trial, along with our dreams and everything we believed in. We felt that Hallmark had attacked the essence of who we were and had attempted to extinguish our spirits. Watching our lives on trial was nothing less than observing the attempted murder of our minds and hearts.

And now Judge Carrigan had substantiated what we believed was right.

I thought about how the Hallmark lawyers had tried to prove that Steve and I and Blue Mountain Arts did not exist and how if Hallmark could not use the look of our cards, their cards would have to be just a blank sheet of paper. These two points were absurd, but they had been particularly worrisome to me. I had been afraid that Judge Carrigan might believe these arguments because of how eloquently they were presented.

It seemed that Judge Carrigan saw beyond the words recited by the actors. He saw through the legal maneuvering and technicalities. He understood the truth. He recognized right from wrong. What a man! What a judge!

My first reaction, upon reading the court order, was a waterfall of emotion. I clutched Steve's arm for strength. My life, so intertwined with Steve's, passed before my eyes. Would our victory enable us to return to simpler times of love and creativity? Or would we be polluted and hardened forever by Hallmark's actions?

I didn't know the answers. I concentrated on the moment, and that moment proved that there could be justice. We reread the detailed court order and danced with joy.

For the next six hours, reporters from magazines, newspapers, television, and radio called us to find out how we felt about the court decision. We couldn't explain why we were feeling so conflicted, but we did explain how honored, elated, and relieved we were, not only for ourselves, but for all artists and all the "little guys" who had been bullied and had not had someone to stand up for them.

Although we had won, our battle had taken an enormous toll on our lives.

We learned that it is vital to protect yourself and stand up for what you believe in, no matter what or who the opposition is; however, filing a lawsuit should be the last resort to accomplish this.

We were thankful for so many things: We were thankful that we had had the stamina and resources to proceed with our lawsuit; thankful for the hard work of our lawyers; thankful for the people who rallied in support of our principles; thankful for the fairness and wisdom of the judge; thankful that we lived in America; and, most importantly, we were thankful for our beautiful family and their unconditional love and support.

chapter twenty-seven

Roller Coaster

As soon as we had begun to celebrate our court victory granting us the preliminary injunction, Hallmark announced that they would appeal the decision. We'd suspected that this might happen, but we still weren't ready for it; I'd hoped Judge Carrigan's word would be the end of it. His word, it turned out, was barely the beginning.

Life had been like a roller-coaster ride during the entire lawsuit. It seemed like Hallmark filed a new motion every day. We thought that they were using the constant requests for paperwork as a tactic or as a way to dwell on minute technicalities and loopholes. It seemed like lawyers could file motions to confuse the real issues or just to explain an idea or word, so that the original accusations—the very essence of the case—were buried beneath everyone's reaction to the latest motion.

The worst part was that if we hadn't answered the motions correctly, and if we hadn't responded to them promptly and accurately, we could have lost the entire case. Every motion they made cost us more attorney fees and pushed us closer to the brink of our emotional capabilities.

The roller-coaster ride wasn't over yet, and it wouldn't be for at least another two years.

After setting the appeals process into motion, Hallmark filed for Blue Mountain Arts to post a four-million-dollar bond. If Hallmark won the eventual lawsuit, they could recover damages that they would incur because of the injunction. When Hallmark refused to show us where they had come up with such an astronomical figure, the court lowered their request and ordered us to post a one-hundred-thousand-dollar bond.

Once the court resolved the bond issue, Hallmark asked to postpone the injunction until after the appeal and final trial. They wanted to continue making their Personal Touch cards, which would effectively nullify Judge Carrigan's order. The judge upheld the injunction, though, and ordered them to stop producing their Personal Touch cards immediately.

Some mornings we received good news—maybe a small victory—but by the afternoon, some other issue would arise that could be bad for our case. Responding to the daily highs and lows of the legal system was exhausting. We couldn't relax for a minute. If we put our heads in the sand, we'd be attacked. Every small victory was bittersweet. Hallmark's resources and energy were unlimited, and ours dwindled dramatically every day.

Despite the victory of the hearing, I couldn't stand to read another brief or formulate another strategy. I detested the entire process and how it controlled our lives. For every legal maneuver Hallmark instigated, we had to go through an ordeal that generated pounds of paperwork. Their tactics magnified our workload. Not only did we have to respond to their briefs, but we also had to find out what they were really up to. In the next months, we learned Hallmark would have the home-court advantage—their appeal would be heard in Kansas City—and they had hired a new battery of high-powered New York lawyers.

In the oral hearing before the Tenth Circuit U.S. Court of Appeals in Kansas City, Hallmark's lead lawyer blurted out an astonishing revelation:

> We copied the idea. We imitated. We emulated. Under the law, there is nothing wrong with copying…an idea.

He went on to say that since it was impossible to define the look of Blue Mountain Arts' cards, Hallmark found it unfeasible not to violate Blue Mountain's trade dress.

Harry boldly stated, "All Hallmark had to do was not put cards together in a fashion that could be mistaken for a Blue Mountain Arts card."

Steve and I were happy that Hallmark finally admitted that they copied us.

The newspapers leapt on the Hallmark attorney's statements. HALLMARK ADMITS COPYING CARDS, BUT SAYS IT'S LEGAL was typical of some newspaper headlines.

As was the norm in this lawsuit, no sooner had one thing been said or done than something else came along to upset, add to, or renege on what had just taken place. But what happened next had to be one of the crazier turns of events.

Hallmark reversed its position!

"We deny it. When the case goes to trial, we will deny the allegations," stated Mr. Hucker, Hallmark's Vice President for Public Affairs. Now the headlines read:

HALLMARK CONTRADICTS ITS LAWYERS, SAYS IT DIDN'T COPY BOULDER CARDS

"They can't say that now," Harry said to reporters. "There were too many people there to hear it." Harry accused Hallmark of "weaseling out" of their admission.

As unbelievable as all this was, the media tempest caused by Hallmark's attempt to explain away its own lawyer's words was simply a sideshow while we waited for the Court of Appeal's ruling.

On January 14, 1987, John Stossel, an investigative journalist with the ABC television news show *20/20*, and two wonderful producers, Bernard Cohen and Mark Golden, arrived in Boulder with a camera crew. After receiving complaints against Hallmark from storeowners, artists, and card companies, they decided to investigate and report their findings. The crew spent a couple of days following us around.

Early on their last morning with us, they walked up the mountain path behind our house with Steve and me. It was a clear, crisp day, and Steve and I sat on a huge, flat rock overlooking Boulder, as we often did, with our yellow notebooks and sketchpads on our laps. The cameramen steadied their cameras when suddenly two deer pranced behind us and stood near our rock. The cameramen captured the spiritual, moving scene.

It started to snow, and after the crew recorded the falling flakes, they left for all parts of the country to speak with artists, salespeople, storeowners, and dozens of people we'd never heard of.

Their stellar investigative abilities led them to find a former Hallmark salesman who admitted that Hallmark *did* have a policy of buying competitors' cards; he even showed John Stossel a Hallmark memo that proved it.

Although Hallmark sent a video of Mr. Hockaday denying all accusations, when the *20/20* team visited Hallmark in Kansas City, Hallmark's security officers refused them access to the building. But that wasn't the only roadblock they put in *20/20*'s way. The show was scheduled to air two days before Valentine's Day, but a week before the date it was supposed to be shown, we received news that the show had been postponed. According to a story in the *Kansas City Star*, a *20/20* producer claimed that Hallmark executives had been "writing letters and protesting with lawyers." The producer asserted "they are stonewalling it a bit to see what kind of pressures they can bring to bear to stop [the show] before it gets going."

Each week the program was delayed. The *Kansas City Star* television and radio critic Barry Gorun quipped:

> Judging from Hallmark's reaction, the company would be just
> as happy if the segment was scheduled for the Twelfth of Never.

I was beginning to realize the depth of Hallmark's influence, and the breadth and scope of it terrified me. Six years later, the tobacco industry reportedly impeded CBS and *60 Minutes* investigations, an incident covered in the film *The Insider*. The primary difference was that the tobacco companies were apparently successful, at least initially, in stopping CBS, while *20/20* heroically forged ahead and aired our story anyway.

Finally, on November 4, 1988, as she introduced the *20/20* segment called "Card Wars," Barbara Walters said:

> If there were a greeting card made about the next story, I
> think you might find some of the language unprintable.

It was miraculous how *20/20* had packed so much information with such accuracy into a twenty-minute story. They had gathered information from people all over the country. The segment even included Mr. Hockaday's video denial. Their hard work and determination resulted in an exposé that accurately portrayed what was going on in the greeting card "war."

The *20/20* journalists were sensitive, justice-bound people who were brave enough to run the show. ABC and its then owner, Cap Cities, did not give in to pressure to "kill" the story. They deserved all the accolades and high ratings the program received. They stood by the truth, but I don't think that it was easy for them.

Several weeks after the show aired, one member of the *20/20* production team confided in us that he didn't want to do tough, investigative stories anymore. He said that they were just too exhausting, and he would rather do light, informative stories that didn't present so many hassles.

The media went crazy over the allegations and reversals and soap-opera-like plot twists. Even Johnny Carson made a joke at Hallmark's expense during his "25th Anniversary Show" monologue.

The lunacy accelerated. In June of 1987, out of nowhere, the prestigious Society of Illustrators, a New York-based nonprofit group whose members have included such famous artists as N.C. Wyeth, Norman Rockwell, and Frederic Remington, filed an *amicus curiae* brief supporting Hallmark's position. Any organization can file an amicus brief that outlines information on particular aspects of a lawsuit to aid the court in its decision, but this brief dumbfounded me.

Why on earth would a society of artists support Hallmark? Not only was this confusing, it was embarrassing. The brief asked for a reversal of the preliminary injunction on the grounds that "specific styles shouldn't be monopolized by one artist. A style of artwork cannot be owned...the Society has no particular interest in the greeting card industry..."

The artistic style, of course, meant little to our case. We'd said over and over that our look didn't consist solely of a single illustration, but the sum of the parts of the whole card. Once again, though, our lawyers had to assemble a counter-brief to argue our side.

As we read our counter-brief, Jared studied one of the twenty-one illustrations the Society had attached to the amicus brief. "Mommy, look what it says on this painting!"

I peered at the illustration, a Mark Chickinelli magazine cover, that the Society claimed resembled an Andy Warhol painting. The illustration was stamped, "Property Of Hallmark Cards Creative."

"That's it," I said to Steve. "That's why the artists' group was against us."

Steve called Harry, who told us that Jim Hicks, the sharp lawyer who worked for him, had also noticed the stamp. I sighed. Now we would have to incur more legal fees on motions, briefs, depositions, and investigations into Hallmark's connection with the Society of Illustrators, but it would be worth it.

Our investigation revealed some rather interesting relationships. Not only had Hallmark recently donated some two-hundred-thousand dollars to the Society, making it the Society's largest contributor, but it appeared to us that the Hallmark lawyers actually wrote the amicus brief. If the "independent observer" writing the brief is somehow related to one of the parties involved in the lawsuit, it must clearly specify this relationship. In fact, the Society's brief had stated that it had no connection with Hallmark. And all this would have been kept secret if we hadn't noticed the stamp on the illustration.

Hallmark tried to turn it around by accusing us of mudslinging and asked the Court of Appeals to deny our motion to strike the Society's brief. We, in turn, issued an answer in another brief.

Harry told the *Christian Science Monitor*, "It is difficult to think of a more plainly bad-faith tactic than to file a supplemental brief under an assumed name, falsely disguised as a friend of the court."

After many more briefs, counter-briefs, and boxes of document requests, the court sided with us, threw out the amicus brief, and Hallmark was ordered by the court to reimburse us the cost of this particular legal challenge.

My head spun. Doubts plagued me. Would this rigmarole ever end? By now, it was late August 1987; almost eighteen months had passed since I had seen the cards in the mall, and the ensuing battle still wasn't over.

For the next year, we continued defending ourselves against more ridiculous motions and accusations, while simultaneously preparing ourselves for the upcoming jury trial.

On May 24, 1988, the appellate court affirmed Judge Carrigan's decision. This ruling was another resounding legal victory for us.

Then Hallmark filed a petition to the United States Supreme Court by presenting a long brief that was bound into a booklet. We then responded with a brief that was equally as long, and likewise bound into a booklet.

For months we waited in suspense, and finally on October 17, 1988, the Supreme Court denied Hallmark's petition. That meant the preliminary injunction would be upheld pending trial.

Steve and I were elated when we heard the news. The highest court in the nation had upheld the appeals court and Judge Carrigan's decision, which meant it would be very hard for Hallmark to beat us in a trial. The Supreme Court, by not hearing the case, in essence had let stand the lower court opinion that Hallmark had indeed violated our rights.

Our precedent-setting case is now cited in law textbooks because of its impact on protecting the look of an artist's work.

But it still wasn't over. To prepare for the upcoming trial, we added another local trial attorney, John Purvis, who practiced law in Boulder and had a great reputation. John's personality differed greatly from both Dave Hill's and Harry's. He looked like a Western movie cowboy— ruggedly handsome, tall, and charming—and his sense of humor and persuasive intelligence gave him boundless charisma. Together with Harry, our group of rustic lawyers was in stark contrast with Hallmark's slick team. With the Supreme Court brief and our team of lawyers, we would be confident and ready for our trial.

Earlier that year, my brother, Robbie, had gotten very involved in our case. He read thousands of pages of briefs as well as all the background material that had been generated. He wasn't a lawyer—although I think he certainly could have been—but he acted like an attorney when he spoke to Hallmark executives on Blue Mountain's behalf. He called me soon after the Supreme Court's decision.

"Hallmark wants to settle before trial," he said.

We had to get special permission for Robbie to represent us, and it was arranged that he would speak on our behalf in the settlement negotiations.

"Negotiate with them," we said. "But we still need to prepare for trial."

Over the next few months, Robbie spoke with Hallmark executives daily. He worked day and night, not only to get a settlement that would stop them from copying us now and in the future, but also to be sure that they weren't trying to trick us in some way. This was not an easy task. He understood the importance of writing an ironclad agreement—any ambiguity would give Hallmark an opportunity to take advantage of us and other artists if they wanted to. When he wrote that they couldn't apply pressure to the stores or us, he looked up the word "pressure" in the thesaurus and cleverly listed all the synonyms.

Robbie insisted on negotiating directly with Mr. Hockaday because he was the top man at Hallmark, and he trusted that his word would be followed. It started to feel as if Hallmark might actually capitulate, and right before the trial date in late October 1988, Robbie called us with exciting news.

"Hallmark's agreed to our terms," he said.

I didn't believe it. "They'll probably back out," I replied.

"No, not this time. We have to sign some papers, but other than that, I think we're there. It's done and it's very good. It'll ensure that for ten years Hallmark won't interfere with your business in any way."

Harry wanted Steve and me to give final approval to the consent decree that Robbie had negotiated. Then, as is customary when two parties sign an agreement, he wanted us to shake hands. I knew that I couldn't do that. I couldn't shake hands with Mr. Hockaday or anyone from Hallmark. Maybe I just wasn't a team player, but I didn't think of this as a sporting event where two teams shake hands after a game. I felt strongly that Hallmark was not sorry for what they had done and that they were only sorry they had gotten caught. If they had admitted to copying us when we first wrote to them, and apologized for it, I would have forgotten what they had done and immediately forgiven them. We would have saved three years of agony. Instead they chose to deny they had copied us. I wondered what made people so arrogant.

No, I'd never shake their hands, even if it meant the settlement would not take place. Fortunately, Robbie was allowed to take our place.

It was a Friday afternoon, and the consent decree had to be signed by Hallmark and us, and then delivered to the judge for his signature. Robbie found out that the judge was attending a conference in Arizona. He was afraid to wait until Monday in case something happened to one of the participating people, so he asked Harry, John Purvis, and the Hallmark representatives to fly immediately to Arizona.

That Friday evening, they found Judge Carrigan reading near the pool at his hotel. Many of the hotel guests were swimming, and as Robbie and the lawyers, decked out in suits, approached Judge Carrigan, they surely must have looked out of place.

Judge Carrigan quickly signed the consent decree and told both sides that they needed to get along. The lawyers left the hotel and Robbie called us.

"It's over," he said. "The lawsuit is officially over, and we got everything we wanted."

It was over. We won a victory that would help all artists protect the look of what they create. We won a victory that would enable stores to carry whatever products they wanted. And we won the right to stop Hallmark from imitating our cards. Robbie had negotiated a masterpiece, for which we are eternally grateful.

In the settlement document, Hallmark consented to the following items:

1. Stop publishing the Personal Touch line of cards;
2. Discontinue the use of the Personal Touch name;
3. Take steps to repurchase Personal Touch cards from Hallmark stores;
4. Not to exclude Blue Mountain Arts from the front one-third of the Hallmark stores and permit storeowners to put our cards anywhere they wanted;
5. Not to pressure or coerce any stores to remove or not carry Blue Mountain Arts cards;
6. And not withhold or threaten to withhold any lease, license, or new store opportunity by pressuring the store to not carry Blue Mountain Arts cards.

* * *

After the consent decree was signed in 1988, Hallmark acted honorably and adhered to all the terms, and we have had no further problems with them.

We were victorious, and I was extremely proud. But this legal battle had cost us three years of our lives, and in the process, we had lost much of our idealism. No consent decree would ever return that to us.

chapter twenty-eight

An Interlude

Though Steve and I had won our court battle with Hallmark and that part of our life was over, we needed a break from everything.

For the next couple of years, we didn't spend as much time on Blue Mountain Arts as we had in the past. Fortunately, our faithful, outstanding directors and the people who worked for them ran the company, consulting us about only the most major decisions.

My book, *To My Daughter, with Love, on the Important Things in Life*, became a hardcover bestseller, and Warner Books published it in paperback along with another book I had written to my sons. Blue Mountain Arts survived our two-year hiatus.

We were full-time, fun-loving parents, attending every school party, school trip, and athletic or musical event. I became a member and then president of the Board of Trustees of our children's school. We reveled in the closeness of our family.

Two years later, we spent the summer in Boulder. We went to our office and realized how much we had missed Blue Mountain Arts. Our stalwart General Manager, Bob Gall, our talented head of Art & Editorial, Cliff Scott, and my mom had kept the core of the Blue Mountain Arts' family together, and we realized what excellent directors they were. The employees trusted them because they were honest, fair, and truthful to the people who worked for them, and it was once again proven to us that these are the most important attributes of a good manager.

We were happy to see all the employees who had been there for so long (and most are still there).[1]

More than ever, we appreciated the fine group of people who worked at Blue Mountain Arts and who interacted on a daily basis as a family. We talked to them, and with pride they told us what they were doing at Blue Mountain Arts.

At the warehouse, we smelled the fresh ink of new cards that had just been delivered by the printer. We waved to the guys riding around on forklifts, and we watched a demonstration of the latest packaging machines.

At the creative department, we watched the artists paint mountain scenes, and Steve missed his paintbrush and paints. We spoke to the editors, and I missed my pencil and yellow notebook. Steve and I loved every aspect of designing our products and we wanted to get back to doing this again. We knew that we were ready to return "home." And we did with a burst of enthusiasm.

Steve and I were interested in expanding our book division, with a goal to publish more books on varied topics. We hoped that Blue Mountain Arts would become a book publisher that could stand on its own, in addition to being a greeting card publisher.

Hank and Helene Steinbuck, who had come to my aid at the first National Stationery Show I'd attended back in 1970, had recently retired from their careers and joined Blue Mountain Arts in the marketing and sales departments. We promoted them to co-directors of sales and marketing of the book publishing division.

Helene and Hank's wild zeal spread throughout the company, and all of us were energized. We expanded our distribution to many new

---

[1]Amanda Abel, Ruth Ackermann, Beverly Barkman, Rachel Billingsley, Kevin Binder, Patty Brown, Gail Bybee, Kim Carpenter, Cathy Catanzano, Barbara Collins, Lorri Collins-Gutierrez, Nethelda Derr, Chuck Durbin, Sandra Dutton, Mari Beth Fitzpatrick, Pat Funkhouser, Robert Gall, Rhoda Geiger, Shirlee Goetz, Faith Gowan, Audrey Grisham, Barb Harvey, Elizabeth Hayward, Pat Hudson, Jody Kauflin, Pat Kettering, Carl King, Pam Kvarnstrom, Mike Levine, Romie Lundquist, Helen Lynch, James Lytle, Mindi McDermott, Virginia McPhail, Sharon Maes, Kristi Mockerman, Gary Morris, Teri Padget, Douglas Pagels, Mary Ann Pape, Mary Parker, Lynn Picard, June Polis, Norma Pollard, Mark Quire, Bronwyn Richardson, Jane Roche, Charlene Rogers, Winnie Sanders, Sharon Schultz, Cliff Scott, Kim Singh, LaVonne Stermer, Jack Truesdale, Patti Wayant, and Marty Wilk.

countries, and sales increased in the United States as well. Within several years, Helene and Hank increased book sales over tenfold.

My mom decided to retire at the end of 1997. In May of that year, we had a magnificent party in New York City celebrating and honoring her for her twenty-four years as Blue Mountain's sales manager.

Alan Greenberg and Winnie Sanders presented to my mother, on behalf of all the sales reps, an exquisitely engraved silver platter.

Alan is president of our best rep group, Splash Sails, Inc., which continues to represent Blue Mountain Arts nearly thirty years later. Winnie, the national sales coordinator, retired after working for Blue Mountain Arts for twenty-five years. My mom and she had a close relationship, and they both referred to Winnie as "June's right hand." Winnie was in charge of the sales support systems, trade show coordination, special accounts, and other sales-related functions.

At the party, an outpouring of love and respect was expressed for my mom in warm speeches delivered by Al Maslia, owner of a chain of stores named Social Expressions, a longtime customer of Blue Mountain Arts; Blue Mountain employees; sales reps; and my brother, Robbie; as well as in a poem I read to my mom. But the highlight of the evening was Mom's five grandchildren taking the podium and speaking about their grandmother and how much she meant to them.

Mike Levine, who had worked for Blue Mountain Arts for over nineteen years, was promoted to national and international sales manager in 2000. He was now in charge of all the Blue Mountain sales representatives and the sales support staff. Mike had been a loyal, hard-working, regional sales manager and was ready to take on this important role after my mom had retired.

Blue Mountain Arts was well on its way to becoming a mature, established company that not only continued to lead, but also was expected to lead. We loved it!

Steve and I started to think of many ideas for new cards and books, always trying, with Cliff Scott and the Art & Editorial Department, to enhance Blue Mountain's creativity. Though we kept the look that had made Blue Mountain Arts recognizable, we also branched out. We designed a new line consisting of occasion-specific cards—Happy Birthday, Get Well, etc.—and we experimented with gorgeous handmade papers, which we incorporated into new books and card lines.

Poetry manuscripts poured in from all over the world, and we tried to use as many of the poems on our cards as we could. Many people wanted me to critique their poems, but I have always refused to offer advice or edit anyone's work; the kind of poetry we receive is so personal that to criticize it would negate the writer's feelings.

Steve turned his interests to computer graphics and began designing and programming stereograms: three-dimensional images that we called "5-D." Steve received a patent for this original program. (A stereogram looks like a random design until you let your eyes relax and a multidimensional picture pops out.) He made his beautiful drawings and photographs into stereogram posters, cards, and books, and even included poetry in many of them. This became a huge fad, and Blue Mountain Arts once again was at the forefront.

We continued to learn and grow with each new venture. Little did we know that the biggest one of all was just over the horizon.

Listen to your customers!
Understand your customers!
Make things as easy as possible for your customers!

chapter twenty-nine

Bluemountain.com: Our First Electronic Greeting Card

"Oh, no!" I shouted. "We forgot to send Jared a birthday card!" It was May 11, 1996, and Jared would be celebrating his twenty-first birthday. We owned a greeting card company, and we couldn't even remember to send our own son a birthday card.

"Let's call him," Steve said, and I shook my head.

"He never answers the phone!" I said. Like most college students, Jared was never in his room. I missed him, and now there was a chance that we might miss his birthday the next day, something we had never done before.

The events to follow, all inspired by the simple act of our forgetting to send Jared a birthday card, would ultimately become the beginning of yet another new and exciting chapter in the life of Blue Mountain Arts, ultimately setting off a major Internet craze: the electronic greeting card.

"I've got an idea," Steve said, and he disappeared into the room in our house filled with stacks of books that we called our "library." He switched on the computer.

The previous summer, Jared had come home and taught our younger son HTML, the language used to create Web pages, and he, in turn, had taught Steve. Steve was now using what he had learned to make Jared's birthday card. After fiddling around with a Java program, he asked me to look at what he had designed.

I couldn't believe my eyes. The computer screen was black and gold, with maroon and blue stars zooming about. Jared's name and "Happy Birthday" danced around all over the screen. Steve told me to click the mouse anywhere, and when I did, the background turned beige and the colors of the floating designs changed to blue, purple, gray, and pink. Jared's name even grew larger as it seemed to approach us. I'd never seen anything like it. Steve was amazing!

I asked him how he did it. He explained that he had programmed an "applet," an interactive Java program designed to download quickly and play on a browser.

"See?" he showed me, beaming. "You can put your name in and it shows the art with your message on it. There are so many tools that enable you to do things with graphics, and I can't believe nobody is using them!"

Despite my awe, computers were never my forte; to this day, I still write with a pen and paper—although I love e-mail. But this particular use of the computer was quite appealing.

Steve posted the birthday card on the Web and e-mailed the URL to Jared.

Since Jared checked his e-mail several times a day, we knew that this would be the only reliable way to reach him on his birthday. I smiled at Steve. I was proud of him for programming and designing such a unique, interactive birthday card for our son, and I had a feeling that he'd found a new outlet for his creativity. His boyish enthusiasm was infectious.

Where Steve saw a hobby, though, Jared saw much more.

"You have to build a website for this," Jared said on the phone the next day. He loved the card, and he recognized the potential in his father's ability. "Can you customize it for anyone? People will absolutely love to receive cards like these on the Web. It could be a Blue Mountain website."

"Yes…" Steve said, as hundreds of ideas flooded his head.

Our younger son had already made sketches of the website's layout, and Steve followed his ideas when he opened the site later in the year.

Steve had been planning to create a Blue Mountain Arts homepage since the previous summer, but the concept of interactive electronic greeting cards had not crystallized until he made Jared's birthday card. Steve had surfed the Web looking at the homepages of large interactive learning companies. "I found one awful page after another. On one website I waited two minutes for a picture to download, and then I realized it was just a picture of a very ugly building!" he told me later, and I laughed.

Such gross misuse of graphics on the Web so annoyed Steve that he decided to show what could be done artistically.

"I'll make greeting cards on the Web that everyone can send for free," Steve said.

Free? I wondered…

Jared always loved the entrepreneurial aspect of Blue Mountain Arts, and his mind for business continually astounded me. Steve and I have good instincts, but we learned through trial and error. Jared, though, soaked up everything about business like a sponge.

During Jared's third year at Princeton University, he started his first Internet company called American Information Systems (AIS), one of the early Internet service providers in Chicago. We could route the bluemountain.com website through the AIS servers, Jared told us. That way they would get some business and Steve could continue to make cards. And most importantly Jared and Steve would get to work together.

Steve disappeared into the library again, working eighteen-hour days animating, designing, and programming for the website. His talents made him perfectly suited for this kind of work. Every day, he came up with new and fantastic ideas for cards. He practically lived in a used bookstore where he would buy old books about various holidays, Eastern art, and ancient Chinese texts one day, and books about exotic animals, Irish designs, and the *I Ching* the next—anything he could research to use on new cards. The owner must have thought he was crazy. And his family wasn't so sure about him either. His ability to hyper-focus on one thing for days, nights, weeks, or months made me wonder if he would ever pay attention to Blue Mountain Arts publishing company or me again. Our daughter thought that perhaps he was going through a midlife crisis and would come out of it soon. But he was very happy so we just let him be.

Steve went to the zoo to take photos of a baby rhinoceros with its mother, and to a wolf preserve, where he took hundreds of pictures of wolves in the rain. He sifted through thousands of images of animals, flowers, trees, and other nature scenes to use in illustrations and animations for cards. I especially loved his two hugging polar bears against a backdrop of snow.

At one point, he recruited one of the more computer-literate people from Blue Mountain Arts to help him part-time. Faith Gowan, our art director, animated some of the illustrations from our paper greeting cards and made them into electronic greeting cards using the program Steve had designed.

Finally, on September 24, 1996, bluemountain.com debuted online with twenty-nine electronic greeting cards. The website was extremely easy to navigate and use. All the electronic greeting cards were carefully designed by Steve to download very quickly—in ten to fifteen seconds— so they worked with the slowest computer modems. Even computer-illiterate people, like me, found it extraordinarily simple to send Steve's cards.

Steve had followed a lesson that we had already learned: Serve your customers and make things as easy as possible for them.

The homepage categorized the cards under the headings: "Friend," "Happy Birthday," "Love," "Graduation," "Thank You," "Support," and "Thinking of You" in a large, colorful text style. One click on a category heading brought you to a category index page, and with one more click, you were viewing an animated greeting card. On the same page as the card, there was an easy-to-use form that enabled the user to personalize and send the card to a friend. Right from the start, the user-friendliness of bluemountain.com was one of its most appealing aspects.

The website featured four "interactive applets" similar to the card Steve had sent Jared on his birthday. The user could personalize the cards with names and messages that were inserted as part of the interactive animation. These cards utilized Sun Microsystems' new

"Java" programming language that had only been incorporated into the final release of Netscape's 2.0 Web browser six months earlier.

Every card was animated, including those with poems. One showed a seagull flying across a dramatic blue and pink sky with my love poem "In the morning" in the foreground. The animated illustration was so beautiful that I couldn't resist selecting more of my poems for the website. We had a wide, family-oriented selection of themes from the start.

Steve designed seven very unusual cards in which he adapted photographs of animals, such as eagles and wolves, into "animated images." In addition, he converted more Blue Mountain Arts paper cards into animated cyberspace cards, including two by Kristin Sheldon, two by Ashley Rice, six with my poems, seven with poems by Douglas Pagels, and one of Shakespeare's sonnets.

The "animated images" were created using a new, animated GIF feature that also had just been introduced to the Web that year. Steve carefully designed the electronic greeting cards so that the users with older browsers were also able to view and send the cards.

Most of the cards were accompanied by music that was programmed, arranged, and played by Richard James, the creative musician we had worked with for many years. The website utilized MIDI sound files, which allowed users to play electronic music without the need to download large files. The MIDI format even played on some of the older browsers.

Steve had submitted the site to a number of search engines so people could find it, and several days after launching bluemountain.com, the Boulder *Daily Camera* newspaper published a front-page article about our e-cards:

> Blue Mountain Arts, which specializes in "relationship-oriented" cards bearing poetic messages, opened a site Wednesday on the World Wide Web that offers e-cards at no charge. Computer users with modems can personalize the cards and send them instantly to computer-connected friends and loved ones.

Boulder is a fairly plugged-in town, and the college population and high-tech industries contributed to a higher-than-average number of people with computers and modems. Now, of course, most people have access to the Internet, but in 1996, the World Wide Web was often regarded as a "geek" or "techie" medium.

On September 25, 1996, the day after the site was launched, people sent fifty cards from the bluemountain.com site; on September 26, the day the article came out, approximately two thousand cards were sent!

The expansion occurred like this: If a thousand people sent cards, then another thousand people would get online to pick up the cards, and then they might choose to send cards, too. If each of these thousand recipients sent three cards, then there would be three thousand new recipients. If each of these new recipients sent three cards, there would then be nine thousand recipients, and so on.

In the Internet industry, they call this "viral" growth. James McQuivey, an analyst for Forrester Research, later wrote, "They [bluemountain.com] basically invented viral marketing."

A few days later, Steve got an e-mail from a man in Fort Collins, Colorado. "Someone in Boulder sent me this card," he wrote. "I love it! I'm sending it to all my friends around the world!"

"Oh, shit," Steve said to me, eyes wide. "This is going to grow like you wouldn't believe. It'll expand like a chain reaction all over the world. This is going to be bigger than we have ever imagined." Steve had always brilliantly understood trends and applied meaningful, accurate numbers to projections; his prediction scared me because I knew he was always right!

On October 3, the day another newspaper article was published, four thousand cards were sent from our website; on October 27, four days before Halloween, seven thousand were sent; and on the day of Halloween, nearly thirty thousand cards were sent, causing the servers to crash and the website to temporarily shut down. The most popular Halloween card was an animated, winking jack-o'-lantern designed by Steve.

We hadn't done any publicity, aside from a brief announcement that the site had launched. We didn't advertise anywhere. (Other Internet companies spent many millions of dollars on ads.) People just came to the site, and it all happened so fast. We later learned, over and over again, that one day in cyberspace is equivalent to years on Earth.

To handle the enormous volume expected during the coming holiday season, Steve decided to expand the website by creating "mirrors" of the website on two of our servers in Chicago and on an additional server in another location. He asked Jared for help with this.

"I know someone at school that I think can handle the job," Jared said. And for the first time, we came face-to-face with the unusual culture of high technology.

Tung-Hui Hu, a gifted friend of Jared's, had entered Princeton University when he was fourteen years old, and now, two years later, Jared hired him to build a server for bluemountain.com. Tung-Hui ordered the parts, built the server in his dorm room, and found a hosting company in Virginia to which he could hook it up. He built it so it could handle the millions of hits and cards that would move through it daily, and he did it all from his dorm room after classes!

In addition to creating the cards, Steve programmed all the Web server software and the custom database that handled the personalization and formation of the cards. He wrote over five thousand lines of computer code. In his quest for perfection, he kept logs of every error that occurred on the website. He scrutinized each one so that he could correct it. This was one of the main reasons why people found bluemountain.com cards so reliable and accessible. He even configured the computers to alert his wristwatch pager when an error occurred; the beeping woke us from a deep sleep on many occasions.

Needless to say, all this took time. Steve slept about four to five hours a night and worked on the computer during his waking hours. He was having a lot of fun, but he wasn't able to do anything other than bluemountain.com. We saw him for dinner, but the rest of the time, if we wanted to talk to him or do something with him, we had to go to our library, shut off the computer monitor, and wave our hands in front of his face. Of course he still accompanied us to all family events, but as soon as we returned home, he was back on the computer.

I've always envied the fact that Steve can just shut out the world and so thoroughly concentrate on something important to him. It doesn't matter where he is or what's going on around him. During these times, he simply doesn't notice anything other than what is going on in his mind. His level of accomplishment astounds me. I think it would have taken at least fifty people to complete what he did all alone in our library.

At the time, most industry experts, as well as the media, said it was necessary to raise at least ten million dollars to launch a successful website. With Steve's hard work and vision, bluemountain.com managed to become one of the most popular sites in the world despite having, I am sure, the lowest budget of any large website. To this day, when people ask, "How many millions of dollars did it take to start bluemountain.com?" I point to Steve. "It took him," I say.

It is important to lead with a clear and consistent vision.

chapter thirty

Number One

Every time we went to restaurants, Steve approached waiters, busboys, bartenders, and other diners—anyone who might possibly speak a language other than English—so he could expand bluemountain.com's repertoire of international cards. At our favorite coffee shop, owned by Hamdi and Reyhan, a wonderful couple from Turkey, Steve discovered that the twelve people working there were from eleven different countries. He asked each waiter to write "Happy Birthday" in his or her native language while I embarrassingly stared into my cappuccino.

Less than six weeks earlier, Steve had been creating dancing pumpkins for a little hobby site; now we were about to set up several new servers. It had taken us many years to build Blue Mountain Arts' audience, but within only a couple of months bluemountain.com had a worldwide, multilingual, multicultural audience. It was absolutely unbelievable. Whenever we wore a bluemountain.com T-shirt or hat, people would stop us and tell us how much they loved sending our electronic cards. There was almost universal recognition of our dot-com company, something that has yet to be achieved in the thirty-four-year history of our paper company.

Every day, Steve created new cards. He was truly in his element. He also used the site to promote special causes he believed in; for instance, he created Thanksgiving cards featuring facts about Native Americans. Since he's always believed that American schoolchildren don't learn enough about the true history of our continent, he used the website to teach them about Native American inventions, foods, and traditions. We also later used the website as a forum to promote causes, such as breast cancer and diabetes awareness.

In the early days, we knew we'd include Thanksgiving and Christmas cards, but the immediacy and ease of e-mail allowed the users to request new cards on a daily basis. One woman chastised Steve for missing St. Lucia's Day, and after some digging, he discovered it was a major national holiday—in Sweden. So he created a St. Lucia's Day card. In the coming months, he would create Independence Day cards for practically every nation in the world, Zoroastrian cards, Kiss and Make Up Day cards, and what seemed like cards for events for every day of the year. Steve's philosophy was that one e-mail letter suggesting a card for a certain occasion represented the views of about one thousand other people who didn't send an e-mail.

The response from our audience overwhelmed us, but one particular correspondence stood out above all the rest. A Canadian man sent us an e-mail that said, "I am sending a card with Susan's love poem on it to propose to my girlfriend in Jakarta. I hope she accepts." Ten minutes later, he e-mailed us again and told us that she had accepted. Just imagine! A man from Canada sent a card on a website in the United States; it was routed through the servers in Chicago and sent to a woman he loves in Jakarta. Within minutes, she received and sent back her acceptance of his proposal.

This new method of instant communication was mind boggling and would change everyone's lives. Our website instantly brought people together from across hemispheres, although sometimes the immediate feedback had other effects. Steve created a card for Indian Independence Day, which happens to be the day after Pakistani Independence Day. Unfortunately, he didn't know that, and he failed to make a card for Pakistani Independence Day. Hundreds of furious Pakistanis wrote that we'd insulted them by recognizing India and not Pakistan. Steve quickly designed a card for Pakistan, and within minutes, it was on bluemountain.com and people started sending it.

In the month of October 1997, one year after opening the site, 1,623,722 cards were sent from bluemountain.com. Word of mouth moved at the speed of light, and the technical side started to suffer from the volume of traffic. After five new servers crashed around

Christmas, Steve and Jared realized AIS just couldn't handle the volume anymore. AIS had every employee working night and day to keep the servers running, but we weren't their only client, and that wasn't a fair situation for either of us.

Once again, Jared's friend Tung-Hui Hu came to the rescue and designed and built us our own network of servers to handle the volume. At that point, the small bluemountain.com staff resembled those servers: We just couldn't handle the volume any more. But we didn't know any more about Internet companies than we had known about greeting cards when we had first started. So, just as we had in the early silk screening days, Steve, Jared, and I called on our friends for help. Together we created the oddest hodgepodge of employees in the industry.

We agreed that we needed someone to manage the technical aspects of the company, so we asked a respected professor and dean of UC San Diego to send us the smartest person he knew. He sent us Mark Rinella. I'll never forget going into the office one day in early 1998 and seeing Mark on the floor. He had a screwdriver in one hand, his puppy in the other, and all kinds of metal and plastic computer components surrounding him. He was making the computer servers by hand. This sure was a company starting from the ground up. Mark would work close to twenty-four hours a day for the next couple of years keeping the site afloat.

Though Steve had answered all the e-mails in the first few months, he didn't have time to handle the thousands of letters that poured in every day. I called Marjorie Shaevitz, one of my best friends, who became the first electronic postmaster of bluemountain.com (Postmaster Pat). She sorted and answered e-mail, set up a system for other postmasters to follow, and alerted Steve to any important technical bugs the users found. I called my college roommate, Myrna, to help select specific melodies as background music for each card. Karen Bidgood, our proficient assistant, edited cards, wrote copy for various projects, and created personalized press releases. The following year, she wrote daily horoscopes.

Bluemountain.com now needed someone who could check in with the servers on a daily, minute-by-minute basis. Mark Rinella called a local Internet company who recommended a young, smart Vanderbilt University student named Jason Taylor—a techie version of Brad Pitt. Jason was majoring in math, physics, and computer science while working two jobs. He later went to the MIT Media Lab to do research on developing quantum computers as he worked toward his Ph.D. We hired Jason, and for the next three years he managed the monumental task of keeping our networks and servers running, often working on them until four in the morning. We were astounded that he was able to accomplish this because he had so many other responsibilities.

Now that we had a technical staff that could handle the heavy traffic, we needed to expand the art staff to keep up with the demand for new cards. Steve called a temporary artist agency and talked to an insightful person named Dena Bloom Meeder. She sent us Susie Acheson, a Web designer who started working for us part-time in late November and became our first full-time graphic artist in January 1998. In addition, Matt Rantanan, a computer graphic artist who had assisted Steve during the previous year, started working full-time on the website.

In January 1998, Media Metrix, a leading Internet audience measurement service, reported that bluemountain.com had 3.3 million unique visitors (8.7% of the total Web audience).

At that time, the website expanded to about two hundred electronic greeting cards, including the extremely popular animal characters designed by Karen Lyn Morse, more of the clever, creative writings and illustrations by Ashley Rice, and works by several other artists and writers, such as Dr. Natasha Josefowitz and award-winning country singer Donna Fargo.

Up to that point, in addition to Steve and Jared, the website had only employed a handful of people borrowed from our paper company, plus a few outside contractors.

Then the rest of our family jumped in. In addition to trying to hold everything together, I'd been writing or choosing music for the cards as well as selecting new card artists. Our daughter—who's as art- and science-minded as her father—worked on various bluemountain.com projects during the summer. She then took six months off from college and orchestrated the engineering, programming, business development, and creative designs necessary to expand new features, such as voice customization and gift attachments, to the electronic greeting cards.

Our youngest son animated cards and also wrote clever captions to go with photographs of animals, which became some of the more popular cards on the site.

Despite our extra help, though, Steve still worked way too much. Every day he switched back and forth between programming and artwork, creating new cards and updating old ones, and working out bugs and investigating glitches. While Jared got things done by delegating responsibility and managing a team, Steve preferred doing things himself. He would usually be in our library surrounded by piles of papers and books, typing furiously on the computer, doing everything from animating butterflies to rearranging indexes.

Steve learned from Blue Mountain Arts that it is important to lead with a clear and consistent vision, and he constantly conveyed this vision to everyone who worked for the website. They knew that the site must help people keep in touch with one another, be creative, and remain easy to navigate, fun to use, fast to download, and accessible to all computers.

Steve loved his new hobby and, apparently, so did everyone else. Mark moved the server base from Illinois and Virginia to Arizona, and then to California's Silicon Valley in an attempt to handle the ever-expanding traffic. This enabled Mark to keep the servers processing the enormous number of Blue Mountain cards sent by people around the world.

On May 19, 1998—one year and eight months after Steve launched our website—*Time* magazine announced that bluemountain.com was the top "shopping site" and the tenth most-visited site on the Web— up there with AOL and Yahoo. The top shopping site, and we didn't even sell anything!

Seven months later, in December of 1998, there were 12,315,000 unique visitors, (21.7% of the Web audience) to the site. In a little over two years after it was founded, our website had grown to become one of the most-visited websites in the world. At this point, everything was so exhilarating, and we realized that there was a certain power in instantly reaching this many people. If there was something very important to say, this sure would be the way to get it out to the whole world quickly.

By the end of 1998, bluemountain.com had a total website staff of ten full-time and six part-time employees. The new people included two project coordinators, Marejka Shaevitz and Catherine Bergman. One of our most dedicated artists, Vanessa Garcia, worked as a volunteer without pay because she was on a tourist visa from Mexico. She built the Blue Mountain Spanish-language website in three months all by herself. Susie Acheson became the art manager, and she hired a talented group of artists in San Francisco. Mark Rinella managed all the technical people. Jared managed the business employees, including some top-notch salespeople. Bluemountain.com was growing to be quite an organization.

We added more of our fifty-plus-year-old friends to our ever-growing staff. Frank Lee, who'd been a physicist in the defense industry and had received a Ph.D. in Physics from Princeton at the same time as Steve, began programming interactive cards and expanded the Chinese site. Steve's brother-in-law, Ken Leshner, formerly a top managing programmer at a major bank, came out of retirement to program Web server software. Our old friend Roger Ben Wilson, who'd worked at Blue Mountain Arts in the early 1970's, left his defense job to help us hire top programmers, webmasters, and website testers.

Steve's and my technical and creative friends were all over fifty years old, on the verge of retirement, and looking for new interests; Jared and his friends were a crop of young whiz kids. The chemistry between the groups was amusing to watch. While the younger group seemed a little more arrogant, cocksure, and know-it-all, the older employees just "went with the flow." They, like Steve, saw this as an enjoyable diversion, a constructive outlet for their creativity. They had the patience and ability to work on long-term projects. And since many of us hadn't grown up with computers, I think we appreciated the historical significance of our project more than the younger employees did.

Jared and his friends rarely seemed content with anything. Ideas flew fast and furious. Their technical know-how stunned me, but their fiscal acumen was minimal and they often lacked a sense of practicality. Bluemountain.com felt like a family of patient parents and their precocious children.

Our electronic greeting cards had become the most popular form of communication on the Web other than e mail.

And that's when our electronic house of cards began to crumble.

chapter thirty-one

Bluemountain.com v. Microsoft: Same Story, Different Players

Before you read this chapter, I want to make a quick disclaimer: Steve and I don't spend all our time suing people. In fact, after thirty-four years in business, we've only been directly involved with a few lawsuits. It just so happens that our lawsuits were highly publicized and involved some heavy hitters.

We love our company, and we would do anything to protect it regardless of how hard the task might be. So when Microsoft introduced software in 1998 that we believed had the effect of interfering with the delivery of our electronic greeting cards, we jumped to bluemountain.com's defense.

Two years after Steve launched the site, a representative of Microsoft had come to visit our bluemountain.com office. Steve sensed that something strange was going on. The Microsoft employee asked about the future plans for bluemountain.com. Unbeknownst to us, the same man had visited Jared in Boulder the week before. He had been as vague with Jared as he was with Steve. Later on we would discover that Microsoft had identified our e-greetings as a "killer app," and they wanted to get into the business.

"I think that Microsoft is trashing our cards," Mark Rinella told Steve one day.

Mark had tried receiving our cards using the new Internet Explorer mail program called Outlook Express, and it treated our cards as junk mail.

Coincidentally, Microsoft issued its junk-mail filter within weeks of opening its own free e-greeting card site. The reigning monarch of the Information Age had engineered a program that had the effect of trashing our electronic greeting cards, thus preventing them from getting delivered to the recipients.

We immediately called the Microsoft representative who'd visited us, and he said a bug in Outlook Express caused the problem. Microsoft would fix it right away.

The next day, November 20, Microsoft rescinded what they had told us the previous day; they said they wouldn't fix the problem until they came out with their next edition of Internet Explorer, which could be at any unspecified time in the future. Less than a week later, we discovered that WebTV, a subsidiary of Microsoft, blocked the cards as well. All this at the start of Thanksgiving and Christmas, the busiest greeting card season of the year!

The ramifications of Microsoft's actions were enormous. It seemed to us that what they were doing was analogous to someone holding up a mail truck and blocking the delivery of letters.

After sending a letter to Microsoft to no avail, I found Gary Reback, a smart, aggressive lawyer who was familiar with Microsoft's past activities. We hired him and he quickly filed a complaint against Microsoft on December 8 that asked for a temporary restraining order to stop them from "disrupting, retarding, or otherwise inhibiting delivery or receipt of Blue Mountain greeting cards." In other words, they had to stop selling or distributing any software that included the junk mail filter until they fixed the filter so our cards would get through.

Restraining orders most typically involve cases of domestic abuse or relatively simple commercial disputes. Asking for a restraining order in this dispute against one of the most prominent software manufacturers in the world was a bold move and was not guaranteed to succeed.

But Gary wanted to stop Microsoft in its tracks before it damaged our company any further, and we accepted the risk.

The court granted us a temporary restraining order on December 21, 1998, ordering that Microsoft enable us to design our e-mail notification messages to bypass the junk-mail filter, that they notify us of any changes in the filter, and that they post a warning on the Microsoft website regarding the filter for every user who chooses to download the software.

After the court issued the temporary restraining order, we saw how such a simple request—that Microsoft allow our mail to get through their filter—could get twisted beyond recognition.

Microsoft claimed that their filter junked their own cards as well as ours. But fortunately, our lawyers had hired an expert to investigate the filters, and they discovered that Microsoft's cards did get through…at least they did until, at some point between our discovery and the first hearing, the filter suddenly started blocking Microsoft's cards, too. The filter blocked their cards, but only after we said it blocked ours.

My head spun. "Not again, not again…" was the refrain that played in my mind, but oddly, at the same time, I felt a little detached from these proceedings. My anger surged when I listened to Microsoft's lawyers speak, but Steve and I just weren't as emotionally involved this time around as we had been with Hallmark. I suppose that's partly because we had been through it before, partly because our livelihood wasn't at stake (we still had the "paper" publishing company, as we called it, after all), and partly because we now expected this sort of thing to happen. It seemed to us that large companies often worry about and spend enormous amounts of time hurting or trying to outdo their competitors. Not only does this waste energy and resources, but it stops them from concentrating on what their strengths and missions are.

Still, what felt like Microsoft's utter meanness grated on me. Although I thought that Bill Gates was brilliant and I appreciated his remarkable accomplishments, I didn't like the way Microsoft seemed to approach business competition.

On January 28, 1999, the court awarded us a preliminary injunction that stated:

> ...Microsoft Corporation...shall be enjoined and restrained from distributing, licensing, and/or selling, directly or indirectly, any product (including any and all types of software) including without limitation, any commercial, public, trial or beta versions of software that include any electronic mail "filter" which impedes in any manner the delivery of Blue Mountain greeting cards or notification messages to the intended recipient's standard electronic mail in-box.

The judge said:

> I do find it beyond coincidence, and I do find it difficult, if not impossible, to accept the assertion by the Defendant that those individuals developing the filter were unaware of the electronic greeting cards aspect of Microsoft's business...So I do believe that there was some intent on Defendant's part—if not outright targeting—of Blue Mountain or similar outfits that were in competition offering electronic greeting cards.

Less than one month later, Microsoft posted an unusual press release on its website. Due to a preliminary injunction ruling, it said, Microsoft Corporation would be removing a "popular anti-spam filtering feature." Linda Norman, the senior corporate attorney for Microsoft, was quoted as saying, "This ruling is particularly unfortunate for consumers who will be denied the ability to choose for themselves an innovative new technology to manage the high volume of unwanted commercial e-mail they routinely receive online."

Steve visualized a mental picture of us—little Blue Mountain Arts—bullying Microsoft. The image was laughable, especially since we hadn't said what they claimed. We didn't want them to get rid of the junk mail filter. We just wanted our cards to go through—a request that according to our experts and even WebTV would have involved nothing more than putting our name on the list of acceptable senders. We had specified that they could keep the filter, as long as they ensured that our cards wouldn't be automatically blocked. And here was Microsoft saying we had strong-armed them into giving up a valuable technology.

Several weeks later we encountered a weird problem that could only occur in the Internet age. The following message had begun being passed around on AOL:

```
Subject: fwd: BLUE MOUNTAIN CARDS VIRUS ALERT!!!!
Date: Sat. 27 Feb. 1999
     Just received a call from family. A friend of
theirs opened a card from Blue Mountain cards and
system crashed.
     Do not open Blue Mountain cards until further
notice. Virus has infiltrated their system....Pass
this on to anyone you may know that uses Blue
Mountain.
```

This was a hoax and not true at all. People all over the world sent this message to each other and posted it on newsgroups. In two weeks the message became so widespread that we received thousands of e-mails from confused website users.

The power of the Internet had suddenly turned against us. But we came up with an idea to reverse the tide. At that time, people were sending almost one million cards from bluemountain.com every day, so we put a statement on each card saying that the website was safe. Eventually through our input on the Internet, people found out that this had been a mean hoax, but not until it had caused us a lot of trouble.

We put the hoax behind us and now we had to prepare for the trial against Microsoft. Fortunately our lawyers took care of most of the details for us.

As fate would have it, we never went to a final trial with Microsoft. A month before our trial date, something happened that would alter the course of bluemountain.com forever.

If your reason for starting a business is to make money, you may succeed, but it will be far more difficult than if you begin your endeavor because you love what you are doing.

*   *   *

In confusing, hurtful times, turning to loved ones is a major source of comfort and clarity to help overcome problems.

chapter thirty-two

E-Insanity

As soon as people learned about the zillions of "eyeballs" that bluemountain.com attracted, Jared began receiving calls from the movers and shakers of the dot-com industry, venture capitalists, and investors.

In 1998, bluemountain.com had expanded its staff to support the website. The servers and computer systems had to be constantly upgraded, and new artists and programmers had to be hired. By 1999, there were approximately eighty people working for the website. For every bluemountain.com greeting card sent by e-mail, we lost about two cents. The website was becoming far too expensive for us to support.

At this time, the cards were free, and the website was non-intrusive. Most other sites required names, e-mail addresses, home addresses, and even phone numbers—all designed to build a database that would then be marketed to solicit more business. Blue Mountain was the only popular website that was non-commercial, did not gather a database of e-mail addresses, and did not even use "cookies." Moreover, we flat-out refused to make our audience pay for cards; the service had been free from the start, and we wouldn't put a price tag on it now.

Thus with no fees, no tracking of user information, and a minimal amount of ads, bluemountain.com seemed to epitomize the most impractical way to run a company.

As the website traffic increased in volume, Jared left his position as western sales manager of Blue Mountain Arts' paper company to develop a strategy to help pay for the spiraling costs of the website.

"We should sell advertising," Jared suggested. Steve blanched. He hated the idea of someone logging on to our site and seeing an obnoxious pop-up window on the screen. But we needed some income to pay for the website. So Jared hired a sales force and a sales manager to sell advertising. It would consist of "banner" ads that would generally display after a card was sent so it wouldn't bother the receiver of the cards.

Jared whizzed around the country talking about the latest tracking technology to potential partners and other content providers. He thought it was revolutionary that companies would consider spending significant amounts of money just to be able to reach the viewers of a website. Jared and his staff started to generate income, but it wasn't enough to cover our ballooning costs.

Though Jared pursued advertising revenue, he thought that e-commerce was the long-term solution to generate value from our "eyeballs." He felt that the most sound business model included expanding bluemountain.com into gift-related items. Since so many people who buy greeting cards might also be interested in buying flowers, Jared thought that an inexpensive, fast, online, quality florist would be the ideal sister site to bluemountain.com. He founded a new company called Proflowers.

Jared traveled to flower growers all over California and sent Steve and me hundreds of beautiful roses to see which were the best. The unique concept behind Proflowers was that the recipient would get flowers directly from the growers. Because of this, the flowers would be more consistent, fresher, and last longer than those delivered from flower stores.

Within a short period of time, he hired his first employee and a systems designer and computer programmer, who programmed the entire Proflowers website fulfillment system all by himself in just three months. Jared met with FedEx to set up shipping arrangements to ensure customers would have next-day delivery, and Proflowers was in business. We agreed to place an ad for proflowers.com on the bluemountain.com website.

Jared asked another one of his college friends to develop the e-commerce infrastructure that would allow bluemountain.com to rapidly set up new gift categories on the website. Just in time for the

1999 holiday season, danschocolates.com was launched offering the most delicious, natural chocolates that I had ever tasted. We also sold plush animals on this site, the most popular being an adorable, royal blue bluemountain.com teddy bear whose look was designed by our younger son.

Our daughter worked on unifying card sending and e-commerce by enabling users to attach real gifts, such as flowers, chocolates, and gift certificates, to the electronic greeting cards. Thus, you could send a gift to someone knowing only their e-mail address. This was one of the visions for the future of the website.

By the end of 1999, bluemountain.com was positioned to become a leading gift portal on the Internet with incremental advertising revenues; however, we were very far from breaking even.

To everyone in the industry, though, bluemountain.com's enormous audience spelled one thing: money. I soon realized that in the upside-down world of the dot-coms, profits didn't mean half as much as exposure, a business philosophy that has never failed to confuse me. In the end, of course, that philosophy was wrong, as proven by the dot-com crash. On Friday, April 14, 2000, Wall Street experienced its biggest one-day fall in history, ending a week in which U.S. markets lost two trillion dollars in value.

Many industry leaders presented Jared with business plans and ideas that predicted huge financial successes for bluemountain.com, but we knew that traffic didn't equal profits. You're just not going to get that many people clicking on that many links and buying that many products. These people were just reiterating what most people believed at the time.

But there were also exciting visionaries in the industry, people who wanted to use the Internet as a source of communication and information, not just as a source of cash. Around this time, we met Jerry Yang, a handsome, intelligent young man wearing a rumpled shirt, chinos, and a rubber Mickey Mouse watch. He, too, had created something new for the Internet: Yahoo! Jerry typified the first generation of Internet company founders. Like Steve, they innovated constantly, and they worked around the clock to implement their ideas. But surrounding these creative founders was a mass hysteria and greed that formed the Internet bubble.

Like any time in history when a new industry or technology is introduced—the seventeenth century Dutch tulip craze, the start of railroads, the California gold rush, the invention of the automobile, and now the lure of the Internet—people who want to be rich (or get richer) try to get a piece of the action. It seemed like everyone wanted to be involved in the dot-com world. This type of frenzy often brings out the worst characteristics in people.

After two years of providing an enjoyable service to millions of fans, we finally had to face the reality of the dot-com craze. Most companies thought: "If we just keep spending and spending and spending, and we create a big audience, then we can sell to the highest bidder and walk away with a bank full of cash." We didn't like this philosophy.

The concept boggled my mind. Why, I wondered, would you want to spend so much time building a company just so you could sell it? The answer, of course, was again money. And getting rich, in my opinion, is the worst reason to start a business.

We had spent half our lives building Blue Mountain Arts, a company we loved and believed in. We created cards because we wanted to help people around the world communicate and to express ourselves creatively. We started our online venture for the same reasons.

We made greeting cards because we liked making them. Steve loved creating the animation and programs, just as we had loved creating our silk-screen posters together.

If your reason for starting a business is to make money, you may succeed, but it will be far more difficult than if you begin your endeavor because you love what you are doing.

And if you're doing something that fulfills a need or provides a service, you're accomplishing something you and other people like and want—that's the philosophy Blue Mountain Arts and bluemountain.com had always lived by.

This philosophy may sound idealistic, and I suppose it is, especially since, by December 1998, bluemountain.com had lost a lot of money.

We could no longer pretend that bluemountain.com would somehow come out all right in the end.

There were three possibilities that could keep bluemountain.com alive in the future:

1. We could take venture capital money and go public;
2. We could sell the company or merge with a bigger company; or
3. We could continue running the company until we ran out of money (which would be very soon)

Obviously, the third option wasn't an option at all, although it was what Steve would have preferred. He knew giving it up—either to stockholders, venture capitalists, or another company—would mean he would be losing his hobby, and we all knew that bluemountain.com would not be as meaningful without him. We wanted Steve to be comfortable with any decision. This was really "his baby," even though he joked that his baby had grown into a monster that had outgrown the house.

We worked through the unappealing cycle of choices. No matter which option we chose, we soon changed our minds because none of the answers seemed right. We'd decide to sell the company, but then we'd feel reluctant to let it go. So we'd consider taking it public, then we'd realize we weren't suited to working with the people we'd need to work with to take the company public. Then we'd wonder if we should just shut it down entirely, but that would mean all Steve's work would have gone to waste and the people who used the site would be so disappointed. Then we'd come back to thinking that selling it would be the best option. The loop kept going on and on, around and around…When you have three choices you don't like, how do you ever make a decision?

Though taking the company public had a strong downside, it was also somewhat appealing. Steve could still run the creative side of bluemountain.com, and we thought we could stay on the board and still have some modicum of control over the website's direction.

We started to prepare for this scenario. The first thing we wanted to do was to ensure that our employees would have a sizable chunk of the stock options, so we hired a well-known Silicon Valley law firm to work out a stock-option plan.

Three months passed, and we could not get the lawyers to complete the work, so we had to discharge them.

Then we hired a new lawyer who was from another large Silicon Valley law firm. Another two months passed, and we couldn't get this lawyer to complete a stock-option plan either. At this point we were concerned that our employees would not believe that we were trying to make a stock-option plan, because so many other companies had these in place immediately after starting their businesses.

Everyone in the dot-com industry had high-powered, aggressive, scary lawyers from high-powered, aggressive law firms—except us. To compete in the dot-com industry, it seemed as if companies had to have these lawyers, but they were obviously not what we needed.

In our phone book, we had crossed out the names of so many lawyers we had wasted time talking to. It seemed like every day we would either add or subtract names. Finally we decided that we should hire a lawyer who was not associated with a big law firm and who would listen to what we had to say and pay attention to what we needed. We hired Jared's Denver lawyer, Jeremy Makarechian, who worked alone. Jeremy wrote a stock-option plan within a week.

Meanwhile, dozens of people offered us advice on "going public." Rule number one in attracting investors, they said, was that founders are considered crazy and must therefore leave the company. They told us that no one would invest in a company if the founders still controlled it. We wanted three seats on the board of bluemountain.com—one for Steve, one for Jared, and one for me—but they said the most we could have was two. We were told that investors would want to have "their people" on the board and to give some of them a substantial percentage of the company. We seemed to be losing our company more and more each day.

Though all these professionals told us giving up control was the only way, we had good friends, Marion and Herb Sandler, who told us a different story. They had taken their banking business public and not only stayed on the board, but were co-CEOs, *and* their company was in the Fortune 500. They were the only people we knew who defied the notion that founders are crazy. After all, Marion argued, who could possibly understand the company's interests better than the founders? Investors like successful companies, regardless of the founders. The Sandlers also countered many other things we had been told.

We respected the Sandlers. They were down to earth, and we trusted them completely.

Despite the mounting problems, we continued on the path of going public and hired an executive search firm to help us find a CEO. After talking with some high-profile, egotistical candidates, none of whom agreed with our vision of bluemountain.com's future, we were introduced to a man we genuinely liked.

When the time came to negotiate the contract, though, his lawyers made so many demands that were unacceptable to us and that seemed so one-sided that we realized we weren't up to this kind of negotiating. So now we couldn't even hire a CEO we liked.

At this point, we began to realize that going public probably wasn't right for us. Everyone wanted a piece of the bluemountain.com pie. Everyone wanted to make a deal. We liked simple business operations where, with hard work and creativity, one could succeed. We detested "deal making," and Internet businesses were consumed with deal making. We knew that we were in way over our heads.

In addition, our youngest son would be going to college soon, and we wanted to spend more time with him during his last two years at home. Going public would have occupied us all day and night, and we knew we wouldn't have the time we wanted to be with him.

Even exploring the possibility of going public strained us to the limit, physically, mentally, and emotionally. Our cell phones rang constantly everywhere we went. When we weren't on the phone with a lawyer, we were thinking about the next conversation we'd have with one.

Steve and I were utterly incapable of living in that world of wheeling and dealing. We couldn't go public.

So we started to wrestle with the idea of selling the company. Jared met with an endless string of investors, venture capitalists, bankers, and owners of various dot-com businesses. Some of these people were quite serious and others had bizarre, nonsensical interests and deals. In one meeting, we met with a well-known investor from Japan who spoke honestly and frankly about what he wanted to do with bluemountain.com. He got right to the point within minutes without beating around the bush, and offered to shake hands on a deal right then and there. We liked him, but we weren't mentally ready to make an agreement so quickly.

We also met with a well-known head of a major dot-com company who came to see us. He inquired about buying our company, but Steve said he didn't think he was interested in selling. "Fine," said the man without blinking. He then told us that he would just make his own card website.

I would share more specific stories, but the faces and meetings blend together in my mind. The one thing we knew for sure was that we would not sell the Blue Mountain Arts paper company. It was quite surprising to us the number of people who didn't even want our paper company. Their dot-com heads surely were screwed on wrong.

Reality set in again as we realized that if we sold bluemountain.com, the new owners wouldn't keep up the site the way Steve had because they wouldn't understand what Steve had created. We didn't want to risk fracturing the staff or distorting the mission of the company, regardless of the size of the offer. Everyone had worked so hard to build bluemountain.com that it had become a part of us all.

We felt so bad for Steve. The decision to let go of the company tortured him. He'd created something he loved, and he wanted to keep it, but he knew he couldn't. Usually, Steve is extremely decisive, but now he changed his mind daily, depending on the latest bad news. Several wonderful advisors spent time with us trying to help us, but we were too emotionally drained to sort through or carry out their recommendations.

I finally phoned my brother, Robbie. He could tell by my voice that I was in a lot of anguish, so he immediately got on a plane and came to visit us. He tried to find out what Steve, in particular, wanted to do. He saw our agony in dealing with the lawyers, potential CEO candidates, venture capitalists, and the nonsensical proposals made to us on every front. Robbie tried in a nonbiased way to help us sort things out and restore our serenity and sanity. After talking with him for two days, it became very clear that we did not want to be part of the dot-com business life any longer. He offered to help us in any way he could. By the end of his visit, we knew that he already had helped us in the most important way possible, by enabling us to realize our "truths." Now we just had to follow them, and we knew this would be difficult.

Jared showed us projections about how many chocolates and teddy bears we would need to sell to make ends meet, and it boggled our minds. We again explored the possibility of selling the company, and we found out that, in this world, you don't just talk to owners of various companies interested in buying. You can't do your own negotiating, and we had already proven that we weren't even close to being up to the task anyway. Luckily Jared had already interviewed a number of investment bankers to advise us and chose three for us to meet with. To our surprise, there was one we liked: Javier Rojas from Broadview. Javier was a practical, down-to-earth oasis of soundness in all the dot-com craziness.

A year before this, out of the many companies that had contacted Jared, there actually had been one potential partner that seemed quite reasonable. Jared had met with the CEO and chairman of the board of Excite@home, an Internet portal company that wanted to work or merge with us. They wanted bluemountain.com because electronic greeting cards were an important application for high-speed bandwidth. It also fit in with their current advertising revenue plans for their media properties, such as the Excite portal. By combining with bluemountain.com, they would become one of the three most trafficked sites on the entire Internet. Excite@home was not at all interested in e-commerce, which is where Jared felt the true value was, so they would let us preserve the independence of his proflowers.com and danschocolates.com. Jared had thought this company would be a good match for bluemountain.com, but at the time we weren't interested in selling. Now, however, when Jared mentioned Excite@home again and suggested that we meet with them, we reluctantly agreed. Javier set up a date for us to meet.

But, as usual during this time in our lives, we changed our minds again. We weren't up to meeting with anyone. On top of that, we started to get cold feet about selling the company. I called Javier and asked him to cancel the meeting at the hotel we were planning to go to. We wanted to get away, think about things, and get some rest before making a definite decision. We took the children to the hotel on the beach and decided that come hell or high water, we would make a decision by the end of the weekend.

At the beach, we again discussed our options, but we told Steve that he had to make the final decision.

"But you guys have worked so hard for this!" our younger son said. He and our daughter looked distraught.

"Dad, you can't give up all the work you've done," our daughter said.

Steve nodded. He looked so downtrodden and worn out. He was weary of the cell phones, the servers, the deal makers, and the deals. In all the years I had known Steve, I had never seen him so disturbed. None of this was worth it. I wished it would end. The pressure got to all of us, and we even started to bicker because we couldn't figure out what to do.

"What do you want to do?" I asked him. I knew what I wanted. I wanted the insanity to end instantly, but we couldn't seem to find the right path to take.

Looking back, I can see the irony of our dilemma. Here we were, in 1999, surrounded by start-ups who wanted nothing more than for the biggest companies in the industry to come banging on their doors to buy them. We didn't want to sell, even though those same industry leaders were banging down our door. But we had to.

It was the love, support, and words of our family that helped us figure out what to do. Again we learned that in confusing, hurtful times, turning to loved ones is a major source of comfort and clarity to help overcome problems.

We went back to the beach and tossed a football to one another.

Though I had called Javier to cancel our meeting with Excite, that night there was a knock on our hotel room door. It was the CEO of Excite. Either he never received Javier's message that we canceled the meeting, or he decided to come despite the message. But since he had taken a plane from the East Coast to California for this meeting, we invited him in.

We ordered dinner in the room and, after speaking with him, realized that we actually liked him. He seemed to understand the mission of bluemountain.com. He had a creative background, and we talked almost as much about Thoreau as we did about business. Then he told us that he and the board of directors were ready to make an offer to buy bluemountain.com. We informed him that we absolutely wouldn't sell the paper company, which was fine with him because he didn't want it anyway. When we asked him what Steve's role would be, he assured us that Steve would still be actively involved at the highest level, and he proceeded to talk about the terms.

If we sold bluemountain.com, the whirlwind of the last few years would finally be over. Could we get out of the dot-com frenzy before it made us completely crazy?

So, yes, we would sell. We now needed a lawyer to speak to the Excite lawyers, and as we had demonstrated many times before, finding the right lawyer was not an easy task for us. Specifically, we needed to find a lawyer whom we liked and trusted and who would be capable of negotiating with very smart, assertive lawyers. We called Harry Melkonian, our lawyer from the Hallmark case. He recommended a good friend of his, Jay Grodin, with whom he had practiced law in the past. Jay kindly offered to take us under his wing and assured us that whatever he couldn't do he would hire other lawyers to do. And this debonair gentleman was true to his word. Jay supported and assisted us in every way possible. He hired Scott Hodgkins of Latham & Watkins, a Los Angeles law firm, and we also called my brother to help negotiate with the Excite lawyers.

Even though we started negotiations for the merger in August, we had a difficult time ahead of us, as we had to lead the company down two tracks at once. Until the deal was closed, it was always possible that it might fall apart and not happen. Thus, Jared had to proceed with building the business models for all the different visions for the website.

Around the clock, Jared, Steve, Robbie, the investment bankers, our lawyers, and the Excite lawyers passed papers, e-mails, phone calls, agreements, and contracts back and forth. Our daughter got involved in the legal language and wisely edited a document that Excite wanted her and Jared to sign. She has such a keen, scientific mind, which helped her to analyze the detailed, legal wording.

Fortunately Ed Guzik, our methodical and practical CFO, had kept impeccable records for over ten years, which greatly helped speed up the merger. He took charge of bringing order to the chaos by cutting through much of the bureaucracy. Ed and his staff organized the vast amount of paperwork consisting of thousands and thousands of pages of documents, contracts, historical records, and new records. He also worked diligently with all the involved parties. What a complicated process it turned out to be!

As one might expect, negotiating with a large public corporation was a convoluted process. At one point, Excite presented us with a document clearly stating that Steve could not tell the bluemountain.com employees what to do, nor could he even make suggestions. In fact, it actually forbade him to even talk to the employees.

When we saw this we were livid. I couldn't understand how Excite could do this to Steve. Didn't they realize how important he was to the site? We didn't want to have anything further to do with Excite. We called Robbie, our children, and our lawyers and told them the deal was off, and we truly meant it.

But calling off the deal meant that once again we were faced with the prospect of hiring a CEO and going public. We spoke to the same people as before, and we faced the same exact problems as before. Again, we did not like this path. We believed it was doomed to failure, and we knew our limitations.

So about ten days later, when two Excite executives came to our house to say the offending language was a mistake and that they did want Steve to be involved, we had to accept their apology.

On October 1, 1999, at 3:00 A.M., all the contracts were agreed upon and finally, in late December, Steve, Jared, our daughter, and I signed our names in what seemed like at least a million places on the various agreements, and the deal closed. The merger documents were thousands of pages long, but they added up to one thing. In a phone call, Robbie repeated the same words he had uttered after our turbulent experience with Hallmark in 1986: "It's done; it's over."

We called our family into the room to share the good news.

"It's over!"

Conclusion

When we merged bluemountain.com with Excite@home, we were offered far more money than we could ever fathom. Even though Excite soon went out of business and we ended up with considerably less, it was still a "dot-com" amount. The night the sale closed, we felt like we should celebrate. Our family went to the local candy shop and purchased five candy apples. Truthfully, this was all we wanted to buy. We were lucky to have already earned enough money to live a very comfortable lifestyle, and we didn't need or desire anything.

For us, though it was a difficult decision to sell the website, it all came down to one, simple question: What mattered most? To Steve and me, the answer was clear. As always, what was most important to us was our relationship and our family, followed by helping others, being creative, and following our Blue Mountain Arts' dreams. The circus atmosphere that seemed to accompany the business side of the Internet industry mattered very little.

We thought about the money we would get and the responsibility associated with it. We have learned through our own experiences that having enough money for the basic necessities is essential. Of course, it is always nice to be able to live comfortably and indulge yourself occasionally, but beyond that, more money cannot buy a good or happy life. However, it can be used to enhance the quality of other people's lives.

We realized that we would now be able to finance our own projects, which could help others. And, in fact, that is just what we started to do. Steve programmed and developed a new website, starfall.com, a revolutionary, free, online interactive learning community to teach children how to read.

I wrote the book *One World, One Heart*, which promotes understanding, peace, and tolerance for all people and has been distributed free to the public. We have given out over six and one-half million copies. We plan to continue funding projects that will have a positive effect on people.

As I write this, America is looking back on the burst bubble of a thousand dot-coms, salvaging what it can of the last great gold rush. It turned out that Excite didn't want Steve involved in bluemountain.com after all. Though Steve was initially hurt and disappointed, his new venture, starfall.com, has been enormously rewarding, especially as he hears more and more about the millions of children who are learning to read from using his new website. Again he's managed to wed art and science by creating a unique and meaningful website.

Steve and I are still creating greeting cards and books, and we spend as much time with each other and our family as possible.

I continue to write poetry and music, and I've spent the last three years completing this book.

Maybe you can identify with some of the feelings and experiences that Steve and I had. Everyone is plagued by self-doubts, problems, and naysayers. I hope knowing that someone else feels the same way you do will help you not to feel so alone.

In this section of the book, I've attempted to share our lives so that perhaps our story and the lessons we learned can help you follow your dreams.

Do what you love
Control your own life
Have imaginative, realistic dreams
Work hard
Make mistakes but learn from them
Believe in yourself but know your limitations
Ignore all the naysayers
Plow through obstacles and failures
Turn your dreams into a reality

AUTOBIOGRAPHICAL
STORIES

Old Friends

We were friends
when we attended school together
Since then
we have followed different paths
living in different places
We grew apart
yet we grew together
Our years of sharing
and discussing
every thought, every idea
and every experience
led us to know each other
so very well
No new friend could ever understand
us as we understand each other
Though we don't see each other often
our friendship is as strong as ever

Some of the people who read early drafts of *Blue Mountain* told me that they enjoyed the story of how Steve and I started Blue Mountain Arts but were not as interested in the personal details of our lives. Others said they wanted more biographical information and asked me specific questions about my formative years.

Though Steve's and my personal life together is an integral part of our careers, the lessons we learned when we started our company are not unique to us and can apply to anyone reading this book.

I feel that my early life and experiences are very important to how I developed as a person, a mother, and a poet, but they are not necessary for understanding the story of Blue Mountain Arts.

That is why I decided to include the anecdotes that most influenced and shaped my personal life in this separate purple section of the book.

Chapter I

A Child of the 1950's

I was born in 1944 and grew up in the country town of Peekskill, New York, a small, close-knit community of eighteen thousand people. It was the ideal place to be in the 1950's.

The small, wooden homes, little front porches, and clean streets could have been pulled from any newsreel, and the scenery was spectacular, with colorful maple trees bordering the glistening water of the Hudson River. We lived only ninety minutes upstate from New York City, yet we might as well have lived nine hundred miles from there for all that we had in common with the metropolis. Peekskill was considered a hick town, despite the fact that we all had New York City accents.

Downtown Peekskill consisted of a few bakeries—offering the best rye bread and brownies anywhere in the United States, a supermarket, several diners, a stationery store, clothes shops, pharmacies, a Woolworth's, a fish market with wood shavings on the floor, and a butcher shop. My favorite store lured in its customers by leaving barrels of five-cent sour pickles on the sidewalk, a delicacy to which I'm still addicted.

All the kids knew one another's parents, siblings, homes, jobs, and hobbies. I was acquainted with and understood so many people. To this day, when I meet someone new, often this person will remind me of someone from my hometown.

My instinct for finding common ground with a wide variety of people grew out of living in Peekskill. Friendships transcended the differences in skin color and religion. This was unique, especially during the 1950's. That was where, for the first time, I learned that people are all similar on the inside. We all crave love, friendship, respect, and understanding.

Peekskill produced some people who ended up with life sentences in jail. On the opposite end of the spectrum, Peekskill High School graduated the future governor of New York, George Pataki. We used to skate on the Pataki family's frozen pond in the winter, and in the summer we picked and ate apples from their orchards.

The vast majority of the residents were blue-collar Americans who wanted nothing more than a secure pension, a healthy family, and to own their own home.

Aside from a few lawyers and doctors, my schoolmates' fathers mostly worked in factories, government jobs, and stores. Several of my friends' mothers worked as seamstresses, aides in the local hospitals, and salesclerks, but most did not have jobs outside the home. It was a status symbol for a woman to say, "I don't have to work." Men and women were proud to brag that the women ran the home and the men earned the money.

Gathered in our sunroom every Friday night, my family watched *I Remember Mama* on our little black-and-white television while eating chestnuts or my mother's homemade chocolate cake. There were only three television networks—ABC, NBC, and CBS—and the types of programs they showed fell under several basic categories: westerns, variety shows, and family sitcoms.

The popular shows such as *Father Knows Best*, *I Love Lucy*, and *I Remember Mama* portrayed happy families. Many of the images were superficial: ditzy Mom in the flared skirt and cinched blouse, cooking or dusting; Dad in his armchair reading the newspaper or outside mowing the lawn; and clean-cut kids playing practical jokes on one another. They showed only the banal aspects of life, never getting into the real issues every child or parent faced.

The sitcoms, movies, and magazines showed smiles across the country, but the news told a different story. McCarthyism blossomed in the 1950's, and racism was rampant. Despite their seemingly comfortable material lives, many people seemed afraid: afraid of communism, afraid of anyone who looked or acted differently from the majority of Americans, afraid of contemporary music, afraid of anything that represented change. Most people seemed to be asking "What will the neighbors think?" instead of "What would make us happy?" The pretty houses all in a row were only a defense against some very real troubles.

The huge gap between parents and children prevented a lot of honest communication. My generation, the inventors of rock 'n' roll, hated the strict rules our parents placed on us. I was an honor student and a serious worker, but I still had to be home on the weekends by eleven o'clock, and going out at night during the week wasn't even an option. I would be grounded for breaking any of my parents' rules.

But the positive side of growing up in the 1950's was that we knew exactly what we were and were not allowed to do. We had to accept this, and there was no confusion over boundaries. It was for me an uncluttered, innocent time where my dreams were free to grow, and my internal freedom helped me escape the rigid atmosphere.

My home, on the middle of a steep hill, was an old, gray, two-story, wooden house with white shutters, and it featured all the delightful nooks, crannies, and creaks that a child could want. We had a metal glider on our front porch, a sunroom with a bamboo couch, and two very narrow stairways, one going up to our bedrooms and the other going down to our unfinished basement, which contained huge oil tanks for the furnace. My brother, Robbie, and I performed circus tricks for the neighborhood kids in our basement when we weren't complaining bitterly about our evening chores.

Park Street, the old, red brick, two-story elementary school that I attended, was about a mile from my house. The school had about an equal number of black and white students, and we didn't notice each other's color as we attended classes and played together.

Every day as I walked home from school, I would stop in the tiny candy store and put three pennies into the bubble gum machine. If I was lucky enough to get a dotted gumball, I'd receive twenty-five cents' worth of candy. When I'd win, I'd eat all the candy as I walked home, concentrating on not talking to strangers.

When I was in elementary school, I learned two lessons I'd carry with me forever: First, positive reinforcement encourages children to dream and instills in them a desire to live up to their dreams; and second, kids aren't stupid. They listen to what adults say and know when grown-ups are being hypocritical.

My classes were often overcrowded. Because my teacher believed I was such a good reader, she selected me to help her teach reading to other students in the class. I loved helping the students and was proud that the teacher singled me out and praised me. When someone believes in you, it helps you to believe in yourself. I tried to live up to her expectations, and when I found that I enjoyed the accomplishment, I created my own personal expectations of doing the very best at whatever I did. This experience probably encouraged me later to read books to younger children during "story hour" at the Peekskill library.

I received my first bite of the acting bug when I starred in an elementary school play. As I stood in line, waiting for my cue, I talked with the person standing in back of me. My teacher yanked my blond pigtail and said, "Susan, shut up! You're too noisy!" I held back tears and quieted down immediately.

A few seconds later, someone's mother said something to the teacher and pointed at me. The teacher replied, "Oh, yes, Susan's absolutely adorable, isn't she? She's a great girl."

In one minute she'd switched from hurting me and yelling at me, as if she hated me, to telling someone how much she liked me. Which was true? I didn't become distrustful at that point, but the incident made me aware of the duplicity of others. It's amazing what teachers really teach their students.

I have never been either as hot or as cold as I was during the different seasons that I lived in Peekskill, but regardless of the weather, we always had fun. In the fall, we raked the leaves from our yard and the street and made huge forts out of them. We would then hide in the forts and eventually break them down and throw leaves at one another.

I was a tomboy and enjoyed playing hardball and touch football with the older boys. I especially loved baseball, and I was quite good at it. When I was in the fourth grade, I wanted to be the first professional female baseball player when I grew up. However, when I was in sixth grade, all of a sudden I noticed that the boys my age had become much stronger and bigger than I was. When they pitched the ball, it was much faster than when I pitched it, and I became afraid of getting hit by a fast pitch when I was at bat. I tried to make myself stronger, but no matter how hard I tried, I couldn't keep up with the boys, especially the older ones. Soon after discovering this, I stopped playing baseball with the boys. The only time I ever played baseball again was in PE class, but it wasn't fun because back then most girls didn't play very well.

During the 1950's there was no such thing as Little League baseball or softball for girls, so it wasn't a popular sport for girls to play. Today, anyone who wants to play sports on a team can do so. My daughter has been on softball, soccer, baseball, and tennis teams, and she cannot imagine a time when she would not have been able to do this. I have been the manager and coach of my children's Little League teams. I believe that sports help girls become stronger physically and mentally, as well as more self-confident.

In the winter, especially on "snow days" when school was canceled, we would sleigh ride down the steep Peekskill hills. One of us would look out for cars, and the rest of us, one per sled, would each hold on to the sled in front of us, like cars on a train, and speed down the hill.

We would go headfirst and then slowly hike back up the hill to do it all over again. We would go up and down the hill many times, and then we'd collapse in snow forts and bombard each other with snowballs.

My hobbies included collecting rocks, toads, turtles, and sticks that I whittled, and playing marbles and flipping baseball cards with the boys. I wrote and sold a little three-page newspaper, which reported on the neighborhood and had very bad two-line jokes in it. This was my first dabbling in writing. When it rained or was too cold to play outside, I loved to read.

Every day in the summer as the sun descended past the hillsides, Mom called me to dinner. More often than not, she couldn't find me because I had climbed high up in a tree to the branch I called my tree house, my favorite spot to read a book or just dream.

By my senior year in high school, I'd read most of the works of my favorite authors: John Steinbeck, F. Scott Fitzgerald, Ayn Rand, Hermann Hesse, Sinclair Lewis, Upton Sinclair, Tennessee Williams, Fyodor Dostoevsky, Jack Kerouac, as well as numerous other authors. Reading allowed me to escape into alternative worlds, where I met characters like Dagny Taggart, Carol Milford, and Siddhartha. My voracious reading sparked my creativity and dreams, and I continued to write my own stories and poems.

I had a happy, carefree childhood until one day, when I was around eleven years old, I discovered that my family had been having serious financial problems.

In my favorite clothing store, I had seen a navy-blue sweater that I wanted to buy. My parents said no, and I didn't understand why, so I argued with them. Later that night, I heard my parents talking with a lot of emotion. Creeping down the narrow stairs above the kitchen, I listened as my mom choked out words through her tears.

"Sue doesn't know we can't even pay the oil bill. Some of her friends can buy new sweaters if they want. She just doesn't realize we can't afford it! How can a kid know that?"

I'd never heard my mom cry before. Her tears and the sound of my father's consoling words brought tears to my own eyes; one fell on the bottom step, echoing so loudly I was sure they'd heard it. I ran back to my bed and swore that in the future I would be self-supporting and I would try never to ask my parents for anything ever again.

I hadn't even thought about whether my parents could afford the sweater, nor did I realize how badly my parents would feel about not buying it for me.

From that night on, I observed my parents more closely. I saw firsthand how my Dad's lack of work and his inability to pay bills destroyed his self-esteem. I painfully watched how hard my mom worked to support the family and hide the fact that we didn't have much. She did a great job because I had never even thought about money before this incident. I had a family that loved me, I lived in a comfortable house, and I had my own bedroom. I had everything I needed.

In sixth grade, I wanted a tape recorder to record my favorite music (this is still a hobby of mine). I recruited a friend to help me mow lawns, and in three weeks, I earned enough cash (seventy-five dollars) to pay for my professional tape recorder. I was so fond of it that I didn't want to let it deteriorate, so I regularly changed the black rubber belts and oiled and cleaned the mechanisms. With my friends, I wrote and recorded plays and a radio program, and I recorded hundreds of hours of music from the radio. I was proud that I was able to figure out a way to earn money to buy the tape recorder and keep my promise to myself that I would not ask my parents for money to buy things.

I attended Drum Hill Junior High School for three years. During this time I became less of a tomboy and more of a student. My favorite subjects were writing and math, each for different reasons. Writing was something I had to do, and I loved it. It was creative and fun. Math was something that was definite, with answers that were either right or wrong. I found this quality soothing.

Always looking ahead, I couldn't wait to be grown up enough to go to high school, where it seemed that everyone was cool and had a good time.

Chapter II

High School Years in Peekskill

Over three miles stood between Peekskill High School and my house. We carpooled to school, and often with my ears throbbing from the freezing winter weather, I walked home after my last class. I liked high school; the mix of students exposed me to many different kinds of people. Even though there were only one hundred and eighty-six students in my grade, Peekskill High was a true Steinbeckian "slice of life."

Most days after school, my friends and I went to the Marathon, a soda shop with fifteen rows of Formica booths. It was the focus of Peekskill High's social scene. The hangouts were the best part of Peekskill, crowded with boys and girls sipping ice-cream sodas and chattering. After leaving the Marathon, we went home, watched *American Bandstand* on TV, and called one another to discuss who we'd seen dancing together. Because there was a shortage of telephone lines, for a while my family shared a party line with several families. I imagine these strangers weren't too happy with my tying up the phone for hours talking about Justine and Kenny and Marathon gossip.

Before I was in high school, everyone who liked the outdoors would play together after school. We would meet in the street and play hide-and-seek, war, touch football, or baseball with whoever showed up. When I was in high school, cliques of students developed: those who planned to go to college, those who wouldn't go to college, and those who would drop out of school when they were sixteen years old. No matter which clique a person was in, though, we all attended the same parties.

About one-third of Peekskill high-school students went to college, and many were the first members of their families to do so. Most of us were expected to pay for a good part of our college expenses by working or through scholarships, and I knew I'd have to pay my entire college cost. That was quite a task, considering I could only work on weekends and during summer vacations.

I had numerous jobs when I was young, but one I had when I was fourteen years old opened my eyes to a new world. I was hired to sell magazine subscriptions over the phone to random people whose names were taken from the phone book. I was given a script to read, and together with all the other women in the office, we probably called one thousand people every day. Our boss was a fast-talking, short, young man, and our office was cluttered with splintery, wooden tables, telephones, scripts, and telephone books. On my first day, to my surprise, I found that I was the only female in the office who didn't have her hair in curlers. Everything about this office seemed strange.

At the end of each day, our boss would gather the names of the people who ordered the magazine subscriptions and go to the homes to collect the fees.

After a month, I arrived early to get my first paycheck, but the door was locked. I looked through the window, and instead of a cluttered office, I saw immaculate wooden tables. I waited for an hour, but no one showed up. I went home and called the office, but the phones had been disconnected.

Our boss had left town without paying the rent or his employees. Later on we found out that people never received the magazines they had paid for. This early experience in the business world taught me always to doubt situations that don't look exactly right. Unfortunately, it was a lesson I would have to learn more than once.

My next job was working in a bakery, tying boxes of cookies with string that hung from spools attached to the ceiling. My fingers were so uncooperative that I quit after two days before I could be fired. My next job, as a waitress in a diner, was no more successful. I made terrible malteds, got orders confused and got mad at myself, spilled orange juice on customers, and snapped at male customers who told me I was cute. From these experiences, I learned how important it is to know your limitations. I have very little patience, and one of my more frustrating limitations is not being able to do tasks that involve any kind of spatial dimension. I couldn't learn to tie the cookie boxes, nor could I deal with flirtatious and rude customers, so I knew I couldn't continue in these jobs.

Then I moved on to the clothing department at Big Scott, a discount department store. After folding sweaters for two weeks, I begged the manager of the store to let me work in the music section. I've always loved music, and plastic 45-rpm's had just replaced the old, breakable, glass 78-rpm records. The disc jockeys played Elvis Presley, Jerry Lee Lewis, The Platters, and Fats Domino. Rock 'n' roll was new, and I asked if I could make the record department more current. I talked to young customers, decorated the window with the weekly Top Ten record list, ordered rock 'n' roll and folk music records I liked, and Big Scott's record business flourished.

I found that my rapport with customers increased tenfold because we all cared about music. Now that I was working in the record department, I did a good job, and I was having fun. I realized how important it is to find a job that you enjoy. I got my first raise from $1.00 an hour to $1.10 an hour, and I was so proud.

After working at Big Scott for a year during the summer, holidays, and weekends, I got a better-paying job at a pharmacy as a cashier. I worked there every summer for the next three years. There was a steady flow of people buying beer, as well as pharmaceutical supplies. I added up items on the big cash register and then packed them in large, brown paper bags. I must have looked at the clock a thousand times each day, waiting impatiently for each workday to end. This job was so tiring.

As I got older I realized that, culturally, life in Peekskill was dull. I'd read all the books I wanted to in Peekskill's library. With no museums, bookstores, or colleges to provide intellectual stimulation, everything centered on our social lives. By ninth grade, most of us dated every weekend; our thoughts and conversations revolved around the opposite sex. Boys drank and got into brawls, and the police broke up the noisiest parties. At night we hung out at Sorrento's, the pizza joint. Tucked away in the corner by the bar stood a beautiful Seeburg jukebox with shiny chrome columns separated by colorful sections of glass. It was always surrounded by kids listening to Tony Bennett singing "I Left My Heart in San Francisco," waiting their turn to spend a quarter to play their three favorite songs.

After pizza we often went to a girlfriend's home for a sleepover, where we'd stay up all night talking and having pillow fights.

In the summer, on our days off from work, we sat on blankets at Sprout Lake, swam out to the rafts, and sunbathed with foil reflectors (this was before we knew that the sun could cause cancer).

I collected empty Coke bottles and turned them in to the food stand for five-cent refunds. At night, we went to carnivals, drive-in movies, block dances, and parties. If anyone was lucky enough to own a '59 Chevy or Ford, three of us, six of us, ten of us—it didn't matter—would all pile in and go for long rides in the country.

By the time I graduated from Peekskill High School, I knew that life at home would never satisfy me. Many of my friends longed to get married right after high school, to start a family, and buy a house. Quite a few of them did so and were happy. Although I hoped to find someone to love, what I wanted most was to be a career woman. I wanted to be independent, to make my own mark on the world, move to New York City, become a writer or journalist, and see my name in lights. But first things first.

I had saved money from working, but not enough to pay for my entire three-thousand-dollar college education. Rider University in Lawrenceville, New Jersey offered me a scholarship, which I immediately accepted. The scholarship, a college loan, and the money I had saved from working would pay for the dormitory, textbooks, and tuition at Rider, plus any clothes I needed. I anxiously looked forward to the next chapter of my life.

Chapter III

Hypocrisy in College Sorority Life

My freshman year started out great: I was elected vice president of the class, was on the honor roll, and had a very active social life. I loved being in college—living with friends, talking to classmates in the student union, and meeting new people almost on a daily basis. I was one step closer to being on my own, one step closer to having complete freedom. Looking back, I realize that, to me, college was more of a people-learning environment than an academic one. Although I was enlightened by reading assigned books, I hardly remember any classes I took. But I do remember, in vivid detail, so many interactions with students.

Almost all the students joined a fraternity or sorority at Rider because that's where they would live and socialize for the rest of their college years. The sisters at the most popular sorority went out of their way to be friendly toward me and other girls they "rushed." They exchanged smiles and nods as they secretly chose the new freshmen they wanted as sorority sisters.

Nancy White, a beautiful, dark-haired, angelic woman with bright green eyes, had made me feel like one of the most important people on campus—or on earth, for that matter.

Until she saw my Star of David necklace.

She asked me if I was Jewish, and when I answered that I was, she said that I didn't look it.

Nancy leaned in and said, "Jews are not allowed in our sorority."

"What are you talking about? What do you mean I can't be in your sorority?" I demanded to know, raising my voice in the women's bathroom. She fidgeted with the collar of her blouse and peeked in the mirror over the sink.

Nancy explained that it was a Christian sorority. She told me that this rule was in the sorority charter and in the charters for two other Rider sororities as well. She told me that there was a nice sorority down the block for Jewish girls.

"We can still be friends," she said weakly.

I couldn't believe I had been friends with someone so phony.

I emptied a glass of water on her hair and stormed out of the bathroom after loudly cursing at her.

I'd witnessed bigotry before, but even in a town as provincial as Peekskill, I was never the victim of such bald hypocrisy. I joined Delta Phi Epsilon, the "Jewish sorority," and while I was there, I took pride in the fact that we were the first sorority on campus to open our membership to both Christian and Jewish sisters.

I felt particularly close to some of my sorority sisters because we shared one of the decade's most memorable and traumatic events. The next year, when I was a sophomore, I was walking into the student union with some of my sorority sisters when I heard a voice boom over the loudspeaker: "The president of the United States has been shot. I repeat: The president of the United States has been shot."

I don't think there's a person in this country who was alive then that doesn't remember exactly what they were doing when they heard the news of President Kennedy's death. The normally bustling campus halted, stunned into silence by the announcement. I left the student union in a daze to retreat to my room, and as I sat on my bed, trying to process the news, my roommate Myrna burst into the room crying.

"How could this happen?" I asked. We all asked that question, again and again: How could this happen?

Five of my sorority sisters and I drove to Washington, D.C. for Kennedy's funeral, and everywhere I went, people cried openly. Some people walked the streets of the nation's capital in a stunned daze as others scrambled for a glimpse of the funeral procession. Frightened by the thought of the coffin, I stood on the street corner with my eyes closed. I felt warmth for the people who cried in sympathy together over our great loss.

The death of our young president opened our minds to the idea that larger, more important things happened in the world, things that dwarfed our little daily dramas. We would never again be the happy-go-lucky teenagers we had been, confident that the older generation would lead the way for us, assuaging our worries and supporting our dreams. President Kennedy's assassin killed our innocence, as well as our president.

Because we shared the emotions of this tragic event together, we expected that we'd share the same attitudes and emotions in all future situations. But that would not necessarily be the case.

A couple of years later, some of my sorority sisters disappointed me as much as the prejudiced women who had rejected me during my freshman year.

The problem at my sorority started when two Christian sisters wanted to put a Christmas tree in our living room, right next to the Chanukah menorah. Myrna and I thought the idea was great; they should be allowed to celebrate their religion just as we did ours, but no one else agreed with us.

"It all starts with a Christmas tree, doesn't it?" a sorority sister cried, near tears in her anger. "So Delta Phi'll just become Christian like all the other sororities, and once again there won't be a place for us!"

I started shouting. "All prejudices are disgusting! You're just as bad as the sororities that wouldn't let us be members!"

The debate heated up.

"Two crazy whores!" someone screamed, and then everyone started talking and yelling. In the melee, I felt something hot hit my face; one of my sorority sisters had flung her lit cigarette at me. I stood up and, with my strong baseball arm, pitched the cigarette back at the girl, only twenty times harder.

Myrna and I ran to our room and locked the door. How could my own sorority sisters act this way? We knew that some of our sisters agreed with us, but we couldn't understand why they were so afraid to stand up for what they believed in.

We knew we were right, but couldn't convince anyone else. Feeling powerless frustrates me more than anything. I can deal with disappointment, anger, and failure, but I've never been able to come to grips with that sense of utter hopelessness that occurs when circumstances are beyond my control.

An hour later, someone knocked on our door. We didn't respond. Then we saw a note slip under the door:

> Dear Sue and Myrna,
>   Since we're the first sorority to be open to all religions, if we set a good example, maybe the Christian sororities will open up and let Jewish people in...After listening to both of you, we realize that two wrongs don't make a right. We should have a Christmas tree as well as a menorah.

Three friends had signed the note. A moment later, another note, signed by two more friends, slid under the door. By two o'clock in the morning, we had received fifteen notes of apology and support.

The next day Myrna and I called for a vote, and by a three-to-one margin, our sorority decided to allow members to celebrate any holiday they believed in, and decorate accordingly.

This small civil rights victory helped assuage the anger I had harbored since my freshman year regarding the exclusion of Jewish girls in Rider sororities. And it also brought back my faith in people.

Love

Love is
being happy for the other person when that person is happy
being sad for the other person when that person is sad
being together in good times
and being together in bad times
Love is the source of strength

　　Love is
　　being honest with yourself at all times
　　being honest with the other person at all times
　　telling, listening, respecting the truth
　　and never pretending
　　Love is the source of reality

Love is
an understanding so complete that
you feel as if you are a part of the other person
accepting that person just the way he or she is
and not trying to change each other to be something else
Love is the source of unity

　　Love is
　　the freedom to pursue your own desires
　　while sharing your experiences with the other person
　　the growth of one individual alongside of
　　and together with the growth of another individual
　　Love is the source of success

Love is
the excitement of planning things together
the excitement of doing things together
Love is the source of the future

　　Love is
　　the fury of the storm
　　the calm in the rainbow
　　Love is the source of passion

Love is
giving and taking in daily situations
being patient with each other's needs and desires
Love is the source of sharing

　　Love is
　　knowing that the other person
　　will always be with you regardless of what happens
　　missing the other person when he or she is away
　　but remaining near in heart at all times
　　Love is the source of security

Love is
the source of life

Chapter IV

Love at First Sight

In 1966 I was a senior at Rider University in Lawrenceville, New Jersey. I was dating many men, but I did not really like any of them very much. One of my more interesting dates was Sidney Limon, a boy whose only positive qualities were his looks and his enrollment at Princeton University, which was fifteen minutes away from Rider.

One night, Sidney took me to a "mixer," which was the Princeton graduate students' term for "party." I sensed someone watching me as Sidney and I danced. I looked up to see a set of piercing eyes, with an intense, curious, intelligent gaze.

We introduced ourselves to each other. He was Stephen Schutz, a graduate student at Princeton majoring in physics.

"Are you dating Sidney?" he asked me.

"Yes."

"I knew I'd seen you before," he said. "I saw you with Sidney last week. You had on black boots and jeans. I remember thinking I liked your long, blond hair."

I blushed and changed the subject by asking him to dance. I wasn't about to let this stranger out of my sight. He was about 5'10" with dark, long, wavy hair; high cheekbones; big, expressive, blue eyes; a strong cleft chin; and a moustache—he was strikingly good looking. A few dances later, when Steve asked if I would go for a walk, I looked at him and forgot all about Sidney. We left the mixer hand in hand.

We wandered around the campus for hours, getting to know each other. Everything about Steve fascinated me; he was utterly unlike anyone I'd ever met. Steve had grown up in a four-room apartment in the Bronx, where he shared a bedroom with his two sisters. He told me that the Bronx was unpleasant and he knew that there must be a better place somewhere. He always planned on leaving there as soon as he was old enough. Every summer, Steve and his family would camp out near the ocean in Montauk, New York, and it was there that he fell in love with the outdoors.

Because of his talent in art, Steve had attended the prestigious public High School of Music and Art in New York City. After high school, he earned his B.S. in Physics at MIT, and when I met him, he was writing a thesis in theoretical physics to complete his Ph.D. at Princeton.

Steve's soft-spoken manner shifted to passionate indignation when he spoke of the injustices and corruption of government, but when he spoke of art or science, I saw nothing but kindness and intelligence in his eyes.

Steve was actively involved in politics. He and several other graduate students organized anti-war groups, and he supported the under-graduate Students for a Democratic Society (SDS). While I championed these causes in my mind, Steve lived his ideas by taking a stand on issues.

I thought of my life at Rider University, which seemed so frivolous in comparison; it rarely centered on anything other than myself and my sorority sisters. We did everything together—ate meals, studied, hung out, went to parties, talked philosophy one minute, and created the model for our dream partners the next. We even each put a list of the qualities our "ideal mate" should have in a glass jar, sealed it, and pledged that we'd open it in ten years. I figured my sisters would have little trouble finding their perfect guys—athletic, secure, witty, handsome, solid providers—but I doubted that I'd find a guy who could meet my expectations.

My list of characteristics included someone who was strong, attrac-tive, intelligent, socially aware, creative, caring, artistic, and with whom I would be equal in all ways. Instead of supporting me, we'd support each other, emotionally and spiritually. I wouldn't live a life that some-one else—my parents, society, or my husband—told me I should live. I didn't think that I needed someone to share my life with to be happy, but I realized how fulfilling it would be if I met the right person.

That evening at the mixer, I admit the thought passed through my mind that Steve just might be the person I had described in the glass jar.

When Steve invited me to see his room, regardless of the implications it might have, he intrigued me so much that I really did want to see how he lived.

"You know the college rule about the door being open enough for a matchbox to fit through?" I asked.

Steve laughed, "Sure, we'll keep it open."

His room was as fascinating as I had imagined. Bach's "Brandenburg Concerto" resounded from a four-foot-high, dark maple speaker that Steve had built himself, which was connected to various stereo components he had wired together. Before this, I'd only seen inexpensive, one-piece units. And he even listened to classical music!

After a couple more hours of talking, I noticed a vivid abstract painting on Steve's wall. He had painted it at MIT. Steve showed me his closet, which was so full of photos, sketches, and paintings that they tumbled out onto the floor. There were scenes of the Charles River in Boston; students at Harvard; charcoals and watercolors of trees, flowers, and beaches; a sketch of a man painting at an easel; photographs of people dancing; a single man walking down an empty street; and my favorite, a photograph of a little boy at the beach with a big, floppy hat falling over his face.

I looked at Steve. Brilliant. Talented. Creative. Handsome. Artistic. In addition, he seemed to seek out his dreams actively, rather than be satisfied with dreaming alone. He loved science, so he rigorously studied it; he loved art, so he filled his closet with his paintings, photographs, and sketches. I wanted to tell him I wrote poems, but instead I only told him I wrote articles for newspapers and magazines, suggesting that he could take photographs for them someday.

We continued to get to know each other when all of a sudden, reality intruded with a resounding thump. Rider had a twelve o'clock curfew, and it was now almost twelve-thirty.

"Great," I said, panicked. "Rider's going to kick me out."

I had good reason to worry. Rules dominated every aspect of dorm life. Boys had to stay in the lobby when they visited us. They could not even come upstairs to the floor we lived on, much less come near our rooms. There was a book in the lobby, right outside the house mother's room. We had to sign in and out every time we left or came back to the dorm, and this was checked constantly. We had a very early curfew during the week, and the lights in our rooms had to be turned out by 11:00 P.M. For special Rider fraternity or sorority weekend parties, we were allowed to stay out until 1:00 A.M., but otherwise we had to be back by midnight. If any of these rules were broken, our parents would be notified, and we'd be suspended or kicked out. The "three strikes and you're out" rule did not apply. It was "one strike and you're out."

"I have to get back right now! I'm sorry, I lost track of time." We held hands and walked outside to Steve's motorcycle.

The night was crisp and clear, and as we got on his motorcycle, I slipped my arms around his waist and held on as tightly as I could.

We rode through the farm country from Princeton to Lawrenceville, my hair blowing as wildly as my thoughts. Here I was, almost twenty-one years old, and I had my arms around a man too perfect to be real.

We arrived at my sorority house shortly after 1:00 A.M., an hour past my curfew. I threw a rock at the window of my room, and my roommate, Myrna, peered out the window. She ran down the stairs to quietly open the door for me. Steve had no idea what we were doing; Princeton, which was an all-boys' school then, didn't impose restrictions on their students the way coed colleges did.

I turned to Steve to say goodbye, wanting desperately to hop back on his motorcycle and ride off into the distance with him. I kissed him on the cheek, ran inside, and tiptoed up the steps to my room so that the housemother wouldn't wake up and punish me.

I stared out the window as Steve sped off on his motorcycle.

I was in love.

* * *

In my dreams
I pictured a person
who was
intelligent, good-looking
sensitive, talented
creative, fun
strong and wise
who would completely
overwhelm me
with love
Since dreams
can be just
wishful thinking
I did not really expect
to find one person
who had all these
outstanding qualities
But then ~
I met you
and not only did you
bring back my
belief in dreams
you are even
more wonderful
than my
dreams

I knew I wanted to see Steve again, but it would be seven months before our paths would cross again.

Myrna and I were eating dinner at our favorite Italian restaurant in Princeton, and as usual, she paid because I didn't have any money. Just as we crossed Nassau Street, a good-looking boy on a bicycle came alongside us and called out my name.

My heart jumped into my throat. The man was a bearded Steve Schutz. Bumping into him while crossing a street must have been fate, and I grabbed the opportunity to ask Steve to my sorority graduation party the next weekend.

The next five days passed slowly. I borrowed a dress from a sorority sister to wear to the party, and Steve arrived on his motorcycle promptly at 7:30 P.M. I received an award and was pleased to be with my friends, but Steve captured all my attention. He didn't fit in with the sorority and fraternity crowd, but he looked so strong and handsome that my infatuation from the first night I met him returned in full force.

There's a part of me that has remained exactly the same as when I was a child and a part that changed after I met Steve. In retrospect, that night changed me a great deal. Steve didn't keep up with the current fads, so he didn't know the fast dances that my sisters and I could dance so well. I was usually one of the people who danced the longest and hardest, but after the parties were over, I felt dissatisfied. I appreciated the importance of fun, but more and more, I became somber and even depressed after a night of partying.

Steve, though, always seemed serious and thoughtful. He didn't go to these kinds of parties, and he avoided the ups and downs that most college kids live by. I admired him for being so independent.

Inside I felt a strong bond with Steve's self-assurance, but on the outside I still blended in with the college crowd. I was now ready to leave behind the more superficial aspects of my social life.

Chapter V

Can You Type?

My senior year was coming to an end. I needed to decide what to do with my life after college, and I thought seriously about what career path I would take.

I reflected on some of my activities that had centered around my childhood dreams. Between the ages of five and thirteen, I had wanted to become a famous actress. I remember how much I enjoyed writing and starring in plays with my friend Walter when I was in sixth grade. (I don't think we had an audience, but we did record these plays on my tape recorder.) I had other fond memories having to do with acting. My grandmother would take me to Broadway plays, such as *Gypsy*, *Annie Get Your Gun*, *Oklahoma*, and *Bells Are Ringing*, and I always pretended that I was the leading actress on stage. I actually developed stomach cramps during every play I attended, most likely due to the anxiety I had about not being the actress on the stage.

When I was thirteen, I had the opportunity to get on a professional stage. I was an apprentice in an old, well-known summer stock theater in Mahopac, New York. I painted scenery, read lines with the actors, found props, and helped with costumes and makeup. For sixteen hours each day I lived the theater, and I loved every part of it—the atmosphere, the smells, the excitement, and even the toilsome work. At the end of the summer, I had a tiny part as a pilgrim in a play. I found it very difficult to act on demand, and I realized that though I loved the theater, acting was not my forte.

That summer I learned that it is important to have realistic dreams. Every person has strengths and weaknesses, and you have to be honest with yourself about them. I could have spent a lifetime trying to become a baseball player in a professional men's league or an actress, but the truth was that, for me, these were dreams that I could never realize.

Thank goodness I was realistic enough not to put too much effort into pursuing these professions, or I surely would have been frustrated and miserable.

As I better understood myself, my career goals changed. Ever since I was old enough to read, I had two interests that seemed to get stronger each year: the first and most important of which was writing. Not only did I love to write, often composing stories, essays, articles, and poems, but I also felt a strong need to do so. Writing poetry always helped me understand my feelings. It was difficult for me to talk about my feelings, but I could explain them in writing. And, unlike acting, it was a very natural and easy process for me.

My desire to become an actress soon transformed into a desire to become an author, a goal more suited to my abilities.

I was also interested in the aging process. I had been a premed major before switching to English during my senior year at Rider. Writers don't need to go to graduate school, but pursuing scientific research would require a Ph.D. When Harvard Graduate School flew me to Cambridge to speak to me, I saw firsthand how the students completely devoted themselves to the pursuit of science, and I knew this was not for me.

What did I really want to do? I was too much of a romantic to spend all my time in a laboratory, which would be necessary if I were to become a scientist, and I didn't have the focus necessary to become a great scientist. But most importantly, I knew that I couldn't survive without writing.

I didn't have time to dwell on what my perfect career would be because I had to pay the bills, so right after I graduated from college I looked for jobs in the newspapers. Back then, the employment section was broken down into women's jobs and men's jobs. I hated all the jobs described in the women's section. Fortunately, two years later, in 1968, the Equal Employment Opportunity Commission outlawed help-wanted ads that were segregated by gender.

I went to an employment agency in New York City. The supervisor told me I'd have to wear white gloves and a very nice dress when I went on interviews. I didn't own white gloves and wouldn't have worn them if I had, but I did put on a dress and went to several potential job openings. The only job I could find relating to biology involved washing out test tubes for minimum wage. I turned the offer down and decided to try to get a job in publishing. The first thing the personnel director wanted to know was whether I could type. The employment agency told me to answer "yes" to all the questions about skills I could perform, and I followed this advice. So rather than being offered a job that entailed writing or editing, I was offered a secretarial job, something at which I would have failed miserably. I truly could not type, I wasn't organized enough to keep track of papers, and I just wasn't suited for this kind of work.

That night I wrote a poem to all my future bosses:

> "Can you type?"
> "No!"
> "Can you file?"
> "No!"
> "Can you take shorthand?"
> "No!"
> "How about simple bookkeeping?"
> "No!"
> "What on earth can you do?"
> "Everything you can!"

After I failed to find a job in the science and publishing fields, my friends Myrna, Sonia, and I decided to take advantage of the teacher shortage and apply for teaching positions in New Jersey. We didn't have teaching credentials, but the Board of Education allowed us to earn them as we taught.

We made an eclectic threesome. I was the introspective brooder who tended to spend my time writing poems and flying off the handle at injustices. I had very fair skin, light hair, and was 5'8", at least five inches taller than Myrna and Sonia. Myrna said I was the "soul" of the group, the one who would have a glamorous career.

Sonia, a beautiful, warm woman, never left the sorority house without every straight black hair in place and every eyelash curled around her big violet eyes. She was the ultimate flirt, and we knew she'd be the first to get married and have children.

Myrna, dark-skinned and petite, never failed to amuse us with her quick wit, which hid her extraordinarily kind and serious side. Her hair, thick and bushy, was as undisciplined and spontaneous as she was. Everyone loved her.

The three of us formed a folk group. Myrna was the lead singer and played the guitar, I sang the low harmony and played the recorder, and Sonia sang the high harmony and played the tambourine. When Myrna and I would go home to visit our parents, we'd take the train from Trenton to New York City carrying a huge bag of laundry with one arm and our guitar or recorder with the other. When we didn't have the train fare, we'd run from train car to train car every time we saw a conductor approaching to collect the tickets. We'd sit in the back of the train and sing and play our instruments during the whole ride. You'd think we would have had sense enough to be as quiet as we could and not bring attention to ourselves while we perpetrated this crime. Looking back, I can't believe how uninhibited, brazen, and obnoxious we were, nor can I believe that we didn't pay the train fares.

My favorite song to perform was an old folk song, "I Never Will Marry," because the words "I never will marry, I'll be no man's wife" truly explained my thoughts. Myrna and Sonia didn't buy into the lyrics. I often think the only thing we ever had in common was a deep understanding and love for one another. Most of the time that's all friends need.

All three of us got jobs as teachers at the same elementary school. We rented a one-bedroom apartment in Lawrenceville, New Jersey, and each morning we commuted forty-five minutes in my yellow Volkswagen, which only started in second gear and had straw sticking out the holes in the convertible canvas roof. On rainy days, we held umbrellas over our heads to keep dry. So much for my glamorous career.

We worked, dated, and enjoyed being on our own, living a kind of extended college life. My sense of dissatisfaction stayed with me, though, and no matter whom I dated, I couldn't stop thinking about Steve Schutz.

I wondered what he was doing and why we weren't seeing each other. I missed Steve and decided that it was time for me to speak to him about our relationship, so I called him. He seemed happy to hear from me and said he'd come by at seven o'clock.

Seven o'clock came and went, and Steve never showed up. I didn't think that I had been "stood up" because I knew that he didn't play games. If he didn't want to see me, he would've told me. By nine, my anger turned to worry. What if he had been in an accident?

At ten o'clock the phone rang.

"I'm in jail!" Steve said, muffled. He had attended a sit-in in front of the Institute for Defense Analyses, protesting the secret war research they did on the Princeton campus. A man had tried to force his way into the building, and Steve refused to move. Somehow, in the scuffle, someone had broken Steve's jaw.

Poor Steve. My hero had been arrested! I wished I could have been with him. Neither of us was afraid to stand up for what we thought was right, and consequently we often got into trouble. We had that much in common. I felt bad for Steve. He was hurt and in jail—behind bars! I felt bad for myself. I was in love with Steve, but I had no idea what he thought of me.

Doubts plagued my mind. If, as individuals, Steve and I didn't know where we belonged, how could we find a place together as a couple? And did Steve even think of us in terms of a couple as I did?

Chapter VI

Window Shadows

I stare out my window
and 10,000 windows stare back —
families, lovers, roommates in each apartment
involved in their own fictions
lights blinking — airplanes, bridges, cars
everyone is running
You cannot even see the stars
I wonder who lives in the window
with the flowers
and what they are thinking
as they gaze through their glass
How can I stand out so as
not to be just another
window shadow?

Fifty black and brown monsters with antennas sticking out their heads marched around the perimeter of our kitchen sink. They only visited after midnight, and whenever I went into the kitchen late at night, I would linger for several minutes and watch this parade. It was entertaining to see how perfectly they lined up, and I often forgot how dirty and scary looking they were as my imagination changed them into marching bands of royalty. It was my very own cockroach procession.

In 1968, Myrna and I moved to an apartment in New York City, where I would be teaching and going to graduate school.

Our apartment consisted of one small bedroom, a tiny bathroom, a living room with a fire escape attached to the window, and a half-kitchen. We bought a secondhand, brown couch for the living room, and I decorated the walls with psychedelic posters and strands of beads, but the bright colors were no match for the city.

One day our apartment was extremely hot, so I left my bedroom window open. When I came home that night, it looked like my apartment had been on fire. There was a thick layer of smelly, black soot all over my bed and walls, the result not of a fire, but pollution.

That same night we were awakened by a crashing sound coming from our living room. It sounded like someone had broken our window from the walk-up fire escape and entered our apartment. I was petrified and couldn't move! We didn't hear footsteps, so after what seemed like an hour, but was only about five minutes, Myrna bravely went into the living room. I heard her hearty laugh and was very relieved to find out that our glass pole lamp had sprung loose from the ceiling and fallen down, shattering glass all over the floor.

Though this had been a laughable accident, it did arise in us a trepidation about living in our apartment, so the next day Myrna's dad paid for the installation of metal bars on our living room window.

And being quite messy, our broken lamp sat on the floor of our living room for a whole year—until we moved out.

Despite the noises of honking horns and police car sirens that woke me up each night, and my less-than-perfect living quarters, I did enjoy New York City life. When I was younger, my grandmother often took me here, and those trips always thrilled and inspired me; I dreamed of living in the city.

Now that my dream had come true, I made the most of it. The throbbing energy of New York City was infectious. It was easy to meet interesting people, and I got to know and understand the "typical New Yorker," who was always in a hurry, always very blunt, and unusually open, outgoing, and bold. New Yorkers truly believe that their city is the only city in America, and I tend to believe them. Walking down the crowded streets of the Village or any other part of the city, at any hour of day or night, bumping into the many intellectuals, artists, and musicians, I could almost believe that the rest of the United States, beyond the Hudson, wasn't as real as Manhattan.

Although New York City was intriguing and exciting, I hated the pain I saw on the faces of so many people. I wanted to try to help disadvantaged children, so I applied for a teaching position in Harlem. Because I had taught school in New Jersey, I was able to teach in New York.

Teaching in Harlem was demanding in ways I had never imagined. I watched dedicated teachers fall victim to cynicism from an ineffectual bureaucracy. Children often came to school hungry. Each class of forty students ranged from children who couldn't read at all to kids reading far beyond their level. Textbooks, scarce and outdated, lay torn in hallways.

One of my most gratifying days occurred when I organized a science fair and almost all my students eagerly made their own fantastic science projects. But there were other days that frightened me. I was once punched in the chest as I tried to break up a fight among a group of girls.

There were also extremely poignant times, like when my five-year-old student Leroy, dressed in a little vest and matching tweed slacks, wouldn't talk to me. Finally he looked me in the eye and said, "My uncle beat up on my mom and I don't know why." All I could do was hug Leroy for a few minutes; we both had tears in our eyes.

One day I arrived at school and saw a group of older students huddled together, causing a louder-than-normal commotion. I was stunned to hear that one of my first-grade students had been raped; after more investigating, I learned that a third-grade boy had raped her.

I ran to the teachers' lounge, hysterical.

"A third-grader raped a first-grader! Give me the phone. I have to call his parents!" I looked around the room for support, but a teacher only sighed.

"Don't get so excited about this," she said, shaking her head. "This isn't the first time that girl's been raped."

"Are you joking?" I asked, as horrified by the teacher's indifference as by the act itself. "I'm going to talk to his parents and the school district."

I couldn't believe there was such violence at school. I had to help this girl and make sure the boy was punished! How could they just sit there and sigh and not try to do something?

"Go back to your class and forget about it," the teacher advised me. "There's nothing you can do."

Though I spent the day yelling and talking about the horrific incident, no one would listen to me, no one would help, and bureaucratic red tape strapped me securely to my desk. But I knew that people who are resigned to disappointment never change things. I was quite disturbed by the incident with the little girl, but it strengthened my resolve to at least try to change things for the better.

Often, Steve would drive from Princeton to pick me up after school, and it would take me a couple of hours to wind down from my day. Steve and I started to spend more time together. We became closer and closer, and we were having a lot of fun together.

But 1968 was ultimately a year filled with one tragedy after another.

On April 4, Steve had tears in his eyes as we listened to the latest news: Dr. Martin Luther King, Jr. had been assassinated. Dr. King was the nonviolent black leader who had founded the Southern Christian Leadership Conference (SCLC) in 1957. In 1964, the Civil Rights Bill passed, and Martin Luther King, Jr. received the Nobel Peace Prize. His gentle, firm leadership had guided thousands of people to lead nonviolent lives and work to change the world through peaceful means. He wanted all races to live together harmoniously; his call for social change inspired all of us.

I couldn't get his speech that he had made five years earlier out of my mind:

> I have a dream that one day this nation will rise up and live out the true meaning of its creed: "We hold these truths to be self-evident: that all men are created equal." I have a dream…

As happens so often in this world, violence brought his life to an end. There was a deep sadness among our friends after Dr. King's assassination.

Then within two months of Martin Luther King, Jr.'s death, the nation was rocked by yet another assassination. Robert Kennedy, the New York senator who had been running for president, was assassinated after winning the California primary. Kennedy had been a champion of civil rights and was trying to stop labor corruption. Many considered him to be as charismatic as his late brother, John. Robert Kennedy's death ripped open the wounds of Dr. King's death and dredged up the devastation of President Kennedy's death five years earlier.

Steve and I were stunned! We didn't know where to go or whom to turn to. It seemed that there was violence everywhere. Nonviolent leaders were being murdered before our eyes. We cared so deeply, but we didn't know what to do. Frustration, anger, and a desire to change the world dominated our souls, while a desire for love, simplicity, and peace dominated our hearts.

I wrote an essay that night about the lies adults tell children and the truths they learn, from kindergarten through college:

> You now have a college degree, and for the first time, you really know nothing. An understanding is incomprehensible in a world built on hiding and painting the truths.

After the traumatic events of the spring of 1968, Steve and I decided we needed to get away from people. We wanted to be alone to cleanse our spirits.

We went to Walden Pond in Massachusetts for three days of camping under the stars in the nearby grass. It was strikingly peaceful. I could imagine Henry David Thoreau living so sparsely at Walden Pond, writing his beautiful essays. We were invigorated by the peace we experienced. Thoreau, who had died over a hundred years before, became the spokesman for 1960's idealists, as his writings defined so many of our feelings that we couldn't define.

Thoreau wrote in *Walden*:

> If a man does not keep pace with his companions, perhaps it
> is because he hears a different drummer. Let him step to the music
> which he hears, however measured or far away.

Steve and I promised ourselves we'd step to our own music. I decided, on the shore of Walden Pond, to do only what I believed was right, regardless of the consequences.

The dream of a peaceful, loving world didn't have to die with Dr. King and Robert Kennedy.

Chapter VII

Our Relationship

Walk with me in love
Talk to me about what you cannot say to others
Laugh with me when you feel silly
Cry with me when you are most upset
Plan with me all your dreams
Share with me all the beautiful things in life
Fight with me against all the ugly things in life
Create with me dreams to follow
Have fun with me in whatever we do
Work with me toward common goals
Dance with me to the rhythm of our love
Walk with me throughout life
Let us hug each other
at every step in our journey
forever
in love

A good relationship doesn't happen by itself. A lot of time and effort is needed to make it work.

Steve and I discussed our future together. Our love for each other frightened him, as did the concept of marriage, which I, too, was intimidated by. Yet I certainly wanted our relationship to continue.

Just as we were talking about this, Steve surprised me by saying that he'd be attending a physics conference in Italy at the beginning of the summer of 1968, just a short time away. He suggested that I date other people while he was gone. We'd see how we felt about each other after the summer. And just like that, he walked away and left me standing there, stunned and devastated.

How could he be so matter-of-fact about being apart from each other and dating other people? I just couldn't accept Steve's nonchalant attitude toward our relationship.

I couldn't speak to Steve about my pain and anger, so I wrote him several poems...

Anger scorching through my body
shaking in rage, the lines tightening in my face
while uttering curses silently in pain
Who the hell are you to cut me off like that?

Steve hadn't realized that his actions and words had hurt me. He said that he was just trying to tell me that he was going to study physics and that he also wanted us both to be happy. He said that he loved me and that after being apart for several months, we would find out how we truly felt about each other. His explanation made sense and I thought that he probably was right. Our love for each other would be tested during his time away, and we'd see how strong it was when he came back.

Steve's parents and I took Steve to the airport for his flight to Italy. I was so sad, and when he kissed me goodbye, he looked forlornly at me. His mother, Ruth, noticed our expressions and put her arm around me.

Barely five feet tall, Ruth had huge, pretty eyes, high cheekbones, and straight red hair. She was a kind, modest woman who had been a compassionate social worker. Ruth was an old-fashioned, hardworking mother who doted on her three children who, in her eyes, could do no wrong. She made sure they ate three healthy meals and were dressed warmly every day. She was going to miss her only son.

Steve's father, Morton Schutz, always wore a brown tweed cardigan sweater and a cap, which was the style in the early twentieth century. He had gone to college and majored in accounting. Because it was during the Depression, he needed a job that would offer security in order to support his family. He felt lucky to start working at the post office, and he stayed there for approximately forty years. "Papa," as we called him, strongly believed in Marxism and had helped found the first Postal Workers Union. He remained politically active his whole life. He was also a true intellectual. He read classical books in German because he believed that the English translations could never quite capture the meaning of the authors' words. When Papa retired at the age of sixty-five, he went back to college to get a physics degree. He and Steve worked on several theoretical physics problems together, as well as statistical applications for our business. They shared many interests.

Steve's parents rarely socialized. They were unconventional humanitarians who, when they were not at work, stayed at home and gave their children complete freedom. They were genuine and honest. I adored them and wondered if I'd ever see them again.

The summer passed in a whirl of fury, emotional breakdown, sadness, and reckless dating. I missed Steve so much. I was worried that he didn't love me and that was all I could think about. I was miserable. I didn't look to see if cars were coming before crossing Manhattan streets, and I listened to Judy Collins' *Wildflowers* album over and over, crying every time she sang Leonard Cohen's song, "Hey, That's No Way to Say Goodbye." I couldn't believe how emotions could so dominate a person's life.

I took a graduate course in physiology and barely managed to pass it. The only bright spot was when I went to California for the first time with several friends.

I'd always had a romantic, glamorized view of California as a mystical land of movie stars and other beautiful people who had nothing to do but walk along the ocean, kicking up just the right amount of water to cool their suntanned bodies.

My friends and I hitchhiked around California and went to Berkeley, where we rented a small apartment. While the air was heavy with dew, everything else appeared light with freedom. Everyone seemed to live outdoors; people of all ages rode bicycles, motorcycles, and skateboards while clad in shorts and T-shirts.

Apartment porches were filled with sunbathing, shirtless men and women wearing halters and shorts. I was amazed to see women mail carriers wearing shorts. In the East, my mail carriers had always been men, and they wore very official-looking uniforms. I thought the women mail carriers were cool.

The first night I was there, my friends and I went to the Fillmore West, a well-known nightclub in San Francisco. The air was thick with marijuana smoke as people openly passed joints from one stranger to another. Crowded bodies danced without inhibitions to the music of Janis Joplin and Jimi Hendrix. I enjoyed this music, but when I went back to the apartment, I listened to softer, more meaningful folk music, which evoked peaceful, inspirational, and loving emotions.

The atmosphere in San Francisco was different from any place I had ever been. It seemed as if San Francisco was experiencing a renaissance of self-expression.

I camped in magnificent Big Sur and saw some of the most beautiful sights I had ever seen, but nothing could distract me from my thoughts of Steve.

I was madly in love with him. When I thought of being a writer, I wanted him to be the first to read my work. When something angered me, I wanted him to be the one to calm me down. I didn't need him to achieve my dreams, but I needed to share them with him.

I wouldn't leave our Berkeley apartment until the mail came each day; I had to know if Steve had sent me a letter. At long last, he sent a brief postcard: "I love you and I miss you."

Not being a man who speaks with a lot of adjectives or who uses beguiling words, I knew this was a deep, well-thought-out sentiment.

So despite the brevity of this message, I was overwhelmed with emotion. I couldn't wait to see him again, and I hoped that one day we could both bask in the spirit of California. Without Steve, even this phenomenal place felt empty and meaningless.

I sent a poem to Steve:

> With you there
> and me here
> I have had no one
> to discuss little things with
> like how the dew feels on the grass
> or big things like
> what's going on in the world
> I have been lonely
> talking and thinking to myself
> I now realize how essential it is to have someone
> to share oneself with

* * *

When the summer ended, I returned to New York City, and all I could think of was seeing Steve. He was back from his trip, but he hadn't called yet. What if he'd changed his mind? What if he didn't love me? Why hadn't he called?

I decided that maybe his sister, Arlene, a blunt and honest woman, could help me figure out what was going on.

"He's running around in circles," Arlene said. "He's not acting right. I know he misses you."

"Well, why doesn't he call or come over?" I asked.

"I think he's either afraid, or he just doesn't know what to do," she said. "Would you see him? He told me you were mad at him."

"Of course I'd see him. Tell him if he really wants to see me he should call me immediately."

As soon as I returned to my apartment, my phone rang. Steve wanted to come over.

I stared out my window, counting every second until his arrival.

He knocked on my door and stood there a moment in his maroon turtleneck and jeans. He handed me a flower just as Judy Collins sang "Michael from Mountains" on my stereo. At first we were awkward with each other, but then our conversation relaxed. We confessed that we'd missed each other desperately and that there had been a big void in our lives while we were apart. We decided to spend some time together.

As we got on his motorcycle and rode to Princeton, I realized the *Wildflowers* album that had symbolized our separation now became the anthem of our love.

We walked along the long, winding, narrow country road to the rustic house that Steve and his friends rented. A forest of oak trees surrounded it, and the brisk weather induced us to gather logs and build a campfire. We spent almost a week there rediscovering each other.

When we ventured out of this paradise, we attended several anti-war meetings together. We felt the anti-war movement was making headway, and we decided to celebrate by painting Steve's car with peace symbols. We invited our friends to the house, gave everyone a beer, paint, and a paintbrush, and drove the dark green 1957 Oldsmobile into the light coming from the porch.

As we painted the car in psychedelic colors and geometric designs, throwing in words like "peace" and "love," I circled the car, admiring our work and pondering the beauty of the car. "Every time we drive down the road," I thought, "we'll be making an important statement."

Then I saw the front of the car. One of our friends had painted "Fuck War" in psychedelic colors.

"You can't put that on Steve's car," I said.

"Why not?"

"It's embarrassing," I said. "I'll probably be visiting my parents soon. They'd die if they saw that."

"Oh, don't be so concerned with what other people think," the artist said. "Take chances in life. There's nothing wrong with saying that."

To my disbelief, everyone agreed. How could they have such honorable dreams for society, but so little consideration for individuals?

I have always believed that if we cared for and respected individuals, then everything else would fall into place. They seemed to believe that changing the system would be enough. Pulling into my parents' driveway with this curse word written on the car would hurt their feelings, and I refused to do that.

"Look, I don't care what you think," I insisted. "You know I'm against the war as much as you are, but I don't want 'Fuck War' on a car I'm driving to my parents' house! So you can paint your car however you want, but take this off Steve's car!"

I don't think the artist had ever heard a woman speak so strongly, and he immediately started to disguise the word by painting a design around it, but what had started out as a great party ended in an argument.

"Great," I thought. "Why do I always seem to be against everyone?"

The car was now beautiful. Steve and I wanted to go for a long ride in our masterpiece. Since we were very much in love with each other, I knew it was time to introduce him to my parents. We decided to take a leisurely drive to Peekskill. I'd never brought a boy home specifically to meet my parents, so as soon as I called my parents, they knew something was up. They usually supported whatever I wanted to do, but my dad was quite conservative, and I didn't think he would like Steve. I knew he wouldn't be thrilled with Steve's liberal ideals.

The moment my Dad saw the rainbows and peace signs on Steve's car, I could see that he intended to put Steve through the wringer. He didn't disappoint me.

"What do you want to be when you're out of school?" my father asked Steve, peering at his longish hair through narrowed eyes. My heart pounded in my chest.

"A physicist," Steve said.

"What if the company you work for is making weapons?"

"I wouldn't work for them."

"Then how'd you live and support your family?"

"I'd get a job doing anything. It really doesn't matter. We'd be happy living anywhere with very little money."

"You believe in nonviolence, right?"

"Yes."

"What would you do if someone attacked my daughter? Would you just stand there?"

Dad ended his interrogation there, satisfied that he had made his point: How could I even think about a serious relationship with such a hippie flake? He exchanged a meaningful glance with my mother.

Later, when Steve had left the room, my parents warned me that if I ever decided to marry Steve, he'd never support me properly and that he'd be inclined to just go off and live in a tent in the woods. I had expected this reaction from my parents. They were only trying to protect their unconventional daughter using a very conventional perspective. But my father's attitude bothered me.

After having dinner with my folks, I decided to go back to Princeton with Steve for a few more days.

Time spent in Steve's house in the woods always invigorated me. Not only could I be close to him, but I also saw how his roommates discussed and made sense out of their own dreams.

One night, Steve hand-lettered and illustrated a political poem I had written. He read it to his roommates during dinner, and we had a lively conversation about it. I was proud to have contributed this writing as a stimulus for such a great discussion.

In this Princeton house, books, music, ideas, helping people, and creativity dominated. I had finally found a place where people didn't play games and lived their lives in an intellectual, honest, and healthy environment. I wanted to live this kind of life forever. But the reality was that I had to return to my job as a teacher in New York City.

Chapter VIII

New York City School Strike

In September 1968, the New York City teachers went on strike over the issue of community control of the school districts. Though I sympathized with the striking teachers, I didn't agree that local control would destroy the districts. Even worse, shutting down the schools would send the students into the streets or leave them home alone while their parents worked. I joined a group of radical teachers who did not strike and continued teaching in order to keep the school open for the children.

There was a lot of crime in the area, which made it unsafe for children to roam around unsupervised. In fact, the children often warned me against walking alone outside the school. Every day, a group of little fourth-grade boys wearing black berets insisted on accompanying me to my bus stop. I adored my tiny bodyguards, and I couldn't abandon them.

One night, someone broke into my school and sprayed the many fire extinguishers all over the school. There was white foam everywhere. We were afraid that if our school was closed, the students might not come back to school, so we took the kids to the auditorium while parents and teachers tried to clean up the mess. Many people helped, and I even observed the principal scrubbing the water fountains. By noon, the school was sparkling and we were able to bring the students to their cold classrooms where the heat had been shut off due to the strike.

In my spare time, I was a reporter for a New York "underground" press, and I covered the thirty-five-day teachers' strike in detail.

One of my published stories appeared in the form of a poem:

New York City School Strike

While shivering in my coat
(why did you turn off the heaters?)
and smelling the stopped up toilets
trying to teach math
to freezing, distracted students
who know that I am not their real teacher
all I can say is
I wish more people cared about
these children, and
to hell with
the bureaucracy of education...

After a tense week of crossing picket lines and trying to teach under extraordinarily bad and unhealthy conditions, including not having electricity, Steve offered to take me to the sand dunes of Montauk, Long Island for the weekend.

Montauk is a magnificent old fishing town on the outer tip of Long Island. On practically every corner, there were little wooden restaurants that served the best clam chowder in the world.

Steve and I talked nonstop.

We motorcycled to the most beautiful sight I had ever seen: mountains of clean, pure sand with only the sky above them, completely removed from civilization. We camped there for two nights, and I felt that there could be nothing in life that was better than this.

I wrote a poem for Steve:

Everywhere rose mountains of sand
making us very tiny
The night wind drew us together
and the crackling fire echoed our souls
We were in the sky

or we were on a desert in the Biblical days
We were Moses climbing the mountain
and when we reached the peak
we were surrounded by
a peaceful barrenness and love
I wonder what other than
nature is significant
and my answer is you
I love you

At the end of the weekend, Steve and I motorcycled back to New York City completely and overwhelmingly in love with each other.

Chapter IX

Our Idealistic Commune

Much to my surprise, my love for Steve dramatically changed my life. I felt a new sense of peace and exhilaration. My dreams suddenly became crystal clear. I would eventually become a writer and work toward correcting injustices in society.

If we lived lives of simplicity, we could show others, by example, that harmony was possible. We would join people who shared our convictions and protest injustice as a group. Several months later, we thought we found a way to do exactly that: We would join a commune.

Sitting on the grass under the tall tulip trees of Princeton, Steve and I gathered with several other people to discuss the peace movement. The date was April 5, 1969, the day before we would all join a Vietnam War protest march in New York City. The cool spring afternoon invigorated our senses as we warmed up to our subject.

"Here we are," one of the men said. "Americans are bombing innocent villages, and no one cares!"

Our leaders had been assassinated, our young men were being shipped off to kill and be killed, and we couldn't do anything about it.

Steve actively campaigned against the war as did forty or so members of the Students for a Democratic Society (SDS). The anti-war movement was very small—amounting to less than 4% of the student population, and only a handful of Princeton professors publicly supported the anti-war viewpoint during that time.

We were in a war that seemed to have no purpose. Supposedly, America was trying to stop countries from becoming communist. Our government said if one country became communist, others would fall like dominoes. Vietnam was considered to be the first domino that would fall. The "domino theory" was ludicrous; Vietnam and China were traditional enemies. And, most atrocious of all, the United States was indiscriminately killing innocent civilians.

"We're burning children with our napalm," Steve said, outraged.

"It's disgusting," one of the other men said sadly.

He wanted to know why people could not see through the government's stories. He wanted people to get along intelligently and sensitively in the world.

"Why don't we form our own ideal society?" this person continued. "A commune where we can all live harmoniously with friends and try to end the damn war together." He truly believed in his ability to change the world.

Another person added that we could share all the money we earned. We'd also share our food and eat our meals together.

"We can get away from current society and create our own society where there's no hatred or wars," Steve said.

"Our children can be taught to be free human beings right from the start," said a friend.

"And they'll be taught to stand up for what they believe in," Steve said.

Ideas were scribbled furiously on paper and we were asked who would commit to living in the commune after we graduated. We all raised our hands in the circle of our friendship.

We'd build a perfect, democratic society, one in which everyone mattered. Our example would prove that a community focused on the ideals of peace, love, and equality—not money, power, and greed—could flourish and succeed.

The next day, Steve and I, dressed in our matching navy pea jackets, joined hundreds of thousands of people—older people, children, students, and hippies—marching along the streets of Manhattan holding one another's hands. I held a sign that Steve had made stating, "You can't get blood out of an onion," and his own sign read, "We must get out of Vietnam NOW." For eight hours we walked while singing "We Shall Overcome." Chants of "End the War in Vietnam Now" echoed along the Avenue of the Americas. Despite our serious mission, my heart swelled. We weren't alone. Other people felt the same way we did. Together we had a chance of making a difference.

That night we returned to Princeton to attend the next meeting of our commune group. Though we had walked many miles during the day, our elation energized us, and we were thrilled to learn that more people wanted to join our commune.

It was suggested that we could pool our money and rent or buy an old house with a big yard. Steve and I had imagined that the commune would be in a bucolic setting, or maybe in Colorado, where there was plenty of land to farm and fresh air to breathe.

Several decisions were quickly made.

It seemed to me that the men did all the talking and that they would earn money outside the commune while pursuing their careers. The women would tend to the daily domestic matters, and the earnings would be divided up equally to support the commune.

One man said that everyone would be making sacrifices, but I wondered what sacrifices the men would be making. I pictured the women cooking and serving meals that we'd all eat together in the communal dining room.

I waited for someone to say something, anything, about this insulting plan. I didn't like causing dissension, and I didn't want these people whom I liked and respected to be mad at me. But I couldn't help myself. I couldn't wait a moment longer and I jumped up, incensed.

"I've always planned on having a career," I said. I wondered why I should be treated any differently from the men in the commune.

Steve looked at me, silently supporting me with his firm blue eyes, but no one else budged. My comments were not met with applause. In fact, my open-minded, peace-loving friends seemed to stare at me as if I'd grown two heads. I could see by the look in some of the men's eyes that they thought I was an aggressive troublemaker and an emotional woman.

The Women's Liberation movement was barely in its infancy. In 1960, only five percent of doctors and two percent of lawyers were women; it seemed that all professional people were men. Women had only won the right to vote forty years earlier, and we still couldn't attend Ivy League colleges as undergraduates. I wasn't even allowed to wear slacks to classes, the college library, or the cafeteria. After being forced in high school to take home economics with the rest of the girls in order to learn how to cook and clean, and being banned from sports such as Little League and courses such as wood shop, I had sworn never to take a back seat to men. I never thought for a moment that I would stay at home and cook for a group of men. I didn't plan to start now.

Despite all our protests for equality and peace, even the sensitive male intellectuals tended to treat women as second-class citizens, and I think many women still thought of themselves as such. What had happened to our dream of an equal, democratic society? Equality was fine in the abstract, but when faced with it on a personal level, it was a different story.

The meeting ended with a call to think about the equipment and money we'd need to run the commune, and nothing more was said about my outburst.

The next day when Steve picked me up from school, he brought the *New York Times* with him. The April 6, 1969 headline read: THOUSANDS MARCH HERE TO DEMAND WITHDRAWAL FROM VIETNAM. We had estimated that there were around 300,000 protesters! The *New York Times* had drastically downplayed the enormity of the peace march and even cited a purported violent incident—one we certainly didn't witness. Frustrated and angered by the day's events, we hoped that the commune meeting in the evening would cheer us up.

The members of our future commune were dismayed by the way the media had made the anti-Vietnam War march into an insignificant event. They were outraged that the peace movement had been mistreated. We were more determined than ever to make our commune a showpiece.

We hoped that our commune would be a way to avoid living in our sick society. We hoped that we would make progress at our meeting planning the details of our commune.

That night we had to figure out how much money we would need to buy the necessities to make our commune livable. We agreed that we would need a very large refrigerator and freezer, two pick-up trucks, a commercial-sized stove and oven, large oak dining tables, and sixteen chairs and beds. One member needed an air conditioner for his allergies.

"I need a stereo," I said bluntly. "I need to have music."

The group mood appeared to indicate that a stereo was a luxury, not a necessity.

I didn't think this was a hedonistic demand. Music made me feel good. It helped me write, and I needed it just like the other member needed an air conditioner.

I felt my ire rise again.

I knew that if we put this to a vote right then, stereos definitely would not be allowed in our commune.

I gritted my teeth. I didn't want to keep disagreeing, but I didn't want anyone controlling my life either. I had to say how I felt.

I told them that just because we would be living in an austere environment didn't mean we had to eliminate fun from our lives. Music was such an important part of my life that this discussion greatly offended me, and I started to obsess about it.

I thought about so many wonderful evenings when Steve and I had gone to little jazz or folk-singing clubs in Greenwich Village, such as the Blue Note or the Village Vanguard. I'd be mesmerized by the intimate performances, and I'd bring home records of these performers. Would I not be able to play these records if I were in our commune?

My mind became deluged with thoughts about music. I did everything with music as a backdrop. I danced to the Platters, the Four Tops, and the Rolling Stones, and I wrote poems and daydreamed while playing Chopin, Dvorak, and other classical music. Mostly, however, I listened to folk music—Peter, Paul, and Mary; Pete Seeger; Tim Hardin; Phil Ochs; Donovan; and Bob Dylan.

Joan Baez was my favorite singer. With her bare feet; long, shiny, dark hair; words on behalf of love and peace; and a voice that completely melted my emotions, she represented a life of song and freedom that we all longed to live. Would I not be able to listen to her music? Folk music illuminated the philosophy that many in our generation, and certainly in our commune, were trying to live by. And now, I wouldn't be able to listen to folk music in my own home because I couldn't have a record player.

Was I really being materialistic? Perhaps a stereo was not an absolute necessity, but it wasn't as if I didn't understand the concept of living on the bare essentials. My family had been poor, but so were most people in Peekskill, so I learned to do without things. If I needed something, I earned my own money to buy it, just as I paid for my own college education and expenses.

It seemed that some of the members were mad because again I was the only person causing dissension in this harmonious group.

The discussion abruptly came to an end, and we started to talk about other topics. But I was not happy and started to feel that I was going to be controlled by other people if I joined the commune.

Wasn't the purpose of this movement to make people free? Weren't we fighting for our voices, trying to make a difference in the world? I felt silenced by the very people who wanted their voices to be heard.

I wanted so badly to make the world a better place, and I believed that creating a familial, communal atmosphere might be a solution. But now I stood face to face with the realization that I couldn't live in any kind of controlling environment, no matter what its intentions were. I wanted to foster my ideals and be free to live my life any way I wanted to. I wanted to love Steve and spend time with him. I didn't want to have people tell me what or how I should conduct my life.

I confessed my worries to Steve about the commune. I hoped my reservations wouldn't affect our relationship, but honesty was a very important component of our relationship, and I wasn't going to abandon this principle now. I told him the truth: I didn't want to be with the commune group anymore.

Although Steve and I believed that the basic idea of people living together with common goals was great, we thought that it would be difficult for everyone to agree on how to live and how to conduct their lives. This really had to be an individual choice—not a group choice.

We decided that we didn't need the commune, and we didn't have to conform to society's wishes for us either. We could have the life we wanted and be individuals at the same time.

"Maybe we can go to Colorado after all—just the two of us," Steve said.

Once again, Steve and I broke away from the majority and pursued what was right for us, regardless of what anyone said or thought. Going against the grain wasn't easy, but our freedom was important to us. We really didn't care who opposed us. The promise of staying true to our dreams remains a predominant part of our lives. Whatever the obstacles, we have always ultimately succeeded in living the kind of life we felt was best for us.

Thank God we had each other.

Chapter X

Mrs. Susan Polis Schutz

When I was younger I dreamed
how marriage should be
a sharing of goals
and lives
a love so strong that
it is always exciting and growing
a blending of two imperfect individuals
into stronger, better people
who laugh more, accomplish more
are happier, more successful
and more at peace
My dream came to be
because you had the same dream as I
and I want you to always know
how thankful I am
for our beautiful marriage
and how much I love
my life with you

On April 13, 1969, I held on to Steve tightly and watched the scenery race by as we rode his motorcycle to our wedding at my parents' apartment in Peekskill.

The tradition of a bride and groom not seeing each other on their wedding day until the marriage ceremony passed through my mind. I laughed as Steve and I drove quickly so we wouldn't be late to our own wedding. We rushed into my parents' apartment, where several of our closest friends and relatives had gathered.

The Peekskill rabbi performed a Jewish ceremony, and we said our vows under a *chupah* (canopy) held up by some of our relatives.

322

After the ceremony, we celebrated at an old, white, wooden, country hotel surrounded by acres of oak trees and grass. We listened to Joan Baez and Judy Collins records on my stereo as we ate dinner.

Steve wore dark green slacks with a light green shirt opened at the collar, a red paisley tie, and a light green jacket. I wore a very short, white, silk mini-dress, and Steve picked flowers to lace through my long, straight hair. My uncle said, "Hey, Sue, if your dress were any shorter it'd be a halter!"

Some of my relatives seemed shocked by the simplicity and uniqueness of the day, but Steve and I thought that we had just had the ideal wedding.

Late that night, Steve and I returned to Princeton to set up our home in one of the old army barracks that had been converted to married students' cottages. Our tiny, new home was sparsely furnished with my old, brown, second-hand couch, a desk made from plywood and bricks, Steve's handmade speaker and stereo, a mattress on the floor, and a refrigerator.

I had about one month more to teach, but I wanted to see if I could secure work for after that. So the next day I began looking for a job. During one interview, I was asked if I had made a mistake when I wrote the date of my marriage on the employment application. The woman looked at me with pity and said, "Looking for a job is hardly a honeymoon."

I thought about this on my way back to our home. According to the dictionary, a honeymoon is a "holiday taken by a newly married couple," and marriage was defined as "a close union between two individuals."

We couldn't afford the traditional honeymoon, but because of the deep, euphoric love Steve and I shared we felt as if every moment spent together was a holiday or "honeymoon."

Our time in Princeton was as idyllic as any newlyweds' should be. We loved being with each other in every way: intellectually, physically, creatively, socially, loudly, quietly...

Steve and I planted tomato seeds by our front door, and by the end of the summer there were hundreds of ripe cherry tomatoes growing outside all six cottages attached to ours. We bicycled around Princeton and sat in the grass yards in front of the cottages studying, reading, writing, and enjoying the company of other newlyweds. We even managed to drive to Woodstock in our painted car to attend the now-famous concert and hear many of our favorite musicians perform. Despite the rain and mud—conditions ill-suited for a gathering of 300,000 people—I was heartened to see how well everyone got along. I don't think anyone realized at the time what a long-term impact Woodstock would have.

As Steve worked on his thesis, I wrote catalog and press copy for an educational toy company and freelance articles for magazines. The first article I ever got published was about making jewelry from seeds and other dried foods. Steve took photographs of me with our friend's daughter modeling the jewelry. I received seventy-five dollars for the article, my first writing paycheck, and I bought Steve a warm, puffy, green down ski jacket. He still has it today.

Steve was almost finished with his thesis, and we discussed our future plans. He wanted to work in Colorado. I wanted to work in publishing, which meant I'd have to live in New York City. We decided to live in Colorado for two years, where Steve would work in physics, and then we'd move to New York for two years so I could venture into publishing. Neither of us would need to compromise our goals, as we would both get to do exactly what we wanted.

Steve was offered a postdoctoral job studying solar physics in Boulder with the Environmental Sciences Services Administration (ESSA), which later became the National Oceanic and Atmospheric Administration (NOAA). Though apprehensive about the prospect of his first "real" day job—he had been a student all his life—he accepted the position. In January 1970, we packed up our belongings and set off on a cross-country journey to begin our life in the West.

Three days later, at twilight, I saw hundreds of cows grazing on one side of the highway; on the other side, a herd of brown and white horses galloped freely along the stark landscape. In front of us lay the small city of Boulder against a backdrop of rocky, peaked mountains, including three beautiful, brown formations in the shape of flatirons. The air smelled so clean, like snow and evergreens, with no trace of car exhaust or humidity. Breathing in that crisp Rocky Mountain air was magical.

After arriving in the most spectacular place we had ever seen, the truckload of all our belongings was delivered to our apartment: our Princeton bookcase made out of red bricks and pieces of plywood, five boxes of books, two speakers, Steve's old portable manual typewriter, my electric typewriter, our old brown couch that continued to follow us around, and the king-sized mattress.

Steve and I were overwhelmingly happy with the beauty of our new surroundings and with our love, but each day, when Steve went to work, we were sad to leave each other. We decided that we would eat lunch together every day.

One day, over tacos and chile rellenos, I mentioned that none of Steve's colleagues came to meet their wives or girlfriends for lunch, and I was concerned that Steve might be missing out on important work-related discussions. He assured me that he would much rather spend the time with me and didn't care if he was missing out on anything.

I wrote stories for national magazines as well as local publications. On my way to lunch with Steve each day, I would stop at the post office to mail my ideas for articles that I wanted to write and check for responses from the queries I had sent out. Sometimes after lunch, I would stop by the funky offices of *The Boulder Express*, a newspaper/magazine that I wrote exposé articles for, to meet with the publisher. And then at night, the time would finally come for Steve and me to be together again.

We discovered that in 1970 there were two types of people living in Boulder—the older, very conservative folks who had lived there all their lives, and the younger people who were either recent University of Colorado graduates or transplants from around the country. They were on opposite ends of the spectrum. I had a run-in with one of the more conservative older Boulder people—a policeman who arrested me for double-parking and being disrespectful. I was sure his dislike for me was because he thought I was a troublesome hippie. On the other hand, the younger Boulderites soaked up the atmosphere the way Steve and I did, relishing each moment of the beauty of the mountains and taking nothing for granted. They were idealistic and cared about peace, nature, and each other.

I joined the local chapter of the National Organization for Women (NOW), one of the earliest in existence. Steve and I joined a food coop, buying sacks of rice and flour in bulk, dividing it up at meetings where we'd discuss our ideals and needs. We looked like most of the other people our age: dressed casually in handmade leather sandals, beaded pocketbooks, jeans, leather-braided headbands, and tie-dyed T-shirts. We felt very comfortable living in Boulder.

In the months following our move to Boulder, we cross-country skied across the Continental Divide, hiked in the mountains almost every day, and soaked up the never-ending, glorious sun. We missed only a couple of days of motorcycling because of snow. In Boulder, it could snow six inches one day, and then the next day steam would rise from the roads as the snow melted in fifty-degree sunshine. But always, the air was dry and smelled clean and fresh. Our lives were romantic, free, academic, and "outdoorsy."

It was during this time I wrote the poem, "Come Into the Mountains, Dear Friend," and Steve came up with the best idea he ever had: the silk-screen poster with this poem and his illustration.

Though we surely didn't know it at the time, this was the beginning of our working together in our joint career.

Soon after Steve started working at ESSA, he was scheduled to attend a physics conference in California. We both loved California and wanted to be there together, so I decided to go with him and try to sell our *Come Into the Mountains* posters. It turned out that this trip was the "honeymoon" we had never taken.

What a divinely romantic place Northern California is.

The old, colorful buildings of San Francisco made the city so dramatic. It had been the heart of many cultural and intellectual changes in the last twenty years. I especially loved the City Lights Bookstore, owned by beat poet Lawrence Ferlinghetti and featuring the writings of Jack Kerouac, Allen Ginsberg, and so many other authors whose books I had read. I admired the intellectual, artsy, "beatnik" rebels of the 1950's, and I knew they paved the way for the next group of young rebels—hippies.

We went to Haight-Ashbury, the legendary haven for runaway hippies. It was a place where kids went to get away from the provincial lives of conservative parents, where they could meet other people who wanted to live their own lifestyles, and where people who believed in love and nature, not war and materialism, gathered together.

Even in 1972, five years after the "Summer of Love," thousands of kids with flowers in their hair roamed Haight Street with their possessions in their backpacks. Yet the innocence seemed to be trickling away. Beneath the colorful shops and psychedelic music, the cafes had fallen into disrepair and pamphlets and literature littered the streets and sidewalks. There appeared to be an increase of drug dealers, who descended on the neighborhood like leeches, and the place was infested with junkies and criminals, making it dirty and unsafe.

The original kids who had made Haight-Ashbury famous as a center for intellect and good intentions had been driven out; some of them went to Boulder.

Steve and I had so identified with the philosophy underlying the hippie movement that watching Haight-Ashbury's demise was like watching our own ideals unravel. We feared that the hippies would be identified only with drugs and rebellion, instead of peace and love. Steve and I wanted to continue the legacy of love that had started in the mid-1960's. We wouldn't let our ideals end up in the gutter among the leaflets and manifestos.

We wanted to understand everything this beautiful state had to offer, so we even went to the famous nude beach, Stinson Beach. Besides freeing one's mind, the hippie philosophy included freeing one's body. I sat back on the sand, watching tall, short, fat, thin, narrow, and wide people walk by. It occurred to me that most people look better with their clothes on, but none of the nudists seemed to notice they were naked. They looked completely comfortable in nothing but their own skins.

I wrote many love poems to Steve during this time, and he created a painting of a beautiful cypress tree that would later be the cover of my book, *I Want to Laugh, I Want to Cry*.

> *In the morning*
> *when the sun*
> *is just starting to light the day*
> *I am awakened*
> *and my first thoughts*
> *are of you*
> *I love you*
> *At night*
> *I stare at the dark trees*
> *silhouetted against the quiet stars*
> *I am entranced into a complete peacefulness*
> *and my last thoughts*
> *are of you*
> *I love you*

I had sold hundreds of posters in California, and as soon as we returned to Boulder, our goals became clear. We wanted to be together at all times. We wanted to write, illustrate, and design works that we hoped would help people to better understand their feelings. Blue Mountain Arts would become the vehicle for us to reach our career dreams, and our love for each other and our family would become the vehicle for our personal aspirations.

From this point on, Steve and I started to spend a lot of time creating new posters and, ultimately, greeting cards and books while building Blue Mountain Arts. That part of our story, including our many obstacles and successes, is described in detail in the first part of this book. So I will skip ahead to the most important and best part of our lives: the births of our children.

Chapter XI

Pregnancy and the Beautiful Birth of Our First Child

Today I woke up
feeling strange
but special
For the first time
in my life
I thought about the fact that I
could produce a baby
Out of me
from him
a little baby
Unbelievable
Sure many of my friends
have had babies
but I never thought of myself
as a man's wife
or a child's mother
I am just me, leading
my own life
and in love with him
But today, I pictured
a child building sand castles
and it belonged to us

Steve and I had been married for five years when the thought of growing our family finally entered our minds. Steve always loved kids, and now that we could support a child financially, he was ready to start a family.

But I was conflicted. We'd created such a perfect life. Would a child topple the scales and throw off our balance of married life and work? Steve and I spent every moment together. Would a child separate us? We kept late hours, ate sporadically, and worked all the time. Steve and I lived with and for each other. How could a third person fit in? What if I didn't have enough love for two people?

My friends only compounded my confusion. Some of them already had children and said they hadn't really felt complete until they had children. Why, I wondered, can't women feel complete on their own? When I had children, would I be expected to give up all I had worked for to run a household? I knew Steve would never ask that of me, but still I worried. My career took so much work; how could I concentrate on raising a child, too? I had spent my entire life saying I only wanted to build a career, never a family. Had I really changed that much?

But there was something very alluring about having children, and I was thirty-one years old...

After weighing the pros and cons of having children and my personal readiness, I came to the conclusion that bringing forth a new life would be an absolute miracle. In this unstable world, love is important, and having a baby would mean there'd be someone else to love... someone else with whom to share the world...and someone else to teach kindness and love.

Steve and I decided we'd try to have a baby.

I was excited and I was terrified, but I reasoned that, since the lore was that it took at least a year to get pregnant, I'd have plenty of time to get used to the idea.

Toward the end of our next round of trade shows and sales trips, I grew more and more tired. I stayed behind in the hotel room a few times while Steve went to the show.

Once I got back to Boulder, I went to the doctor thinking that I had mono, but he gave me considerably different news. I wrote a poem about my discovery:

The test is positive
It's what?
It's what?
It's what?
Me?
No, it must be wrong
It must be wrong
My name is
Susan Polis Schutz
I'm a writer
I'm not grown up enough
to have a baby

I'd never had contact with babies. I'd never even met a baby, for that matter! My college friends always told me they could never see me as a mother. And here I was about to become one. As usual, I worked out my confusion on paper and started a journal of my feelings, which later became a book titled *Someone Else to Love.*

I didn't like how I felt when I was pregnant. I needed to take naps, I felt weak, and my body kept doing things I didn't understand. When I went to the doctor, he kept me waiting for what seemed like hours.

I wondered who this little person would be. How would I take care of him or her? I was afraid to buy anything for the baby until we met because I thought it might be bad luck.

Despite my apprehension, though, I also looked forward to sharing this child with Steve. "Will our baby have sky-blue eyes that examine and understand and melt with sensitivity like his father's do? Will our baby get lost in his own genius, concentrating on and deciphering new subjects like his father does?" I wrote.

We would help our baby to be independent, to be a happy child of the mountains, loved by family, friends, and animals. Though we would love, teach, and cuddle our child, we would still devote time to each other and Blue Mountain Arts.

By my fifth month, I had all my energy back, and we went on a trip to New York City. Because I felt so well, I found it hard to believe that there was a real, live baby growing inside me. I soon lost my waistline, and a few weeks later, I was holding my jeans that had split apart together with a diaper pin. I couldn't bear to give up my jeans.

In the sixth month, the baby moved; in the seventh, I heard its heartbeat. The moment I heard that tiny heart fluttering, so quietly and fast, I started to believe that I was actually going to become a mother.

Though I was happy, I noticed some disturbing things about my friends and acquaintances. I looked undeniably pregnant by that point, having since discarded my jeans in favor of maternity clothes. Suddenly, no one spoke to me as they had before I was pregnant. I was no longer a career woman or an attractive adult woman. I was first and foremost a pregnant woman; no one could see past my big stomach to my mind. When someone spoke to me, it was as if I were their mother; they didn't talk to me about world affairs, writing, politics, business, or any of the things we'd discussed in the past. Instead, they talked about diapers, babies, and family life. Why couldn't they treat me as they always had?

When I went to the doctor for my eight-month visit, another doctor met me in the elevator.

"You're Susan Polis Schutz, right?"

"Yes, I am," I said.

"You own Blue Mountain Arts, don't you?"

"Yes, I do," I replied.

"How do you plan to take care of your baby when you're working?"

I told him about the nanny we'd hired.

"If you're planning to have someone else raise your child, why are you having a baby?" he sneered as he left the elevator.

A doctor was trying to make me feel guilty for wanting to work! How dare he be so condescending toward me and other women who do the best they can for their children? So many families can't afford to raise their children without working; how could he be so presumptuous as to assume anyone who had children had to stay at home?

Yes, I'd continue to work! No, I didn't like being pregnant despite the fact that many women believed pregnancy was one of the best experiences of their lives. I felt a little guilty and confused.

As much as I disliked other people seeing me only as a pregnant woman, by the eighth month I started seeing myself in much the same light. Even though I went to work every day, pregnancy and childbirth occupied my mind, emotions, and physical body. Sharp pains ran down my leg (the baby was touching a nerve), and I often couldn't walk, so Steve wheeled me around the office in a desk chair. I'd gained sixty pounds and looked and felt like a house. My doctor persuaded me to go to Lamaze classes, but the pain of childbirth frightened me; I was convinced that even the proper breathing wouldn't help, so I quit the class.

No, I wouldn't use the popular Lamaze breathing technique. Yes, I would use formula in addition to breastfeeding. Yes, I would use disposable diapers to make my life easier.

I wasn't the earth mother it was so popular to be back then, although I did give up caffeine, alcohol, aspirin, allergy pills, and foods containing any chemicals for the entire nine months. I was going to have a baby, and I'd make my own choices about my pregnancy and the delivery.

By the ninth month, I was a prisoner of my body. My stomach was so huge I couldn't put on my shoes. I couldn't walk at all. If I stood still, my legs cramped. Delighted as I was to have such an active baby, I sometimes wished the baby would kick my ribs a little less often. But "as soon as the baby kicks," I wrote in another poem, "I forget about everything and cannot wait to see it." I was tired, and I hated looking at myself. In one poem, I wrote, "My body is king. I am its helpless servant."

I hoped I would give birth soon. I wanted the baby, I loved the baby, but I couldn't wait for my pregnancy to be over.

About a week later I felt a strange sensation in the middle of the night.

"Steve?" I yelled. He mumbled in his sleep.

"Steve? I think I might—"

His eyes flew open. "Is this it? Are you having a contraction?"

"I don't know."

"You don't know?" he asked, confused.

"It doesn't hurt that much."

"Should we go to the hospital?"

"Our doctor won't be in until morning! I don't want a strange doctor to deliver our baby. Let's wait awhile."

"Are you sure it's a contraction?"

"I don't know!" I cried.

"We'd better time them."

The pains were really quite mild, but they were, indeed, contractions. So starting around 2:00 A.M. on May 11, until 7:00 A.M., we timed the contractions.

Once they were five minutes apart, as the doctor told us, we went to the hospital where we were greeted by a receptionist. She grilled me with many seemingly ridiculous questions, ranging from whether or not I'd had the mumps to where and when I was born. I screamed at her and said that I would answer her questions after I had my baby, that I was in labor right now, and she needed to take me to a room immediately.

It seemed like forever before a nurse wheeled me into a room. My doctor examined me.

"You're going to need an X-ray," he said after a few moments.

"Do I have to?" I asked. "Won't that hurt the baby?"

"Susan, we have to have an X-ray. Your contractions aren't getting closer together, like they should be. We must be sure nothing's wrong."

I relented. It turned out that the baby was too big for my body, and I needed a caesarian section immediately.

They wheeled me into the operating room, and on May 12, 1975, I gave birth to a long, thin, baby boy. He was eight healthy pounds with delicate, light skin; soft, red cheeks; a few wisps of light blond hair; and bubbly blue eyes.

I held Jared in my arms, and with Steve by my side, I wondered why I hadn't liked being pregnant when something so miraculous was the result.

The next day I wrote a poem about the miracle of childbirth, which Steve illustrated. We printed this on beautiful Blue Mountain paper, and it became our birth announcement.

The next few days were a blur of incredible pain around the incision, happiness, relief, and love. After five days in the hospital, the three of us went home to the waiting arms of my mother. For four hours, Steve wandered from store to store buying diapers, bottles, formula, and blankets. We didn't know what kind of store carried baby supplies, how to hold our fragile little boy, or how to diaper him. We were so in awe of this new life, and our responsibility for him, that we were scared of doing something wrong. I absolutely loved this new creature.

I was stunned to find that people—women especially—pitied me for having had a C-section. They said they were sorry I didn't get to see my baby being born. Why did it matter how my beautiful, healthy baby was born? After all, they hadn't seen their husbands and parents being born, and that didn't make them love them any less.

In the weeks after our son's birth, much to my surprise, I still looked pregnant. I think I expected to regain my slim figure immediately, but that wasn't even close to the truth. I had lost only ten out of the sixty pounds I'd gained, and I hadn't recovered my energy. I felt tired, weak, impatient, and annoyed. Any woman who's experienced the postpartum "blues" knows that the word "blues" is an insult. For me, postpartum depression was a physical exhaustion and an emotional drain that only abated with time and rest.

As I grew stronger, our love for our son intensified every day. Every time I looked at him, I loved him more. I thought my heart would burst with joy, and we couldn't stop kissing him. He'd often fall asleep in our arms and we'd hold him for hours.

Asleep in my arms
startled by a noise
he raised his little head
and looked at me
He grinned with love
as his eyelids closed
and he fell back to sleep
I grinned with love
as my eyelids closed
with tears

I called the nanny I had hired before Jared was born and told her that we had changed our minds. There was no way we'd part with our baby. For all my promises never to let a child be the singular focus of my life, Steve and I realized that our baby was the most important part of our lives. Fortunately, we had the flexibility to be able to always have him with us. We moved his crib into our office, and as I described earlier, we took Jared to work with us every day.

At one presentation with five accountants and lawyers—all in suits, of course—our little boy was playing quietly with Legos when an unpleasant odor permeated the air. Steve nonchalantly picked him up, placed him on the rug in the middle of the office, and changed the baby's diaper as the meeting continued. The other men blushed or looked uncomfortable and even disgusted by Steve's "domestic" abilities. I couldn't help laughing. Thank goodness for men who are confident enough in their masculinity that they don't mind changing diapers!

We were lucky to be able to hire people to take care of the domestic chores at home, such as the cooking, cleaning, and shopping, that Steve and I didn't have time to do. Sil Lidia is one of those wonderful people. She has diligently taken care of our Colorado house for over thirty years, starting before either of us had children, and she and her children are like family to us. Without this help, we wouldn't have been able to devote so much time to Blue Mountain Arts and our children.

We took our baby everywhere with us. In the mountains, he sat in a little backpack on Steve's back. When we went to trade shows, he was there loving the attention from all the people who visited our booth. Traveling never bothered him because he never knew what time it was. He always had a smile on his face.

But during one trade show, Jared cried all day and refused his bottle. Nothing we did could cheer him up. Every time we gave him his bottle, he threw up. We took him to a Los Angeles emergency room, and after two hours, a young doctor said he probably had the flu. We weren't satisfied with the diagnosis, so we took him to a local pediatrician who placed him in a nearby hospital where a nurse took him away for several hours of medical tests.

We found out later he had been given a spinal tap to test for meningitis, and an inexperienced resident had poked my baby seven times to find the right spot. The image of Jared being stuck with a needle without Steve or me holding him was unbearable. We had given Jared to a stranger and abandoned him to experience pain all alone! Never, ever again, we swore, would we let him be taken anywhere without our being at his side.

"Take him home," the doctor said after all the tests came out normal. "He's run down from all the traveling he's been doing. Traveling is really hard on babies."

Steve and I couldn't believe that traveling had affected Jared. Contrary to what the doctor told us, we believed babies are perfect travelers. Their needs can be met regardless of location, while adults have to adapt to wherever they are. Different time zones didn't bother our infant because he ate when he was hungry and slept when he was tired. Steve and I made a parental decision. We decided Jared needed some fresh air and sunshine, so we went to Laguna Beach, California.

We fed him apple juice rather than milk, and the next day he seemed to feel better. He was back to his old happy self, soaking up sunshine and playing in the sand. When we gave him a milk bottle, though, he immediately got sick again. Steve and I made the connection: Could he have a milk allergy? And if so, why hadn't the doctor thought of this? We went to the grocery store and bought soy formula for him.

He loved the soy milk. In his own language of "mmm" for milk and "ah-ah-ah" for apple juice, he told us exactly which drink he wanted. And he had no more digestive problems.

After hours of tests and doctors' diagnoses, it was Steve and I who discovered our son's milk allergy.

Our method of raising our baby, which included constant travel with us while we worked, might be different from the way most parents raise their children. Nevertheless, what babies need most is love, and Jared had plenty of that. He had the total love, support, attention, and admiration of two people who dedicated their lives to him.

But to be the best parents possible, we needed more information.

We learned about children's diseases, medical tests, and medicine.

We learned about nutrition and exercise. We never again wanted to rely only on a stranger's knowledge. We sought out doctors and experts for advice, of course, but we would use our own research, common sense, and knowledge to judge if their advice about our precious son made sense.

We took control of parenthood and of our own lives. We decided that we would not return home as the doctor advised. We would continue on the trade show circuit as long as our son continued to be healthy and happy.

After his birth, I reread my pregnancy journal and thought how foolish I had been to think that my capacity to love had limits and that I wouldn't have enough love for Steve and our son both! Love is expansive: The more you give, the more you're capable of giving.

I had worried so much about balancing work and family, and I knew we would have to make constant adjustments to achieve what we thought was right for us. But should we ever have to make a choice between the two, we wouldn't even have to think twice. On May 12, 1975, our lives had changed forever.

I thought
I loved my husband
with all
the love
I could possibly have
But now
a whole new love
(which I never knew existed)
toward our baby
has been born
I am overwhelmed
by the emotional
warmth
beauty
and love
I share with
my husband and our
little child

Chapter XII

Our Ethereal Daughter

We had a beautiful little girl
I want to shout it to the clouds
I want to yell it across the ocean
We had a beautiful little girl
Nine months of worry and discomfort
and there she was
all pink and cuddly
with huge, blue eyes
perfect little hands and feet
tiny rosebud lips
We had a beautiful little girl
I want to shout it across the mountains
I want to yell it through the fields
She is beautiful
She is healthy
She is perfect
Thank you, Daughter
Thank you, God

After experiencing the utter joy of bringing a child into the world in 1975, ten months later I received a startling phone call telling me that my father had suffered a stroke and had just passed away. I was shocked and devastated by this sad event, and I write about it in Chapter Thirteen, Fragility of Life.

Bringing a new life into the world and losing another caused Steve and me to think about what was important to us, and our priorities changed dramatically. Our first priority became—and remained—parenting, and everything else came second to that. To accomplish this, we made several major changes in our lives. We had been working eighteen-hour days, so we tried to solve the time-consuming problems we were having with Blue Mountain Arts and our careers. I describe this in the first part of this book. Now we could concentrate on our family.

We decided that we wanted to expand our family and have more children. On July 10, 1980, our beautiful baby daughter was born. My friend and obstetrician, Dr. Katherine Carson, delivered her, and having a woman doctor made all the difference in the world. She understood what I was going through and let me make all the choices.

Robust and pink-cheeked, our daughter was so healthy that the doctors nearly forgot about her as they attended to me. My own little girl, with a perfectly round face, huge, blue eyes, and fair skin, named after a strong soldier in the movie *Exodus*, slept quietly and peacefully in her bassinet. I wanted to instill a world of happiness, confidence, strength, and freedom in my daughter. I held her and kissed my pledge onto her soft cheeks.

My darling daughter
I am glad that
you were born in an age
when women are
aware of what is going on
and don't always have
to fight so hard to be heard
The world is wide open
for you to be whatever you want
It will be hard
but at least you
will find other women
striving for the same thing
and you won't be called "crazy"
for wanting to achieve your goals
Though full equality
is not here yet
there certainly have been changes
that will make your life as a woman

not so stereotyped and confined
You are living in an age
where womanhood is
finally growing
to be everything
that it can be
and I picture you
my beautiful child
as a beautiful woman
in full control of her life

I was so preoccupied with my daughter that I couldn't stop watching her.

I wrote many poems to my precious daughter to express my love for her, and in 1986, my book *To My Daughter, with Love, on the Important Things in Life* was published.

Some of the poems in *To My Daughter, with Love* were my advice to her on growing up. Some just reiterated my deepest love and support for her, and some wondered about what she'd be doing when she was older.

One of the most important things parents can do, besides give unconditional love to their children, is to teach them what is important in life. I tried to do this.

To My Daughter, with Love, on the Important Things in Life

A mother tries to provide her daughter
with insight into the important things in life
in order to make her life
as happy and fulfilling as possible
A mother tries to teach her daughter
to be good, always helpful to other people
to be fair, always treating others equally
to have a positive attitude at all times
to always make things right when they are wrong
to know herself well

A mother tries to teach her daughter
to know what her talents are
to set goals for herself
to not be afraid of working too hard to reach her goals
to have many interests to pursue
to laugh and have fun every day
to appreciate the beauty of nature
to enter into friendships with good people
to honor their friendships and always be a true friend
to appreciate the importance of the family
and to particularly respect and love our elder members
to use her intelligence at all times
to be proud of the fact that she is equal to men
to listen to her emotions
to adhere to her values
A mother tries to teach her daughter
to not be afraid to stick to her beliefs
to not follow the majority when the majority is wrong
to carefully plan a life for herself
to vigorously follow her chosen path
to enter into a relationship with someone worthy of herself
to love this person unconditionally with her body and mind
to share all that she has learned in life with this person
If I have provided you with an insight
into most of these things
then I have succeeded as a mother
in what I hoped to accomplish in raising you
If some of these things slipped by
while we were all so busy
I have a feeling that you know them anyway
One thing I am sure of, though
I have loved you every second of your life
I have supported you at all times
and as a mother and friend
I will always continue to admire and love
everything about you
my beautiful daughter

The bond between a mother and daughter is composed of a deep understanding of and support for each other, and it is based on an enormous amount of emotion and love. There is no other relationship in the world where two women are so much like one. In my poems, I wrote about the love, respect, and friendship that my daughter and I had and how much fun it was talking and going places with her.

From an early age, my daughter was an ethereal bundle of talent and energy. From science to art to sports, she was always involved in one of her passions, and she always made us laugh with her very funny, cynical humor. I enjoyed being with our daughter and couldn't wait for her to come home from school every day.

When she was older, she taught me the true meaning of being an independent woman. She wonderfully and intelligently conducted her academic, work, and social life without caring about stereotypical roles.

Too quickly it became time for her to leave home and attend college where she'd become a physics and math major. I was sad, but I knew that she was ready.

This is your last year at home
then to college
new people
new environment
new learning
I know you are
more than ready
to absorb the dazzling knowledge
from the ivory towers
of lofty minds
but are you ready
to leave the familiar
surroundings of your
loving home and
small-town environment?

Don't be afraid, Daughter
You are so strong
in your beliefs and values that
you will be comfortable
in any situation in which
you find yourself
because you will be in charge ~
choosing the best aspects
and avoiding the worst
You are ready, Honey ~
Your mind needs new challenges
Your soul needs new like souls
And always remember that
though we will say good-bye for now
your family deeply loves you
Wherever you are
we will be right there with you ~
in your dorm, in the library, everywhere you are ~
in our minds and hearts
I love you

Chapter XIII

Birth of Our Adorable Second Son and Our Enchanted World

When I was growing up, I was unable to imagine myself ever becoming a mother. Now I know that, by far, it is the most important and fulfilling thing I have ever done.

Steve and I realized that to raise healthy, happy, interesting, and stable children, we had to be active, involved, loving, supportive, and available parents. And, believe me, we were! Nothing ever came before our children, and we adored being with them. Business associates, friends, and relatives took us all together as a family, or not at all.

The year 1983 was a great one for us: Blue Mountain Arts AireBrush cards were rated the number-one-selling card line in America, but much more importantly, I became pregnant with our third child.

I was thirty-nine years old, so we decided that this would be our last child. The nine months of being pregnant went by expeditiously because Steve and I were remarkably busy with Blue Mountain Arts and our children.

Dr. Katherine Carson, who had delivered my daughter and with whom I had recently written a book entitled *Take Charge of Your Body*, had retired because she had cancer, but she pledged to me that she would get out of bed to deliver one last baby—mine.

On October 6, 1983, Dr. Carson came to the hospital, issued orders in her usual strong voice, and made sure that I was as comfortable as I could be. It was such a beautiful moment: Steve, my love, holding my hand; my dear friend, Kathy Carson, performing the caesarian operation; and my little son being brought into the world.

This baby boy was special right from the moment he was born. He looked completely different from our other two light-skinned, blue-eyed, blond children, both of whom were born without hair. He had olive skin; thin, black fuzz on his head; very large, brown eyes; two big dimples on his cheeks; and one on the left side of his forehead. He was so adorable.

As he became a toddler, his uniqueness in our family continued to shine. He was always smiling and grinning with a twinkle in his "Polis," almond-shaped, dancing eyes. He had an innate kindness and sweetness encased in a beautiful, happy innocence.

I would often sit for hours in our rocking chair singing made-up songs to him, and he would sing along with me—in tune—and eventually fall asleep. One day, after placing him in his bed, I wrote a poem to him:

Little one
you brighten up
everyone's life
that you come
in contact with
You go to sleep smiling
You wake up smiling
Your large eyes are so alive
with warmth and intelligence
Your dimples
are always laughing
What you say
with your cute baby accent
is so fresh and cheery
You understand so much more
than people think
Love and kindness radiate
from every part of you

You are love and kindness
Little one
you brighten up
my life all the time

When he was four years old, I watched him trying to save the life
of a beetle, and I wrote another poem to him:

My sensitive little son
who looks in the pond every day
in order to take out any bugs that
might be drowning
who cares about every living
person, animal, and flower
as much as he cares about himself
My beautiful little son
whose eyes radiate all the
joy and goodness in his heart
who kisses my hand
and tells me how much he loves me
which is enough love
to carry me
through any day

When he was five years old, I noticed random words hung up on
his bedroom wall. When I asked him what they were, he replied, smiling,
"These are my words of the day. I hang up pretty words that I want to
remember." And he added, "I just love words."

Early on, he was extremely perceptive and noticed things about
people that no one else noticed. If someone was smiling but underneath
they were not happy, he would somehow see this and he would ask them
why they were sad. Even today, he has an uncanny sensitivity for how
people feel. He is a truly selfless person. He also has a beautiful singing
voice and a spectacular way with written and spoken expressions.

Right before he left home for college, where he would major in social and political theory, I wrote him a poem:

My Darling
So understanding
of people's feelings
Deeply concerned
with the health and happiness
of those he loves
Readily shares
possessions or accolades
with those who he thinks need them
A beautiful boy
inside and out
His stylish hair falls gently
on his wide, dark eyes
which bristle with
humor, tenderness, and exuberance
A selfless intellectual
sensitive and loyal
ready to try out new things
and take new paths
while creating a life he wants to lead
as he finds out more about himself
Please remember that
I will always be behind you
in everything you do
with pride and
unconditional love

Chapter XIV

Where Are They Now?

I certainly could fill up a book on each of my children's many virtues and minor foibles if I wanted to. Instead, I prefer to talk about the feelings we have for one another via my poems. I also prefer to describe generalities as opposed to specifics about them because they are people with the right to have a private life, and I don't want to invade that. But I felt I had to speak about them in this book because they are such an important part of Steve's and my life.

I noticed that by the time each of our children was five years old, their personalities and unique characteristics were established and remained generally unchanged throughout their childhood and teen years. They have been honored in school with many awards for academic and personal achievements. But most importantly, they are extraordinarily kind, humble, and loving. They are unique, hard-working, self-contained, self-motivating individualists who have chosen to stand apart from the crowd even though at times it has been difficult to do so. Like all children, they have had their fair share of unpleasant situations, but they became stronger and more confident because of the lessons they learned from them.

Since Jared has chosen to go into a career of public service and his name is well known, I have written in more detail about his life and activities while trying not to give specific details about our other two children who are still in college.

When Jared was eleven years old, he attended a city council meeting and gave a spontaneous, passionate speech about saving a canyon. Because of his speech, the members voted to save this canyon and Jared realized that one person can influence decisions that affect the lives of people. From this moment on, he knew that he wanted to be a public servant when he grew up.

Jared wanted to be out in the world as quickly as he could, so when he was sixteen years old, during his junior year in high school, he applied to and was accepted by Princeton University. In lieu of his senior year, he went to college where he majored in political science (his passion), and most of his activities revolved around world issues.

As soon as Jared graduated from Princeton, he joined us in our ventures, but he also formed many businesses on his own. Jared focused on becoming a successful businessman while he was young, so that he'd soon be able to spend a lot of time on community service and political activities.

He has finally embraced his love for helping people. In November 2000, he was elected to the State Board of Education of Colorado, and I am quite sure it will not be his last elected position.

I wrote him a poem:

*I am so happy
with the direction
that your life
is taking you
Your decisions and actions
are noble and intelligent
I often think about
how you were the same way
when you were a little boy
I hope that you remain strong and in control
of your life forever
Sometimes you will make mistakes
and because you take risks
you will have your share of opponents
I want you to know
that at all times
the proudest mother in the world
is always here
to encourage you*

to understand you
to talk with you
to support you
and to love you forever

At the young age of twenty-six, Jared was doing what he always wanted to do, and that is what I had always hoped would happen with our children.

Our daughter and younger son are still students, so they have a while before they can start to pursue their dreams.

Though I miss my "children," we talk on the phone several times a week and exchange daily e-mails. I have discovered that the relationship between parents and their children changes once the children leave home. No longer do we know what they are doing every minute of the day, nor do we get to see how they are feeling, and I worry excessively about all the negative things that could possibly go wrong in their lives. But they are on their own, and all we can do is hope that they make the right decisions about themselves.

Steve and I devoted an enormous amount of time and love to raising our children. We brought them up in a free and honest atmosphere, where they could be free and honest individualists. They were expected to be kind, loving, respectful, caring, hardworking human beings. We were with them practically every moment and never took a trip or vacation without them. We never pushed them in any way, but we supported whatever they wanted to pursue. Perhaps that is why they each developed their own interests. We took them with us everywhere, including dinners with interesting people (most of the time they were the only children at these dinners), read to and with them, shared our work with them, and exposed them to anything that could teach them moral and intellectual lessons. And, of course, we attended every sports or school event they were ever in.

We encouraged our childrens' creative instincts and always urged them to follow their passions.

Steve and I will not consider ourselves good parents if our children have high achievements but are not happy. If they live their lives according to their own ideals while pursuing their world of dreams, and they are happy, loving, and confident, then we will know that we have succeeded as parents.

One thing I know for sure is that I am extremely lucky to be the mother of these three glorious children.

Chapter XV

A New Phase of Life

From the time Steve and I became parents, our lives were our children's lives, and their lives were ours. Our publishing company, Blue Mountain Arts, was completely intertwined with our family life. I've been very lucky in that most of my dreams have come true. I found the one true love of my life—Steve—and we've been blissfully married for over thirty-five years. I've been able to work with Steve by combining my poetry with his illustrations, and our works have helped people communicate their feelings. Most importantly, I have loved being a parent to our three children.

I continue to love my husband, my children, and my work more than ever. Nature, music, and reading still play important roles in my life, and of course, I will always write. Now that my book, *Blue Mountain*, is complete, my furniture cluttered with ideas for it scribbled on hundreds of Post-It notes and napkins will finally be cleared. And my mind, which has been somewhat obsessed with this project for many years, will be cleared as well.

And at this time, Steve and I are entering a new phase of life.

Our house was a loud and lively hub, not only for our children but also for their friends. It is very quiet now. With no more children at home, Steve and I are putting our own schedule first, something we haven't often done in twenty-six years. We remain close with our children, but now that they are not living with us, our relationship is different.

In the future, we will continue to pursue some of our old dreams; perhaps we will form new ones.

This life is yours
Take the power
to choose what you want to do
and do it well
Take the power
to love what you want in life
and love honestly with your entire mind and heart
Take the power
to walk in the forest
and be a part of nature
Take the power
to control your own life
No one else can do it for you
Take the power
to create your own dreams
and try hard to reach them
Take the power to make your life
healthy
exciting
worthwhile
and very happy

EPILOGUE

Coming Full Circle with *One World, One Heart*

Steve and I were on the East Coast planning to fly to New York City on the morning of September 11, 2001. Needless to say, we didn't get there. And we, like everyone else, were devastated by the tragic events of that day.

We immediately went to be with our children; we just had to be with them during this time.

After we realized that our family was safe, we wanted to do something to help our country, but we didn't know what to do.

In October of that same year, it occurred to me how we could do our small part.

I feel strongly that everyone has the same basic needs and emotions and that we must put aside our differences and come together as one in peace, understanding, and tolerance. It is so sad that people can be so nonloving, hateful, unfair, and violent toward each other.

I wrote poems on this subject, and together with Steve's illustrations, we published a book entitled *One World, One Heart*.

Because of the success of our publishing company, we were able to finance printing and distributing *One World, One Heart* and give it away for free throughout the world, hoping that readers would listen to our message.

We wanted the distribution of *One World, One Heart* to be a grass-roots movement, not a media-hyped one. We did not advertise or do any publicity at all about this book.

Over six and one-half million copies have been sent free to churches, synagogues, hospitals, schools, government organizations, charities, Girl Scout troops, police stations, Salvation Army shelters, firefighters, support groups, senior citizen homes, hospices, jails, colleges, and many groups trying to promote peace. The book is also available on the Web for free.

In 1969, Steve and I started making posters with messages about love and peace. Back then, we had to sell our posters so we could eat. From the sale of our posters Blue Mountain Arts publishing company was developed.

Thirty-five years later, in 2004, we still are trying to promote our message of love, but now we are fortunate enough that we don't have to sell our message in order to eat. This time we can give people *One World, One Heart* for free and hope that it will affect the world in a positive way. We've come full circle right back to where we started.

CREDITS

We gratefully acknowledge the permission granted by the following authors, photographers, publishers, and authors' representatives to reprint photographs or excerpts from their publications.

The *San Francisco Examiner* for "All their life is together" by Caroline Drewes (February 17, 1976). Copyright © 1976 by the *San Francisco Examiner*. All rights reserved.

The Associated Press for "Some card merchants think…" from "Susan Polis Schutz: Entrepreneur in Selling Emotions" by Mary Beth Nibley for the Associated Press (July 17, 1986). Copyright © 1986 by the Associated Press. All rights reserved.

The *Daily Camera* for "[The] introduction to Susan Polis Schutz's first book…" from "Love Is Susan's Message" by Margaret Banman (September 2, 1973). Copyright © 1973 by the *Daily Camera*. And for "Blue Mountain Arts, which specializes…" from "Sentimentality goes high tech: E-cards address cyber niche" by Bill Long (September 26, 1996). Copyright © 1996 by the *Daily Camera*. And for photograph by Laura Galinson from "Blue Mountain Decision Delayed" (October 26, 1986). Copyright © 1986 by the *Daily Camera*. And for photograph by Karen Schulenberg from "20/20 filming" (January 15, 1976). Copyright © 1987 by the *Daily Camera*. Reprinted courtesy of the *Daily Camera*. All rights reserved.

Barry Staver for photographs of Susan and Stephen Schutz. Copyright © 1976, 1979, 1983 by Barry Staver. All rights reserved.

Kim Kulish Photography for photograph from "60's Messages in a 90's Medium," by Kim Kulish, published by the *New York Times*. (January 23, 1999). Copyright © 1999 by Kim Kulish. All rights reserved.

The Estate of Martin Luther King, Jr., c/o Writers House as agent for the proprietor, New York, NY, for "I have a dream…" by Dr. Martin Luther King, Jr. Copyright © 1963 by Dr. Martin Luther King, Jr. Copyright renewed 1991 Coretta Scott King. All rights reserved.

A careful effort has been made to trace the ownership of selections used in this book in order to obtain permission to reprint copyrighted material and give proper credit to the copyright owners. If any error or omission has occurred, it is completely inadvertent, and we would like to make corrections in future editions provided that written notification is made to the publisher:

BLUE MOUNTAIN ARTS, INC.
P.O. Box 4549, Boulder, Colorado 80306

We welcome your comments regarding this book at our special Web address: http://www.sps.com/dreams